Praise for *Exploding*
and Zombies

"This a love story. A double love story, to be exact. It's the story of science and faith, two lovers who had a falling out that resulted in a bitter rivalry for the last few centuries. And it's the tale of a youth pastor who loves God and his teens too much to give up on them. Like a good relationship counselor, Andy Root calls into memory the shared story of science and faith, showing us that they have more in common than we first suspected."
—**David M. Csinos, Atlantic School of Theology, founder of Faith Forward, and coauthor of** *Children's Ministry in the Way of Jesus*

"Too few of today's youth have had productive ways of engaging science and religion modeled for them because youth workers largely feel ill-equipped to do that. Sound familiar? Then this book is for you. Root's oh-so-real fictional encounters display the tensions youth face between the messages they imbibe about science from culture and the lives of faith they acquire from their families and youth groups. He unpacks these tensions and shows a way forward without avoiding the hard questions or delegitimizing accepted science or orthodox Christian faith. The dialogue between science and religion is an important one for our culture in general—all the more for youth. Please see that the youth ministers in your community get a copy of this book."
—**Jim Stump, senior editor, BioLogos.org**

"Early appetizers in this book whet my appetite for a main course that was immensely satisfying to both mind and soul. I've long held that too many persons positioned to shepherd young people do not think faithfully or critically about their practices. With *Exploding Stars*, Root offers next-level nutrition to so many who are still desperately undernourished as thoughtful ministers."
—**Dave Rahn, senior ministry advisor, Youth for Christ USA**

"With the skill of a master storyteller, Root once again pokes at the boundaries of ministry practice and theology, pressing us to see beyond our constrained, artificial limits to precisely out where young people (and their pointed questions) live. If all the universe is bound up in relationship, as Root urges, this fundamental face-to-face relationality becomes a key that unlocks the mystery of the connection between faith and science—without doing away with that mystery. Thankfully, we can finally kill the false rivalry and instead put faith and science in dialogue. Now, instead of fearing these conversations with young people, I can't wait to start them!"

—**Brad M. Griffin, youth pastor, director of the Fuller Youth Institute at Fuller Theological Seminary, and coauthor of** *Growing Young*

"Andy Root's new book offers youth workers (and everyone else) an exemplary study around debates in science and theology anchored in everyday narrative encounters with youth, reminding readers of the need for this crucial engagement for our future. Root's creative, practical, theological response weaves a theology of relationality and salvific ministry, emerging from a personal, Triune God and sustained through the everyday work of ministers. Root's theological response easily warrants our consideration for its originality and depth, standing alongside any other theologian working in the fields of science and religion. Andy engagingly provides historical reconstructions that reveal the humanity of many famous scientists and sound theological reflections around issues like the Big Bang, the immensity of the universe, the place of evolution, and even how we read Scripture. A text very accessible to anyone in ministry, this book breaks new ground, setting a hopeful table where young people, both enthralled by science and engaged in faith, can find new conversations."

—**Dean G. Blevins, Nazarene Theological Seminary**

"Andy Root tells the truth: you can't keep faith and science apart. Evolution, the Big Bang, and other scientific topics have revolutionized the way we understand ourselves, yet the church remains unprepared to deal with them. This is especially so in

youth ministry, where kids in the midst of deep intellectual formation wonder how faith can possibly make sense in light of an evolving, 14-billion-year-old cosmos. To this question Root brings his gift for storytelling, his love of science and philosophy, and his abiding concern for the pragmatics of ministry. The result is a moving, exhaustively researched, and imminently useful guide for youth workers who want to welcome science into their ministry but don't quite know how."
—**Paul Wallace, astrophysicist, lecturer in physics and astronomy, Agnes Scott College, Decatur, GA, author of** *Stars Beneath Us*

"One might not expect a book entitled *Exploding Stars, Dead Dinosaurs, and Zombies* to be a work of serious theology that rigorously engages scientific and historical research—but this is exactly what Andrew Root has achieved. It would not be an exaggeration to consider this book *the* youth ministry book on science and theology. As a highly regarded theologian of youth ministry, Root here brings the specific developmental and spiritual realities of young people into conversation with some of the most challenging questions surrounding the intersection of faith and scientific knowledge. Root is refreshingly and unapologetically theological in his engagement not only with specific scientific theories but with the socially constructed metaphysical edifice of science. Root's work is exceptionally well-researched and—just as importantly—remarkably accessible; one need not hold a PhD to follow its arguments (though even academics will be challenged by them!). *Exploding Stars* is a gamechanger, deserving a place on the bookshelves of not only all youth ministers but anyone seeking an intellectually honest and spiritually sensitive engagement with science and theology."
—**Sarah Lane Ritchie, University of St Andrews, Scotland**

"*Exploding Stars, Dead Dinosaurs, and Zombies* is an exceptionally important work for youth workers ministering with today's emerging generation of young people. It's important because it will profoundly impact the youth minister who commits to really engaging the thesis of this book. It's important because the content in this book is at the core of how young people are thinking about faith in a world of science.

In a postmodern world, which declares that we can't really be sure about anything, Root's critical realism rooted in orthodox Christian history and thought rings profoundly true and Christocentric. This book led me to contemplate the astonishing mysteries of the cosmos, the reality that we are even alive as human beings created in the image of God. And it inflamed my passion to follow Jesus Christ in ministry shaped by the relationality of God's own being and divine action. I loved this book."
—**Mike King, president and CEO of Youthfront, author of** *Presence Centered Youth Ministry*

"Thanks to this resource for the church, the long-suffering rivalry between faith and science can take a historical and deeply theological turn. Root ministers to us through these pages, inviting us to imagine a world where everything from particle physics to P. Diddy is pertinent to youth ministry and where faith and science must be reconciled if youth ministry is to have anything to do with Jesus."
—**Abigail Visco Rusert, Princeton Theological Seminary**

"Once again, Andrew Root comes to the rescue of youth leaders trying to 'keep it real' with young people. If the title alone doesn't stop you in your tracks, its basic premise should: instead of fearing the scientific knowledge that permeates young people's world, churches should embrace youths' God-given curiosity to question, explore, and investigate the world God made. *Exploding Stars, Dead Dinosaurs, and Zombies* helps youth leaders bring science and theology together as conversation partners, not sparring partners. This book will change what you talk about in youth ministry."
—**Kenda Creasy Dean, Mary D. Synnott Professor of Youth, Church and Culture, Princeton Theological Seminary, author of** *Almost Christian: What the Faith of Our Teenagers Is Telling the American Church*

Exploding Stars, Dead Dinosaurs, and Zombies

Exploding Stars, Dead Dinosaurs, and Zombies

Youth Ministry in the Age of Science

ANDREW ROOT

FORTRESS PRESS
MINNEAPOLIS

EXPLODING STARS, DEAD DINOSAURS, AND ZOMBIES
Youth Ministry in the Age of Science

Cover design: Brad Norr

Print ISBN: 978-1-5064-4674-5
eBook ISBN: 978-1-5064-4675-2

The paper used in this publication meets the minimum requirements of
American National Standard for Information Sciences — Permanence of Paper
for Printed Library Materials, ANSI Z329.48-1984.

Manufactured in the U.S.A.

This book was produced using Pressbooks.com, and PDF rendering was done
by PrinceXML.

To
David Wood
Your impact and insights have meant much.

Contents

Preface

"I wouldn't have pegged you to write a science and theology book," said my friend. I nodded my head in agreement, and she continued, "And I really wouldn't expect that you could do that through youth ministry." And yet here it is! I actually think the issue of how we engage scientific theories and think about their place next to faith is most important (and probably most interesting) with young people. My hope for those of you who wade into this book is that you'll find some help in engaging in such conversations with youth, but even more so that your own imagination would be ignited and your vision broadened for how God acts in the natural world. Yet, this book isn't easy. We will tackle some big theological ideas. For instance, chapter 10 does the heaviest theological lifting, and throughout you'll be taken into scientific and philosophical terrain. Even so, this book should be read as a story: a youth worker trying to make sense of doing ministry in our time.

In the end, this story is about ministry, but that means it is also a direct theological project. While my friend at first couldn't see it, this project actually fits very closely with the trajectory of my other work. My work has explored ministry as the location of divine action. I've made a strong push for practical theology, and particularly youth ministry, to focus on *divine action*, seeking descriptions of how human forms of agency can be connected to God's agency. Of late, this has taken me deeply into Charles Taylor's understandings of the secular, and how our late modern world makes divine action seem impossible, odd, or at the very least, contested. If ministry is to engage with real people, witnessing to divine action, then coming to grips with science and its claims about reality will be very important to all those doing ministry in our time. At the center of how I've imagined the encounter of divine and human action is *personhood* (I've even called my practical theology a "critical realist personalism"). With less jargon, I've called this "place-sharing" in other works, asserting that the location where persons share in each other's lives as an act of care and love (what I call "ministry") is the place where the living Christ, and therefore divine action, is present. This project will not depart from this focus. I'll explore how the sciences point to the possibility of a personal world, where ministry is a hidden-but-sure force, moving across the universe.

Speaking of persons, there are many to thank for their help in this project. This book is part of a John Templeton Foundation grant called "Science for Youth Ministry," housed at Luther Seminary. Drew Rick-Miller, and all the staff at the Foundation, have been wonderful to work with. This book is only one of many of the grant activities. My co-leaders in the project, David Wood and Tony Jones, have also produced important work (you can find more information about the grant at scienceym.org). Together we believe we've pushed this faith-and-science conversation deeper into the youth ministry world, a place it hadn't been. The grant was originally the brainchild of David Wood, and since working on this project, David has become a close friend. I've dedicated the book to David, because not only was the grant his original idea, but also, over the last decades, his work as much as anyone's has moved this faith-and-science conversation into the life of churches. I'm deeply thankful for our many intellectual conversations and friendship.

Nancy Lee Gauche has also worked directly with us, keeping us in order and providing amazing support. But Nancy Lee has done more for me; she's been my key partner in educating students at Luther. Our partnership has been deeply rewarding to me. Some friends were also kind enough to read the full manuscript and offer comment. Kevin Alton read with a youth worker in mind. My colleague Alan Padgett, who has written important books on theology and science, pushed me in a number of areas. He saved me from some mistakes (though in the end, any shortcomings are all mine). And my dear friend Blair Bertrand offered sharp insight, as he has many times before to my projects. I also need to thank my children, Owen and Maisy, who had to endure too many Einstein stories at dinner. And, finally, to my wife Kara, who, again, read, edited, and made my writing so much clearer. Her talents and support are more than I deserve.

Andrew Root
St. Paul, Christmas Eve, 2016

PART I

(Part Aly)

1.

Introduction: When Ministry Meets Science

If the Internet is good for anything—besides streaming TV shows, movies, and music—it is lists. Top ten lists are everywhere, and about everything. Recently I clicked on one (when, of course, I should have been doing something else): "Greatest Movie Rivals." The list included Happy Gilmore vs. Shooter McGavin from *Happy Gilmore*, Woody vs. Buzz Lightyear from *Toy Story*, Daniel LaRusso vs. Johnny Lawrence from *The Karate Kid* (remember, "Sweep the leg, Johnny!" "Put him in a body bag!!"), Harry Potter vs. Draco Malfoy from *Harry Potter*, Neo vs. Agent Smith from *The Matrix*, Maverick vs. Iceman from *Top Gun*, and controversially, number one . . . (drum roll) . . . Rocky Balboa vs. Apollo Creed from *Rocky*.

If you add sports rivals to your search you'll find more lists with a heightened level of debate. The comment threads often convey that this rivalry is for keeps, as Michigan fans tell Ohio State fans to die a slow death. Rivalries seem an essential part of the human drama; a way we make sense of our world.

We've been living with another rivalry that's had a major impact on our ministry—the rivalry between faith and science. Some people have the perception that science is out to "sweep the leg" of faith, putting our young people's Christian commitment in a body bag. Many of us respond by seeking to avoid the rivalry altogether, never creating space for our young people to discuss how scientific findings affect their faith. Others of us, with the tone of a college football fanatic, have told our young people to pick sides. Both options keep faith and science apart, treating them like oil and water, unable to be mixed.

But, if we're honest with ourselves, keeping faith and science apart is impossible, and both approaches are unhelpful to our young people. Whether we address science and its relation to faith or not, they'll be confronted in a high school classroom, on the Internet, or in a vocational calling with how, or whether, faith and science can relate. And at some point, we'll be asked by a parent or curious young person to help them make sense of evolution or the Big Bang next to the claims of Jesus and the creation account of Genesis. We get the sense that these questions are much more than merely intellectual; they stretch to the deepest level of Christian faith. Essentially, young people wonder if there is a way to think about a God who moves and acts in the world, and yet still be a smart, normal person (this will be the focus of part 1). Can you affirm evolution, the Big Bang, and quantum mechanics and still believe God heals bodies, directs events, and transforms life? In other words, in a scientific world how do we think about divine action? If we care about faith-formation, about actually helping young people live out their faith and encounter a living God in the world, then there is no way to avoid discussions about faith next to big scientific ideas. If we can find a way to explore the intersection between faith and science with young people, we can show them a living God who acts in the world.

But maybe we are overwhelmed by putting faith and science in dialogue because we've misread things from the beginning. On closer examination, we will discover that faith and science are not actually rivals. The history of the birth of science reveals that the church, in fact, had much to do with science coming into the world. The first scientists and those who supported their work were committed people of faith who acknowledged the acts of God. Although we very much live as though the rivalry is real, there is actually no clear line of demarcation separating faith and science, as there is between Vikings and Packers fans.

Science, or "natural philosophy" as it was first called, is a probing of the world. This emerged not in opposition to the acts of God, but as a way to understand the acts of God as deeply as possible. Probing the natural world, it was believed, would help us more deeply understand the creativity of God.

But all this only adds to our conundrum. Those of us doing youth ministry have often avoided the whole faith-and-science discussion, not only because we've been misinformed about this supposed rivalry, but more so because we feel inadequate and confused about the topic to begin with. Our calling, after all, is to minister to young people, not to explain string theory.

The starting point of many of the religion-and-science discussions hasn't helped us. These conversations often begin at a philosophical altitude that makes the air too thin to breathe, scrambling our minds in confusion. Ultimately, it just feels like the discussions are lodged somewhere far from the practice of ministry. We care about discussions of faith and science not for philosophical or intellectual reasons, but for ministerial ones.

That's what this book is about. This book looks at the faith-and-science discussion through the practice of ministry. We will push deeply into scientific and theological discussions, but with a mind on how this affects the practice of ministry itself. I believe that to enter the faith-and-science discussion at the level of the practice of ministry (as opposed to academic theology or philosophy) shifts things.

Our actual lives and experiences are the places where faith and science interact in real ways every day. Cancer, hurricanes and space exploration, viruses and virtual reality—we make meaning and choices guided by science and by faith all the time. These are not hypothetical or distant philosophical arguing points. As we share life with our young people, these are the places their questions and struggles will arise. These are the places we seek to meet them in ministry.

Therefore, attention throughout this project will be on *ministry*. When I say *ministry*, I *do* mean what you do with your young people on Wednesday night or on a retreat, formally leading a mission trip or informally hearing a story from their week. But I also mean something else; when I say *ministry* I mean the very form of God's action. I believe that the way God makes Godself known to the world is as a minister—as one who comes into the world to share in the world, embracing and loving it, caring for it by sharing deeply in it. God creates the world to lovingly minister to it. I think there is a way to think about scientific theories, like Big Bang cosmology and Darwinian evolution, as witnesses to God's ministry in the world.

This book, then, will not only explore how we should think about faith and science next to *our* ministries, but also next to the ministry of God. As a matter of fact, I believe that an important way to see, know, and experience the act of God is to take on the form of God's own action. Our ministries not only do things to the human beings giving and receiving ministry, but they do so because they participate in the ministry of God, connecting our human actions with divine action. Particularly in parts 2 and 3, I'll explore how some of the most central scientific theories and findings witness to *ministry*, and whether the universe itself isn't held together by ministry. It's possible to see the Big Bang, evolution, particle physics and more, as an echo of the ministerial nature of God in the world.

This leads me to give a heads-up about how this book is written. When Galileo Galilei wrote arguably the most important book in the history of science, *Dialogues Concerning the Two Chief World Systems*, he wrote it as a fictional debate, creating characters and circumstances that allowed him to make his point that the earth moves around the sun. When Einstein had his many scientific breakthroughs, they came from a story, a thought experiment, where he'd imagine himself in a fictional situation. In a similar way and as a kind of homage to Galileo and Einstein, I have done the same, creating a fictional youth worker named Jared. Like Galileo, I use a fictional character as a way to explore the significance of the faith-and-science conversation within the practice of ministry. Through his experiences, we will explore how faith-and-science conversations might affect your ministry and make a difference in forming faith in young people. Like Einstein, my thought experiment allows me to think through structures of reality, and in my case, to explore how ministry, theology, and science might come together.

While Jared and the young people we'll encounter are fictional, the circumstances they confront are very real. In actuality, Jared and his young people are a combination of many of the situations and stories that we heard in doing focus groups of youth workers and high school students for our John Templeton Foundation grant *Science for Youth Ministry*.[1] So like Galileo I'm building my characters from real people (one of the missteps for Galileo was when he named a character "Simpleton" and put the Pope's words in Simpleton's mouth. Oops!). I'm hopeful that by using this fictional story you'll begin to imagine how these discussions might impact your ministry, and even spark some ideas for how to stage faith-and-science conversations in your church.

Throughout the book you will find intricate discussions of philosophy, theology, and scientific theory, but always through story—either the story of Jared, or from the history of science, meeting people like Einstein, Galileo, Charles Darwin, Asa Gray, and more.

My greatest hope is that by the time you put this story down you'll see that scientific findings like evolution, relativity, cosmic fine-tuning, and the Big Bang are *not* moves seeking to sweep the leg of faith. But rather, in their own way, these scientific perspectives open up a possibility for us to think again about God's action and how it comes to us for the sake of ministry.

So we now begin the story. Once upon a time . . .

---

1. For more on this study, see the white paper here: http://scienceym.org/downloads/.

2.

When Youth Ministry Encounters
Science: The Story of Jared (Aly's Story)

Jared considered himself a veteran. By this point he imagined
he'd seen just about everything in ministry. By the end of the
year he'd complete twelve years in full-time youth ministry, and
for some reason crossing this marker gave him great confidence.
He felt particularly good about having logged these years in
youth ministry. Nearly every year for the last five or six, he'd
been asked to consider transitioning to another position. The
council at his church gave him every opportunity to become the
Associate Pastor for Formation, broadening his responsibilities
from young people to all people. But Jared felt an overwhelming
calling to youth ministry, choosing to remain the high school
youth pastor. This decision he wore as a badge of honor. Jared
had slowly but surely become one of the youth ministry leaders
in his small denomination, using his new leadership as a way to
encourage others to make youth ministry a long-term vocation,
as he had.

But nine months ago, Jared nearly left youth ministry. The
denomination had pegged him as the perfect person to plant a
new church in a re-gentrified neighborhood of his city. Jared
was honored; the possibilities and freedom were exhilarating to
contemplate. For weeks Jared daydreamed of the opportunity,

only rarely being tripped up by the challenges. Those challenges seemed small compared to what could be, mainly because the denomination was ready to financially support the endeavor. They were ready to give whomever the committee chose every chance to succeed. But this commitment meant the committee was ready to do its due-diligence in finding just the right person.

Before this, Jared always had a philosophy about interviews, something he had fallen into. Actually, retrospect is what made it a "philosophy." This philosophy was: Never prepare for an interview; the less you know the better. This, Jared believed, allowed him to be his most authentic self. And, more importantly, if it worked out, it was a sign that it was the Holy Spirit leading him. This lack of preparation kept his anxiety low and his self-centered ambition at bay.

This approach had worked twelve years ago when he had taken his present job. Never had Jared imagined he'd work in a church; his dream was to own his own restaurant. With a degree in business and hospitality services, he had been the assistant manager at a popular chain restaurant when the pastor of the church he was attending invited him to apply for the open Youth Pastor position. Just six months earlier Jared had started volunteering in the youth ministry, leading a small group and going on the summer mission trip. He was shocked by the invitation to apply, and not really sure it was for him. After all, he had only been going to that church because the girl he was dating had invited him. Jared had met Tanya at the campus ministry during his junior year. They were just friends those years in college. But when they found themselves in the same town they began hanging out.

Jared went into that interview shooting from the hip, freely dreaming of what could be for the youth ministry. The next day he was offered the job. He took it, reasoning that it was better than overseeing midnight appetizers at the restaurant. But within a year not only had ministry become a vocation, but Tanya had become his fiancée.

Jared would use his philosophy again when he interviewed for seminary. Jared had little interest in seminary, just as he'd had little interest in becoming a youth pastor three years earlier. Tanya had just finished grad school and their next move was to start a family. But Jared's pastor wanted him to pursue it, explaining that he could take classes while staying full-time in ministry. The church not only offered him the time for his online and intensive courses, but would also cover the cost of as many as three classes a year. If Jared could get a scholarship, almost all of the tuition would be taken care of. But to get this scholarship he'd need to interview, so dusting off his philosophy, Jared interviewed. Three weeks later a letter came granting him admission, and the scholarship, too.

Jared used this philosophy one more time when he applied to be on the denomination's planning team for their tri-annual youth gathering. Jared had never even been to one of these gatherings when he was interviewed to be one of the three core people on the programing team. Again, his philosophy worked perfectly, and Jared was now a core leader in the denomination's youth ministry.

But this church-planting interview felt different. So different that it caused Jared to question his philosophy altogether; perhaps it was nothing more than a cheap cover for his own insecurity or laziness. Jared realized that if he had a shot at the position, he'd need to know something more than the superficial about the neighborhood. So he decided he'd spend an afternoon walking, praying, and exploring it.

The neighborhood was billed as a mix between upwardly mobile young professionals, mainly in the technology sector, with an *avant-garde* art scene. People often called the neighborhood "Baby Brooklyn," using it as both an insult and a compliment, meaning it was filled with earnest overly educated young adults. As Jared walked the streets, he recognized that the stereotype was mainly true. Much to his surprise, Jared began to feel more confident that this was the position for him; after all, working with young people was his specialty. Excitement gripped him as he recognized that this position would not mean leaving youth ministry, but a radical broadening of it. And that point, he thought to himself, would be the perfect way to start the interview! After all, some of the very youth who had been through his ministry now lived in "Baby Brooklyn," and one of them, Aly, had agreed to meet him for coffee.

They decided to meet at a place called The Rusty Spoon, a coffee shop in the heart (that in many ways served *as* the heart) of the neighborhood. Jared arrived a few minutes early. As he walked through the door he noticed the colors. The floor was an aged Spanish tile of greens and maroons. Many of the tiles wore the marks of decades of traffic, broken and chipped in ways that somehow felt welcoming, like a worn soft pair of jeans. The ceiling was high and spotted with rust, gathered at the edges, and seams of the old, embossed tin panels. It appeared that at one time the whole of the ceiling had been white, but that was hard now to decipher. In particular areas whole sections of the tin had been removed to run pipes for air conditioning and ventilation. Yet like the floor, this seemed fitting.

The walls were covered with paintings and drawings. As Jared examined them it became clear that these were done by local artists, with small white tags in the right corner advertising a price. For a second, Jared thought he should get one, liking the idea that he was the kind of person who would appreciate such things. But after seeing no tag with a price less than $800, Jared gave up the fantasy, choosing a latte instead. A hurried young man took his order as a diligent young woman in turquoise, thick-rimmed glasses made his drink.

When Aly arrived, she was warm but distant. It felt odd to Jared, as if he represented something she missed but wished not to return to. It made him feel old, or at least out of place, or something he couldn't quite put his finger on. She sat down and Jared offered to buy her a drink, but she passed, explaining that she was "off" things like caramel lattes and was now only drinking her coffee black with a teaspoon of coconut oil and tumeric. When Jared said he'd get her a cup, she shot back that she had already had her two cups for the day—saying something about antioxidants, caffeine, and the blood system that Jared couldn't quite follow.

Jared was happy to see Aly. He'd watched her grow up. Aly's dad was a mean first baseman on the church softball team, and Jared had vivid memories of her from when he first arrived at the church. He remembered watching twelve-year-old Aly wandering the dandelion-filled park before the games. He also remembered retreats, mission trips, and confirmation lessons he'd shared with her as the years passed. It was great to sit across from a now twenty-four-year-old Aly. Jared felt a deep sense of appreciation as he recognized that Aly was now an adult.

For the first fifteen minutes, their conversation took them to reminiscing. Aly described how she had loved going to church, stating that her parents loved church and so did she. "It was great," she explained. "I felt safe, I guess, I mean I felt connected." Not quite directly enough for it to be awkward, but enough for Jared not to miss it, Aly thanked him for how much church and youth group meant to her growing up. "It colored almost every part of who I was," she said. Yet, like a snag in the conversation that brought a chill to his body, Jared got stuck on "who I was." It shifted him so off balance that he found himself asking like a reflex, "Who you were? What does that mean?"

Aly froze. It was as if she had come to their meeting with a secret, telling herself when she reached for the door of The Rusty Spoon, *whatever happens keep it hidden.* Now she was outed, and the look on her face gave it away. "Well, I mean it is still part of me . . ." she stumbled. "I mean it was . . . I mean, well, honestly, I'm just not sure about the whole thing."

"What whole thing?" Jared asked, trying his best to catch himself, pushing down any signs of defensiveness, or worse, the existential crisis that his *whole* ministry had been impotent.

Aly paused, and then like someone standing on a tall cliff readying themselves to jump into a cold lake below, she breathed in deeply and jumped. "Well, I mean, I think church is still important; I'm just not sure that there is, like, a God who does stuff in the world. I mean, I understand why people in the past believed that, and that was really true to them. They lived or died because of what God did. But we now know about things like disease and germs and genes. I mean, that's what I studied in college. And now I work with this start-up that is working on the tech end of gene therapy. I guess I confront it every day, that people's genes make them what they are, and maybe with the right technology we can heal some illness or make people better. It makes no sense to wonder if God makes infants sick for some, like, cosmic purpose."

"Wow," Jared responded. "Those are important thoughts." The existential crisis could no longer be completely contained, so Jared asked, "Did you have these questions back when you were in the youth group?"

Aly responded quickly. "No . . . well, I mean, yes." Taking another deep breath, she said, "Yes. I mean, I couldn't have put it like that, and I had no understanding of genes or gene therapy or anything like that. But, I really did wonder a lot, like tossing and turning in bed, about whether God causes things in the world. But I was too young and scared to face the facts, I think."

"What facts?" Jared asked.

"I mean the fact that God is mostly unnecessary. Like, I have this friend, Ronny, who plays guitar here on Tuesday nights, and he says, 'You can't live without science, but you sure can live without God.' And he doesn't mean that as, like, some lame punk statement of rebellion; it just seems true. Like, I know so many people in this neighborhood that have no need for God at all, and yet they do so many good things, marching against corrupt corporations, starting charitable-giving apps, and doing all kinds of ecological activism. And almost none of them do it *for* God, or even think they *need* God."

Shocked by the unexpected direction their conversation had taken, all Jared could think to respond with was, "What about your family?"

"What do you mean?" Aly replied.

"I mean they still believe and go to church, right? I mean I saw them at the late service last week."

"I guess."

"You guess?" Jared asked

"Well, yes, it's surely part of their life, and honestly, both that and my own experience at church keeps me from, like, totally abandoning and turning my back on what I learned growing up. I watched my mom's faith make such a difference when my sister got sick. But then again, it was *science* that healed her. And my parents may have been praying, but they were also driving hundred of miles and cashing in their 401Ks to see specialist after specialist, hoping that science would save their daughter. So it just seems to me that if there is a God, he just creates prob-

lems that science seems to be able to solve. I mean, I have to be
honest, science saved my sister. God just allowed her to get sick
in the first place. Or maybe it is just easier and more logical to
believe it wasn't God at all, but her genes or bad luck."

Good Science, Bad theology

Aly then stopped herself. "I'm sorry, Jared, I know you didn't
come to talk about this . . . I guess I've just grown up."

GROWN UP. Jared thought, *what does that mean, grown up?*

Aly said this with an air of confidence; there seemed to be a
certain bravado in those words.

Jared could only ask, "Growing up means . . . ?"

Aly returned, "It means I know enough now that I can choose
science over God—I think."

Just as Jared got tripped up over Aly speaking about her faith
in the past tense, he felt the same snag on Aly's ". . . I think."
But now wasn't the time to follow that trail. They spent the next
forty minutes discussing the neighborhood.

Jared left "Baby Brooklyn" ready for his interview, but now
with a stab of desperation. And this stab bled a little. He had the
split-second thought that if he was asked to plant this church,
then he wouldn't have to deal with the questions Aly's experience raised in regard to his ministry. He felt the intoxicating lull
that directing our minds toward a future dream or desire can be
to the anxieties and burdens of the present. Jared knew that the
impact of the conversation with Aly would not soon leave him,
but he had little time to consider it. His mind was swimming in
the warm waters of his future ambitions.

3.

When Youth Ministry Encounters Science: The Story of Jared (Martin's Story)

The disappointment had left an almost metallic taste in Jared's mouth. Just two and a half weeks after meeting with Aly, Jared interviewed once, and then again before being passed over for the position. He felt heartbroken and foolish. He had actually allowed himself to mentally move into "Baby Brooklyn," even spent a whole evening searching the Internet for real estate and schools for his kids. He tried his best not to allow the disappointment to show, but he was stunned. The regret not only sat on his tongue, but also wrapped itself around his knees, sapping the energy he had for his youth ministry job. When he would recognize this melancholy, anxiety would follow. *Why am I feeling this way?* he wondered. *I've always loved this job . . . but now, I feel so freaking tired.* He continued going through the motions, but the sluggishness and anxiety was taking a toll. Occasionally his mind would go back to the conversation with Aly, but he had no energy to consider the challenges that her story presented to his ministry.

By the time Jared loaded sixteen high schoolers into a bus for the summer mission trip, the emotions had become less extreme, but his energy had not yet returned. It was a good trip, though Jared felt little of the exhilaration he'd had in previous years. Yet, he did recognize a deep-seated sense of enjoyment of the young people themselves. He wondered if he had felt this before. He was sure he had, but the disappointment had somehow washed away the cluttered ambition that made building a program more rewarding than the young people themselves. It was as if before the wave of disappointment, Jared was driven to build his ministry into a shiny successful city. But now that wave had crashed over him and washed that away. In its place were just the young people themselves—funny, interesting, and insightful in their own right.

By the end of the trip Jared could feel his energy returning, but it was now directed toward just enjoying the young people, as opposed to building them, or the ministry, into something. But Jared couldn't think about this too deeply. When he did, thoughts of Aly returned, and he worried that his shift to just enjoying the young people would leave them in worse shape than Aly in the future.

When Jared allowed himself to think about his conversation with Aly, he imagined that at some point between her youth group days and her residence in Baby Brooklyn she had just let go, or subtracted faith from her life. Jared imagined that science in particular was a kind of formidable crowbar that pried faith from her life. Jared knew there was no way to keep young people away from science, and at a certain level he understood that he himself was as dependent as anyone on its findings and accomplishments. But, he couldn't help it; somehow he blamed science for subtracting faith from Aly's life. If Jared had his way, he'd just keep these scientific tools away from young people. *If they didn't have any crowbars, there'd be a lot less prying apart.*

Of course, he wasn't sure what kind of world he'd live in if this could actually be accomplished. But, if subtraction of faith was the problem, then the tools used to do the subtracting were the culprit.[1]

1. Here I'm leaning on the work of Charles Taylor, who will become very important in the chapters to follow. For more on subtraction, and using it as a misread of our situation, see my *Faith Formation in a Secular Age* (Grand Rapids, MI: Baker, 2017).

These thoughts were racing in Jared's mind as he rested on his bunk after another day on the mission trip. But like being awoken from a dream, he was pulled from his contemplations. "So are you ready for the zombie apocalypse or what?" He realized quickly that the question wasn't for him. Rather, Martin, an eleventh-grader, was addressing Louis, a tenth-grader. Jared quickly looked at his watch and noticed that it was still twenty-five minutes until lights out. So Jared decided to listen in, ready for a laugh.

"No," Louis responded, the tone of his voice signaling concern that he was soon to become the butt of some joke.

"Well, you'd better be," Martin returned with intensity and a pointed finger. "You had really better be."

Martin had been part of youth group since ninth grade. His family had come from a much smaller church because they wanted Martin and his younger sister to be part of a youth ministry. Yet it always seemed like Martin was more into sports than faith. He was a smart and athletic kid, but no honor student or varsity athlete. And similarly he rarely missed a youth ministry activity, but had little interest in leadership. He was always just there. Not necessarily a wallflower, but rarely risking much other than his presence and a few sarcastic comments framed as jokes.

Jared felt like he knew Martin well, but then again he wondered if anyone *really* knew Martin, or if Martin even knew himself. Watching Martin ask his seemingly ridiculous question, Jared felt like he was seeing him for the first time. "Seriously," Martin said, now raising his voice as he directed his question to the full room of six high school boys and Jared. "What are you chumps going to do when the mass extinction comes? Because I promise you fools, it's coming."

Everyone laughed, assuming Martin was joking. "I'm serious, dumbasses!" Martin shot back.

"Hey, watch the language," Jared hollered from his bottom bunk. But now Jared was in the conversation, no longer just a spectator on the fringes. And that was good, because he was taken by Martin's intensity. *Did he really believe this? What was Martin getting at?*

"Martin," Jared said, "I don't think anyone is laughing at you; we just don't know what you mean. What do you mean? Do you believe the TV show *The Walking Dead* is a documentary?"

Martin still had a hard exterior to him, not sure he was ready to let his guard down, but ready to answer Jared's questions. "No—well—maybe. There might not be a true zombie apocalypse, how would I know? But, I am sure a mass extinction is coming," Martin said.

"Why?" Jared asked. "Why are you so sure?"

"Well, besides all the evidence of an ecological crisis, it's just science."

"What do you mean it's 'just science'?" Jared asked, intrigued.

"I mean," Martin said, sensing he was climbing to some intellectual high ground, "It's j-u-s-t science."

"HOW?" Jared shot back with enough force for Martin to remember who he was talking to.

This seemed to mellow Martin enough to take a breath and shift from bombastic pundit to teacher. As Martin began to explain, Jared was now sure this was indeed the first time he had *seen* Martin. He had known Martin for almost three years, spent hours and weekends with him, but only now was Martin truly revealing himself.

"What I mean is that mass extinction is part of the process of evolution. We're living in the time when mammals have excelled on this planet, but only because the lizard era of dinosaurs met its mass extinction. So, okay, you're right, I'm not sure if our extinction will be in fifteen years or five thousand years, but it's coming. That's just how evolution works."

"And you believe all that?" Jared asked, shocked by Martin's ability to articulate this position. "Well again," Martin said, "it's just science."

"And you believe everything science says?"

"Mmm," said Martin, "I'm not sure. But I don't want to be one of those people that doesn't, who is too scared to face the fact that earth is four billion years old and that our lifetime is so short it doesn't even show up on a timeline of the planet. That actually, the whole history of human beings makes barely a blip on the timeline! I want to be brave enough to face that, not be too scared to know that mass extinction is coming."[2]

"What about God in all this? Do you think God will allow or cause this mass extinction?" Jared asked, now more honestly probing for himself than for Martin or the boys listening.

Martin looked as if he'd never really thought about how those things go together. He bit his lower lip. "I don't know," he said. "Honestly, I don't know what God does—diseases, earthquakes, other bad stuff—I don't know. It just, I guess, seems to me that evolution or natural selection makes a lot more sense in regard to what causes stuff. It's actually easier. All you need is a butt load of time, and not, like, some dude doing good or bad things. I mean I still like God; I guess I just think natural selection causes stuff and makes more sense. I guess I'm just down with Darwin, that dude's dope."

The rest of the room laughed.

---

2. "There are 'five to ten million species' alive today, and 'five to ten billion species that have come and gone over evolutionary time.'" Christopher L. Fisher, *Human Significance in Theology and the Natural Sciences* (Eugene, OR: Pickwick, 2010), 238.

4.

When Youth Ministry Encounters Science: The Story of Jared (Sasha's Story)

Jared wasn't sure if the conversation with Martin had reinvigorated him or sent him to the precipice of despair. It had reinvigorated him in the sense of energy; after the mission trip he felt a new verve for his ministry. But the shadow side was that he felt like he had nothing to say in response to Martin. Energy without direction is its own kind of despair, and that's right where Jared was when Trent called asking Jared to have breakfast with him and his daughter Sasha.

Trent was an African American man in his late forties. Jared had known Trent for a while. Trent was the core leader for a fundraiser that the youth group worked with, and Jared always found Trent to be encouraging. Jared knew that Trent worked at the same university that Tanya, Jared's wife, had gotten her master's degree from. But what Trent did there, Jared wasn't sure.

Sasha was a ninth-grader. As she followed her dad into the restaurant, making her way to the booth that Jared sat in, he noticed how tall she had become; she now looked more like a woman than a girl. Sasha was known through the youth ministry for being a brainiac; even as a ninth-grader, she was in many advanced-placement junior and senior courses. Everyone knew that Sasha was considering going to college early, and Jared figured that this might be the very reason they were meeting this morning.

As Trent and Sasha squeezed onto the same bench across from Jared, he noticed just how yellow the restaurant was. It was almost too bright—a kind of artificial sunshine that made Jared a little nauseous. Jared was uneasy, but ready to give the advice he had about Sasha going to college early, even ready to provide his take on schools. Of course there was small talk to begin, led mainly by Trent, who asked about the possible renovations on the youth room and how Tanya was liking her new job.

In the middle of responding, a pimply-faced waiter interrupted Jared, beaming a faux smile above the yellowest button-down shirt Jared had ever seen. Hanging slightly cocked to the right, on the left pocket of the brain-burning shirt was a neon-orange name tag that Jared couldn't quit make out. It was all so bright it hurt Jared's eyes. "What can I get you folks?" the waiter asked, so inauthentically cheerful it was comical. Each of them stammered out their wishes.

As the glowing waiter walked way, Jared knew it was pointless to return to the question. It was all for decorum anyhow. Trent wanted to meet with Jared for some purpose, and this interruption provided just the segue to move into it.

"So, Jared," Trent shifted. "We've been having quite a conversation at our house."

"Oh?" Jared responded, leaning in, ready to offer his wisdom on Sasha's decision to go to college early.

"So you know I'm a physics professor at the university," Trent continued. Jared hadn't known, but feeling that they knew each other too well to admit that, he nodded, wondering if his red face clashed against the bright yellow of the restaurant. "Well," said Trent, "I'm an experimental physicist, and a lot of what I do focuses on engineering issues. What I mean is that we experimental physicists try and create actual experiments to prove—or disprove—the perspectives of theoretical physicists."

Jared just nodded again, holding his breath, as if it would keep the embarrassment from washing over him.

"Actually," Trent detoured, his voice filling with pride, "did you know that I worked on part of the particle tubes at CERN?"

"No!" Jared blurted, trying as hard as he could to hide the fact that he had no idea what *surn* was. Perhaps if he said as little as possible, he'd keep from embarrassing himself. "Yep," Trent said with a beat of confidence. "It was an exciting summer. I loved Switzerland." Jared was trying as hard as he could to put the clues together—*physics, Switzerland, surn, some tubes or something*—he racked his brain to try and figure out what it was. Jared just sat as still as he could, hoping the conversation would pass into some area he could follow. Jared later discovered that CERN was the particle accelerator that got a lot of press a few years back, as people worried it would actually end the world in a physics-induced nova.

"Well," Trent continued, "I used to be preeettty hard on those theoretical physicists. I mean I always appreciated their brilliance, but their self-importance always got me. Like, come on, seeking a 'theory of everything'! I get that, that's science, but if you can't prove it in some observable way, why all the hubbub?"

Jared was even more lost now than before.

"See," Trent continued on his roll, "my focus on the experimental elements of physics, I think, allowed me to keep my faith and my science separate. I worked on particular experiments and I didn't need to think too much beyond that. I mean, don't get me wrong, I had my questions and I knew there were some big contradictions between what I held as true scientifically and what I believed in relation to my faith. But I didn't need to think about it too much. And that worked okay for me."

Jared couldn't believe this. Here again was this damn science thing popping up. But this time he had no idea really what Trent was getting at.

"See, I could do this, until this one," Trent lovingly pointed at Sasha. "It appears," Trent said with a voice filled with pride, "I somehow got myself a theoretical physicist on my hands." Now smiling ear to ear, Trent said, "I don't know how that happened!" He winked at Sasha.

Okay, okay, Jared repeated to himself, using those words to lower his anxiety, thinking, *This is indeed about colleges.* Jared wasn't sure he had any helpful advice about physics programs, and this was the first time he had ever even heard about the difference between experimental and theoretical physics. But he knew that the local Christian college, where he was adjuncting a class once a year, had a strong focus on the natural sciences. Figuring this was the reason for their conversation, Jared interjected.

"I see . . . Well, if Sasha is thinking of going to college early, I would really recommend Kappel. Not only will she get a great science education, but she'll do so in a way that really deepens her faith."

But now something was wrong; the easy disposition of Trent turned stiff, and Sasha who had been quiet but engaged, looked straight down at the table. Jared realized immediately that he had made a misstep.

"That's the thing," Trent said. "Sasha is having a hard time seeing how physics and faith go together. I've always found a way to just move between my faith and my physics, but Sasha, I guess because she's more in the theoretical bend, can't do that. So our conversations have been pretty intense at home."

"Good," Jared said, hoping to find a way to redeem himself from tripping over his assumptions.

"But, Sasha does have some questions I can't answer," Trent said, "so at the least, maybe you could give us some direction?" Jared thought back to how little he had to say to Martin. What could he possibly say to Sasha? It appeared the crowbar of science had struck again, digging out someone's faith.

As Jared anticipated Sasha's questions, the restaurant glow somehow felt even brighter. It was if the chemical insecurity in Jared's brain was mixing with the yellow hue in his mind, turning its nauseating brightness from a nine to an eleven.

Trent finally interrupted the silence. "Ask him," he said, nudging Sasha with his elbow.

Sasha, who had not mustered as much a word in the first twenty minutes of their time together, then unloaded with the articulation of someone ready to skip ahead to graduate school—forget college.

Looking right into Jared's eyes, she said, "My issue is really space, I guess. The universe is so huge and our galaxy is just this little thing, tucked away in this little corner. I mean, when you start to think about how huge the universe is, it is hard to believe that we're really very significant. But, what bothers me is just how the Bible makes this little place that we know is in the middle of nowhere, so significant. The Bible seems to make what happens on this little, almost literally, *speck of dust* so important. Like, the Bible and Christianity actually seem to believe this whole huge expanse of space was created just for us, who are so small."

Jared felt tranquilized, as if a dart was shot from across the room, striking him in the chest. The stunning poison was a mix of shock at how articulate Sasha was, with Jared's own insecurity.

Sasha continued. "And not to sound stupid, but what if aliens show up? From a pure mathematical perspective, it seems possible that there is life out there. I mean NASA is finding planets beyond our solar system that seem to be candidates for life. But Jesus lived on this little planet in the middle of nowhere. So what will we do when aliens show up? Could we possibly still believe in the God of the Bible and Jesus?"[1]

"Wow," said Jared, looking at Trent for some help.

But Trent was the opposite of helpful, returning Jared's look with an expectant, "So, pastor, what would you say?"

Jared's nausea had heightened to full-on sickness; to cope, he decided not to move.

Sasha was now geared up, so she filled the empty space. "I mean, we used to believe that earth was at the center of our solar system and the sun revolved around the earth and that there really couldn't be anything outside of our solar system. But we now know better, so how can religion still make human beings the center of everything? I just don't want to be part of a belief system that is childish enough to ignore science."

These last words seemed harsh, so Trent tried to soften them. "I think what Sasha means, is that she doesn't want us as a church to make the same mistake we did with Galileo."

---

1. We'll go deeper into Sasha's concern about aliens later in this project, but it is interesting for now to see the difference between cosmologists and biologists. Ian Barbour explains: "Most scientists are open to the possibility of intelligent life on relatively nearby galaxies, though biologists seem to consider it less likely than do astronomers or science fiction writers." *Religion and Science: Historical and Contemporary Issues* (San Francisco: HarperSanFrancisco, 1997), 215.

5.

Is Faith for Immature Babies?

It was one of those beautiful years where Christmas had a magical feel to it. The reds and greens could almost be smelled, and every breath seemed to hit Jared with a wave of cinnamon and mint. In years past, the Christmas season had come and gone, almost more with fatigue than wonder. It had actually been a while since Jared had felt the marvel of Christmas. He blamed this on the busy church schedule. The last handful of years the darkness of Advent seemed to speak to him more than the bright glowing candlelight of Christmas.

If you'd asked Jared back in late spring, summer, or even early fall, he would have assumed that this Christmas would be his darkest. Even now, nine months since his voyage into "Baby Brooklyn," the wounds of being passed over for the job hadn't healed. Surprisingly, though, something had changed this Christmas, and Jared was feeling its joy and mystery.

As Jared walked to the front of the candlelit church, taking his seat as a reader, he knew that much of the awakening to the Christmas mystery was because of his children. Sam was now seven, and Svea was five, and their excitement for the season had become intoxicating; this was the first year that their Christmas anticipation was palpable and the magic seizing.

From Jared's seat up front, facing the congregation, he could spot Tanya and the kids. Svea was kicking her legs with exuberance. Every third or fourth kick her butt would bounce off the pew in excitement. Jared tried not to giggle as he watched her, but the happiness welled too much within him to keep the biggest smile from spreading across his face.

But a little bit of nerves also accompanied Jared's Christmas joy. He did, after all, need to stand up and read a long biblical text to a full sanctuary. It was no big deal; he'd done this many times before, but its importance kept him reviewing the passage. He looked particularly for big words, reviewing the names and cities, hoping that with a little more repetition he'd avoid tripping over them. But as he skimmed the text again, he noticed how this coming child was bringing "hope to the world." *A child who brings hope to the world*, Jared thought. *And does this child have something for aliens? And why does this child come to this planet? To this small place, in this Milky Way, in this little galaxy, on this small blue marble?* As Jared thought about these questions he spotted Sasha's dad, Trent, in his usual spot, today in a shiny full suit. Looking down the pew, Jared spotted Sasha sitting quietly with her perfect posture, her left knee flush with her mother's right.

As Jared watched them, out of the corner of his eye he spotted Martin. Seeing him, Jared thought, *And what about mass extinctions? Does this child have something to say to deep time and the waves of extinctions that have come and gone?* Catching Martin's eye, Jared nodded a "hello." Martin returned the nod. "This child" and these questions gave Jared a hollow kind of dread in his stomach, but oddly, the Christmas season—and the anticipation of his own children—was too much to allow that dread more than a passing shiver. The mystery of the season seemed to remind Jared there were answers out there. And the next thing he knew he was reciting the text, feeling the nearness of this child as he read to his own children and all the children of God.

Sitting back down, Jared exhaled the last bit of anxiety and directed his gaze to Tanya and the kids. He hadn't noticed her before, but in the row right behind Tanya, on a pew instead of a bench in The Rusty Spoon back in Baby Brooklyn, was Aly. She was alone.

The service ended and people hustled to their coats, off to their Christmas Eve celebrations. Jared said hello to families and youth, wishing everyone a Merry Christmas. As he did, he felt a touch on his elbow. It was Aly.

"Hey, Merry Christmas!" Jared exuberantly proclaimed.

"Merry Christmas," said Aly, rather flatly.

"Are you here with your family?" Jared asked, curious why she was sitting alone.

"No." Aly's eyes became wet and the rims fought hard to keep the tears back, quivering rapidly. "No," she repeated. "My sister is sick again." With those words her eyelids failed, and two tears escaped each eye, streaking Aly's cheeks. "My parents are with her; it happened so fast and looks pretty bad. Seven years clean of cancer and now it's back, and bad." The sadness took Jared's breath away.

"I'm sorry." It was all he could think to say.

"I just felt like I needed to be at church," Aly said. "I don't know why, I told you last time we met that I don't think I believe any of this, but I really didn't know what else to do. I honestly feel so childish and weak running back here . . . but it is Christmas and my little sister has needles and tubes in her body."

Jared had nothing to say; he just connected his eyes with Aly's and stood with her. After a few seconds, Svea found her dad and threw her body on Jared's leg, rubbing residue of Christmas cookies all over his best pants with her sticky hands. Svea shouted, "Let's go, let's go, Christmas! Christmas! Christmas!"

Jared picked up Svea, grunting as he lifted the five-year-old to his hip. Looking Svea in the eyes, Jared said to her, "This is my friend Aly, and she's had some very bad news about her sister."

Svea eyes pierced Jared's and she said in response, "On Christmas?," her voice at an octave that communicated a deep injustice.

"Yes," Jared responded. "Her little sister is very sick."

In a moment that can only be called precious, Svea took her arms from Jared's neck and lunged toward Aly, placing her little arms around Aly's neck. As she did, Aly cried, closing her eyes to take in the compassion of this five-year-old.

"Thanks," Aly said to Svea. "I needed that; I really did." Jared set Svea down and sent her off to get her coat and find Tanya.

"Call me if you need anything," Jared said.

Aly breathed deeply and wiped the tears from her eyes, using both palms to clear her face. "I will," she said. "I'm sorry about crying, I really do feel childish."

"For crying?" Jared asked. "That seems right to me."

"No," said Aly. "I guess I just feel childish that I ran back to church when things went bad. I don't know if I want to blame God or ask God to do something. I honestly don't believe God does things in our world and yet here I am at church, crying."

BROUGHT TO YOU BY *FAMILY GUY*

Carl Sagan, the great popularizing astrophysicist, narrated and co-wrote one of the most successful PBS shows ever. Actually, it would be the most watched, crushing even Big Bird's *Sesame Street*, until Ken Burns released his documentary *The Civil War*. Sagan's blockbuster was *Cosmos: A Personal Voyage*, which aired in the 1980s. It used cutting-edge special effects (at least for the time) to take the viewer into galaxies, exploring planets and the universe. But the real sign that Sagan's show was a true hit is that in 2014 it was remade.

This time, the show jumped from PBS to Fox, and on prime-time. This was made possible by the show, *Family Guy*. Well, not directly, but *Family Guy*'s creator Seth MacFarlane produced and financially floated the show, believing it essential for teaching us science's true origin story. The reboot was called *Cosmos: A Spacetime Odyssey*. And its narrator was Neil deGrasse Tyson, who claimed that Sagan's original show had been the catalyst for his own scientific passions. The new show premiered March 9, 2014, with about nine million viewers.

The third episode, "When Knowledge Conquers Fear," begins with Tyson walking out into a desert scene, approaching a baby as it lies in a basket, the starry night sky spread above it. Tyson explains that this baby is humanity, and this baby has no idea why the world is like it is. This baby is ignorant and confused. When this baby humanity sees a comet, it assumes war is coming or a king is dying. "Stupid baby," Tyson as much says. But with the Enlightenment, just some three hundred years ago this dumb baby began to grow up. Tyson then takes us into the story of the breakthroughs of Englishmen Edmond Halley and Isaac Newton in the 1700s.

Tyson ends the episode by returning to our baby beneath the sky. Now, he tells us, because of Newton (and the Enlightenment he was part of), this dumb baby is growing up; the baby is, for the first time, understanding its world. Never mind, of course, that Newton saw God deeply within creation with no conception that all the wisdom of the men and women of faith before the Enlightenment was in any way stupid, immature, or backward. Rather, Newton's very motivation was to read the book of nature with as much devotion as he had read the scriptures. But that is far from Tyson's point; his point is that *science is the mature position of the future, while faith is for babies*.

This is what someone like the Aly of our story believes. Even now with her sister sick, she feels stupid for assuming that God cares. She doesn't want to be the kind of person who is weak enough to need some divine being to help her cope. And she's not alone—Sasha and Martin, also, in their own ways, seem to contend that science is the mature position. Faith is for those unable to cope with the stark reality that we are alone in an impersonal world.

To see how we got here we must explore how science became the mature position of those brave enough to face the future, and faith became seen as childish and primitive.

THE CAMBRIDGE DONS

According to Neil deGrasse Tyson, Halley and Newton's big breakthrough was discovering that the universe itself was ordered. The phenomena of the sky, like comets, were actually not ruptures in the order of the universe. Rather they conformed to the laws of the universe like everything else. Newton had shown through mathematical equation that gravity itself was a law that all matter must obey, whether on earth or in the heavens.

"General laws" were the great discovery of this group of professors at Cambridge, often called the "Cambridge Dons," that would radically change our conception of the world we live in.

Things no longer seemed as capricious as before; these laws gave us the very code that consistently allowed us to see the firm order of the universe. And these general laws were embedded not in the narrative stories of a people, but in the numbers and equations that seemed to avoid all the traps of subjectivity and emotion.

It's not that laws were in opposition to God. Israel had long ago discovered its own laws that they too believed ordered the universe. And much like the discovery of the Cambridge Dons, they came with a eureka. It was a eureka of revelation! But what was discovered was very different. Israel discovered the very name of God (Exodus 3). They discovered that at the center of all things was indeed a single personal force, and there were laws that revolved around stories of persons who encountered this personal force, this one true God. And how, after encountering, you should live for this personal force by honoring and attending to persons in the world (by not coveting their possessions, or stealing their livestock, or lying to their face, or smashing their heads in with a rock—i.e., the Ten Commandments, per Exodus 20).

Most of these Cambridge Dons embraced Israel's laws. Newton, while unorthodox on many points, believed deeply that he was only discovering the *natural* laws that God himself had put in place. These general natural laws were assumed to be delivered by the personal hand of God. But now in place, they were ever consistent, and this could be proven with equations—not through personal stories but hard numbers.

This allowed for cracks to begin to grow that would soon become a gully as the centuries unfolded. Attention could now be given to phenomena by attending to only the general laws. There was no need to speak of personal forces beyond these laws. As a matter of fact, attention to the general laws seemed not only to garner advances but was consistently productive. The effect of gravity could be replicated again and again, but the encounter with the personal force called God could not. This God of the law of Israel seemed to appear and then disappear; to answer prayers, but then not; to cause something, and then cause nothing.[1] The laws of nature that Neil deGrasse Tyson so admires were indeed amazing, but their discovery also brought a great shift. The laws of Enlightenment moved us to see the order in which we lived as an *impersonal one*.[2] Where Israel's laws rehearsed and then bent our lives to a personal order of a divine being with a name, the general laws of the Enlightenment required no personal being at all. And soon those following Halley and Newton began to wonder if there was indeed no Great Oz behind the curtain of these laws. Maybe all there was were these impersonal laws and no great mind beyond them running things.

1. This kind of thing made much more sense to our ancestors and even today to those that have experience of the personhood of God, because this is the shape of a personal reality. But once this is ruled out of bounds and science moves to the objective of overruling the personal, then God can seem to disappear. This is Roger Scruton's point in his important Gifford Lectures published as *The Face of God*. The quote here is a capsulation of this thought: "I have suggested that the arguments that we might use to reconcile belief in God with the scientific worldview, however cogent in themselves, raise another problem for the believer, which is the problem of God's presence in the world. Where do we find him and how? The ghost of an answer to that question is this: God is a person, and he reveals himself as persons do, through a dialogue involving those three critical words, 'I,' 'you' and 'why?'. That answer brings us up against another problem raised by the scientific worldview, which is the problem of reconciling our beliefs about persons with the science of the human being." *The Face of God* (London: Bloomsbury, 2012), 23.
2. "In any case, this general parti pris for the impersonal may then spill over onto materialism, as the outlook which 'science' has developed. But it is interesting that this is not always so. Some people who opted for science over religion were later influenced by the sense of spiritual flatness which I mentioned above. They felt both sides of the cross-pressure. Indeed, this malaise seems to grow among educated elites in the late nineteenth century. They turned to various forms of spiritualism, para-scientific researches, para-psychology and the like. In one case, that of Frederick Myers, the two moves were successive; first a loss of Christian faith owing to Darwinism, then a return to the spiritual, but within the bounds of an impersonal framework. He spoke of himself as 're-entering through the scullery the heavenly mansion out of which I had been kicked through the front door.' A spiritual-but-not-Christian (or Jewish or Muslim) position, adopted on something like these grounds, has remained a very widespread option in our culture." Charles Taylor, *A Secular Age* (Cambridge, MA: Belknap Press of Harvard University Press, 2007), 364.

INTRODUCING THE COMPREHENSIVE SOCIAL
PRACTICE OF "SCIENCE"

What Neil deGrasse Tyson and others like him assume when they talk about "science" is not necessarily particular findings or even theories of a particular discipline or approach. Rather, what Tyson and others mean when they say "science" is a *form* of *ultimate* social practice (I'll call it "comprehensive" because it looks to provide a life-philosophy or even religion). Social practices are things certain people actually perform. They are powerful because they direct the ways you act in the world. Of course, people are born into communities of social practice; therefore they may get a head start. But even these natives must actually *learn* the forms of a social practice—they must learn how to practice this form. But because they do, these practices are never done alone, but within a social group that has a history and tradition. The very point of a social practice is to socialize, or, we could say, *convert* a person into a way of life.[3]

There is a lot to say about this, but for now what we can see is that "science," as Tyson and others mean it, is a *comprehensive* practice that provides a way of actually being in the world. When Tyson and others say "science," they often mean it as a form of practice that is superior to all others, almost as if it were its own religion. The core commitment of this comprehensive social practice is "a view of the universe framed in general laws. The ultimate [commitment] is [to] an impersonal order of regularities in which all particular things exist," bound *only* in time and space.[4]

MacFarlane rebooted *Cosmos* not just to make money but with a larger purpose. He hopes it will socialize (convert) people further into the *comprehensive* social practice of "science," helping them learn these practices by being engaged in the stories of "science's" history. This is clearly why, for Tyson, the whole story starts not with the deep time of evolution or even the Big Bang, but with the seventeenth century. It starts here because it's

---

3. I'm leaning here in part on Thomas Kuhn's *Structure of Scientific Revolutions.*
4. Charles Taylor, *A Secular Age*, 362.

during this time of the European Enlightenment that the foot-ings of this new form of "science" are laid (coming to fruition in the nineteenth century). Tyson might think he is giving us an origin story of existence, saying, "This is just how things actu-ally are." But what he is actually doing is telling us the origin story of the social practice of "science." And that story, for good or ill, began in the seventeenth century.

Logically, then, Tyson opposes faith (taking his potshots at it on his NatGeo show *Star Talk*[5]) because faith is also a social prac-tice—which like this form of "science" makes ultimate claims.[6] Maybe because of this, Tyson sees faith as corrupt and deeply misguided. But really what bothers him is that faith's central commitment as a social practice is to assert that the world we live in is not impersonal at all, but rather is a deeply personal place (that there is a personal force called God who minds the whole of the universe).

This irks Tyson and his ilk, not really because any astronom-ical or biological theories oppose this commitment to a personal universe (most don't), but rather because faith's claim that the

5. See episode 9 of season 2. Taylor adds texture: "So then as now, in post-Galilean Europe and post-Scopes trial America, a fragilization of faith partly due to disen-chantment, combined with an internalization of this disenchantment, produces a face-off between 'religion' and 'science' of a strangely intra-mural quality. This is the face-off which figures so prominently in the ex parte 'death of God' story so popu-lar among unbelievers. One party, moved purely by the interests of 'science', that is, finding an adequate explanation for the undeniable facts, squares off against another, mainly actuated by an extra-scientific agenda, that of maintaining cherished beliefs and/or traditional authority." *A Secular Age*, 331.

6. Mikael Stenmark explains in detail: "Religious practitioners either grow up in a religious community or at a later stage in life become a part of a religious commu-nity. The longtime members of the community train the newly converted in reli-gious practice. These newcomers learn how to participate in worship, how to read and interpret sacred texts, how to encounter the divine reality, and so on. Hence we have at least two significant groups of religious people: the old and the new believers. In science too we can distinguish between old and new scientists, although one can-not grow up in a scientific community as one can in a religious community. With regard to this point we find a crucial difference between the two practices. The prac-titioners of science enter the scientific community at a later stage in life and the long-time members of the community train them in doing science properly. They learn the content of the currently accepted theories of the discipline, how to use instru-ments and collect information, how to interpret the phenomena of the natural and social world. Hence, looking at the world with the 'eye of faith' or with the 'eye of science' is something one has to learn. It is part of a social training process." *How to Relate Science and Religion* (Grand Rapids, MI: Eerdmans, 2004), 19.

world is personal chafes against the social practice of his own life philosophy, which he calls "science." So Tyson must speak out against faith as a social practice because he's a high priest of the *comprehensive* social practice of "science," ordained by television. What Aly is rubbing up against is *not the findings or theories of science* but the form of the social practice called "science."[7] When Jared sat with her at The Rusty Spoon she explained this friction well. She told Jared that she just no longer believed that God caused things in the world. She wasn't saying, necessarily, that she was an atheist. She still saw value in the social practice of faith. She was appreciative of how the social practice of faith impacted her family, and she was oddly comforted by the thought that the social practice of faith still existed. She saw how it could help people. But on that early spring day, she was just ready to state that the world was an impersonal place and that the things happening in it were caused by impersonal laws with no real personal being behind it all. This comprehensive social practice of "science," she told Jared, made more sense. It's genes and germs, not God or some other personal force that causes people to get sick.

Yet, on this Christmas Eve, Aly is back, swimming again (even if just for an hour) in the social practice of faith. She's still not sure what caused her sister's sickness to return. But with her own person grieving the suffering of her sister, she can't help entering the social practices of faith that so fronts the mystery of the personal.

This was it; this was the snag of the "I think" that Jared heard Aly say back in Baby Brooklyn. There are those like Tyson, who can foreclose on the utter impossibility of a universe open to

7. Alan Padgett says something similar: "The word 'science' can be used in at least two senses. We might refer to science as an activity or practice. This is the turn that Ludwig Wittgenstein made in his later philosophy, and he was followed by R. Hanson, Stephen Toulmin, and Thomas Kuhn. Such an understanding of 'science' lies at the foundation of the developing field of 'science studies.' On the other hand, another sense of 'science' is a body of received knowledge. In both senses, I will argue, value commitments play a role in the criticism and growth of knowledge. Worldview commitments, therefore, likewise play a (limited) role. But this relationship must not be seen as one-sided. Rather, science and our worldviews are most healthy when there is an ongoing relationship between them, with no member a dominant partner." *Science and the Study of God: A Mutuality Model for Theology and Science* (Grand Rapids, MI: Eerdmans, 2003), 68.

the transcendence of a personal being. But most of us cannot. Even when someone like Aly is able to voice a commitment to the comprehensive social practice of "science," it comes with an openness, an almost sad longing to be able to again claim the warmth (and yet terror) of a transcendent personal being loose in the universe.[8] Someone might say that this longing for the personal is just a trick of our minds, or it could be a witness that there is indeed a personal reality that spreads over the whole of the universe.

Aly is back, but, as she tells Jared, that makes her feel stupid and childish. She feels like a grown adult who goes to the Governor's Ball dressed like a princess, carrying under her arm a coloring book.

WHAT'S THE *TELOS*?

One of the ways to spot if "science" seeks to be a comprehensive social practice is to look at what philosophers call its *telos*, the goal that nearly all those who join the social practice share. As I will explore more below, one of the reasons that the social practice of faith and the comprehensive social practice of "science" seem to be in such conflict is because they are actually siblings (or at least very close cousins).[9] And as siblings, faith is the older brother, who created a space for the younger.[10] Then, as the younger gained strength, he began to see his older brother as a

8. This is what Charles Taylor means by "cross-pressure."

9. Peter Harrison points to the constitution of faith and "science" as social practices. "As I hope is now apparent, science and religion are not natural kinds; they are neither universal propensities of human beings nor necessary features of human societies. Rather they are ways of conceptualizing certain human activities—ways that are peculiar to modern Western culture, and which have arisen as a consequence of unique historical circumstances. So while this historical analysis may not make science-religion conflict go away, it should be clear why it has emerged at this particular time and place." *The Territories of Science and Religion* (Chicago: University of Chicago Press, 2015), 194.

10. "Christian theology provided the intellectual environment out of which natural science was able to develop. By founding a worldview in which reason and order were understood to be built into the world by a rational God, theology helped to create the intellectual nursery in which early modern science was born and raised." Padgett, *Science and the Study of God*, 5.

rival, pushing the older out of the space he had created for the younger.[11]

What is important is to recognize how these social practices share a family resemblance.[12] This family resemblance can most clearly be spotted when we examine their distinct *telos*. *Scientific findings and theories* most often have a *telos* that is somewhat similar to theology's.[13] The particular goal of astronomy, biology, or physics is to seek to discover the truth about the phenomenon they are studying, to articulate through this study the shape of reality itself. (Of course, their methods for getting to this truth are very different, but nevertheless the truth of reality is the goal.)[14] The methods of scientific discoveries and theories rarely seek to say more about reality than can be empirically demonstrated.

But "science" as a comprehensive social practice has a different

---

11. This is the argument that Peter Harrison makes in his book *The Territories of Science and Religion*. I'll be in dialogue directly with it below.

12. "Historians of science have presented much evidence against the myth, however. John Heilbron, no apologist for the Vatican, got it right when he opened his book *The Sun in the Church* with the following words: 'The Roman Catholic Church gave more financial and social support to the study of astronomy for over six centuries, from the recovery of ancient learning during the late Middle Ages into the Enlightenment, than any other, and probably all, other institutions.' Heilbron's point can be generalized far beyond astronomy. Put succinctly, the medieval period gave birth to the university, which developed with the active support of the papacy." Michael H. Shank, "That the Medieval Christian Church Suppressed the Growth of Science," in Ronald Numbers, *Galileo Goes to Jail: And Other Myths About Science and Religion* (Cambridge, MA: Harvard University Press, 2009), 21. Noah Efron adds, "For all these reasons, one cannot recount the history of modern science without acknowledging the crucial importance of Christianity. But this does not mean that Christianity and Christianity alone produced modern science, any more than observing that the history of modern art cannot be retold without acknowledging that Picasso means that Picasso created modern art. There is simply more to the story than that." "That Christianity Gave Birth to Modern Science," in Numbers, *Galileo Goes to Jail*, 82.

13. I, like Stenmark, see a difference between theology and faith here. Following him, I think it is much easier when we stay at the level of academic pursuits to see a connection, or even partnership, between science and theology. Both seek to attend to reality with methods they operationalize. But when we move beyond the conversation with theology to faith, which I would say has its *telos* in the very experience of the personal being of God, we see more complication and potential conflict.

14. This is the epistemic goal that we'll explore in depth below.

telos.[15] Its goal is to embrace the stark truth that there is no personal force in the world. It asserts that big brother's goal of experiencing a personal force and seeing this personal force as *the* cause in the universe is a deluded fantasy. What makes the comprehensive social practice of "science" so appealing to Aly, Sasha, and Martin is that its goal is to "grow up" and no longer see invisible persons. The goal of the social practice of science is to become mature.[16] This is why Neal deGrasse Tyson's baby in a basket is so appealing, but so deceptive. He's not talking about scientific findings, but a practice that sees all answers in "science." Immature people before the Enlightenment might have believed in a divine reason for comets, but we're grownups and know the source of everything.

Philosopher Charles Taylor says it this way: "The story that a convert to unbelief may tell, about being convinced to abandon religion by science, is in a sense really true. This person does see himself as abandoning one world view ('religion') because another incompatible one ('science') seemed more believable. But what made it in fact more believable was not 'scientific' proofs; it is rather that one [practice]: science . . . [as] a mature facing of hard realities, beats out another [practice]: religion."[17]

[handwritten margin notes: "a practice that sees all answers in science" with arrow to "Science Fundamentalism"]

15. When I say "the comprehensive social practice of science" I means scientism. I used it in the singular to echo something like Bacon's Enlightenment Rationalism.

16. Taylor says, "We can see from . . . how much the appeal of scientific materialism is not so much the cogency of its detailed findings as that of the underlying epistemological stance, and that for ethical reasons. It is seen as the stance of maturity, of courage, of manliness, over against childish fears and sentimentality." *A Secular Age,* 365.

17. *A Secular Age,* 366.

6.

"Science," Adolescence, and Growing Up

All three of the young people speak to Jared of growing up and not being childish, moving past stupid fantasies. It is no wonder that the adolescent feels particularly drawn to (and even at times forecloses on) the comprehensive social practice of "science." Their culturally based developmental goal is to grow up, and the social practice of "science" heralds itself as the mature position. To some adolescents this is particularly intoxicating because the social practice of "science" makes the iconoclastic move against the social practice of faith that brought it into the world in the first place.

It is little wonder, then, that some studies have found that adolescence is a particular time when the tension between faith and science is heavy.[1] But this tension is not between faith and *scientific findings and theories*, but between social practices. When we recognize "science" as a comprehensive social practice, this felt tension makes all sorts of sense, particularly in adolescence. Not only is the social practice of "science" iconoclastic, but it also appears to provide direct explanations, with useful outputs.

The modern concept of *adolescence* revolves around *explanation* and *usefulness*. Adolescence is a cultural and developmental time when we're invited to embrace the explanation of things. It

1. See reason three in this report: https://www.barna.org/barna-update/millennials/528-six-reasons-young-christians-leave-church#.V6N4ymW4yHU.

is no longer appropriate *not* to think for yourself; it is time to put away fantasies and be responsible for understanding why things are the way they are.[2] It is indeed a time to grow up.[3] As adolescence has taken this shape through education in technological societies, this move into explanation is supposed to prepare you for some form of usefulness. Adolescence is ultimately a time to prepare to be of use.[4] This perspective has the result of making childhood (and children themselves) useless (an anti-Christian perspective, in my opinion). "To be a child" is an insult meaning you lack or refuse the explanation of things and therefore are useless. In adolescence you are invited to explore the explanations of things so that you might be of benefit to society by growing up to manage people and money, producing advancement and growth for corporation, country, and individual portfolio.

2. Daniel Siegel says, "Creative exploration with an expanded sense of consciousness. An adolescent's new conceptual thinking and abstract reasoning allow questioning of the status quo, approaching problems with 'out of the box' strategies, the creation of new ideas, and the emergence of innovation. Downside: Searching for the meaning of life during the teen years can lead to a crisis of identity, vulnerability to peer pressure, and a lack of direction and purpose. Upside: If the mind can hold on to thinking and imagining and perceiving the world in new ways within consciousness, of creatively exploring the spectrum of experiences that are possible, the sense of being in a rut that can sometimes pervade adult life can be minimized and instead an experience of the 'ordinary being extraordinary' can be cultivated. Not a bad strategy for living a full life!" *Brainstorm: The Power and Purpose of the Teenage Brain* (New York: Jeremy P. Tarcher/Penguin, 2013), 9. Siegel adds, "This period of the teenage years and early twenties is a time of great potential and of great constructive power. The push against traditional ways of doing things and of thinking about reality can yield ways of thinking outside the box that enable new and creative ways of doing things to emerge." *Brainstorm,* 23.
3. Though, culturally, this growing is confused. It remains a liminal stage where you are to seek the explanation of things through education, but with a glass ceiling—there are many ways you remain a minor, or held out of full adulthood. And since the late 1960s this being held out has been glorified as a path to embrace a depth of authenticity. Then, culturally to "grow up" is to know the explanation of things. But since the 1960s we've been in a conflict with what the usefulness of adolescence really means, shifting from collective commitments (like citizenship, etc.) to individualized pursuits of authenticity—being "useful" then means the ability to pursue your own desires. For more on this cultural shift, see part 2 of my book *Faith Formation in a Secular Age* (Grand Rapids, MI: Baker, 2017).
4. To explore more fully how the construction of adolescence has been used in our growing society of unbelief, see my article "Adolescence and the Secular Age of Unbelief," https://perspectivesjournal.org/blog/2017/01/09/adolescence-creation-secular-age-unbelief-2/.

A LITTLE CHICKEN-OR-EGG

The comprehensive social practice of "science" proclaims itself fit for just such a process of growing up because it most fully embracing empirical explanations for the sake of usefulness. It asserts over and again that once we eliminate the possibility that there is a personal force causing things in the world, we are free to find our own explanations that are of use in our day-to-day lives (we can be free from authorities we don't choose). We can forget all this childish nonsense about gods, spirits, and transcendence, and grow up, embracing impersonal explanations and concerning ourselves with only technological usefulness. It is little wonder then that the modern adolescent, to the point of caricature, is perceived as obsessed with questions of *why* and technological gadgets.

So we're stuck with a chicken-or-egg dilemma. It's hard to know if the modern concept of adolescence, revolving as it does around *explanation* and *usefulness*, comes first, or if the social practice of "science" does.[5] But whether it is the chicken or the egg, it's clear that modern adolescence and the social practice of "science" fit hand-in-glove. Whether you're a modern adolescent like Sasha or Martin, or a youth running in the streets of ancient Athens, you nevertheless share a task. All human beings participate in social practices, and all social practices have a *telos*—they have goals that deliver an ethic (what is right and what is wrong action). And because they do, all social practices (whether ancient or modern) call for integration. *To come of age means integrating the* telos *of your social practice.* Your task, whether as an ancient or modern young person, is to integrate your social practice.

The comprehensive social practice of "science" is so captivating to modern adolescents because it promises integration that

---

5. I personally think it is clear that the comprehensive social practice of "science" makes it possible for the conception of adolescence to be at all. It is the development's starting point in the time of the Enlightenment that forges this new conception of youth. After all, it would be modern psychology that would give us this concept of adolescence. This in part is why I cannot follow Crystal Kirgiss's theory *In Search of Adolescence: A New Look at an Old Idea* (San Diego: Youth Cartel, 2015). She takes no consideration of distinct social practices.

delivers a feeling—an ethos—of maturity. And this social practice of science is doubly captivating because it spends just as much energy showing how older sibling faith fails over and again at the integration that "science" promises. It repeatedly asserts that believing there is a personal force causing things in the world is both a bad answer for why things are the way they are—like why the sky is blue—and worse, are ultimately useless—God has no power to bring a cab to your door like Uber does. Even if God exists; God is useless. But GPS technology has almost more uses than can be imagined! Historian Peter Harrison says it this way: "It is the utility of science—the fact it yields practical outcomes and useful technologies—that now provides the basis of its ambitious claims to give us access to a true picture of the world. Science is true, we are repeatedly told, because it works."[6]

Aly, as a young adult, chooses this ethos of maturity because in the end it feels more integrated; it seems to fuse with her work, education, and day-to-day life. Aly believes that to possess this integration is to indeed be mature. It is to have grown up. She recognizes that to integrate your social practice as your own is to be mature. And because we have given over the definition of young people to the modern conception of adolescence, the social practice of "science" will almost always promise an integration that will be interpreted as more mature for youth like Aly, Sasha, and Martin.

HOW IS SCIENCE MATURE?

But if the goal of the comprehensive social practice of "science" is maturity, what does this mean and how is it perceived as scientific? The operations of scientists (those responsible for findings and theories) most often focus in on one phenomenon, using methods of logic and repetition to make a discovery.[7] Again, as we said above, it is to assume that there are firm contingent laws behind phenomena. When this approach moves from a method into a social practice, it makes the assertion that those who can

6. Peter Harrison, *The Territories of Science and Religion* (Chicago: University of Chicago Press, 2015), 182.
7. Particularly, those in the hard sciences.

evacuate all subjective, personal commitments and see things just as they are, are indeed mature.[8] Those who can admit that there are only impersonal laws and structures are mature, and those needing some personal force to cause things are childish. Charles Taylor writes, "For those who take on [the social-practice of science], the noblest, highest truths must have this general [impersonal] form. Personal interventions, even those of a God, would introduce something arbitrary, some element of subjective desire, into the picture, and the highest truths about reality must be beyond this element." Taylor continues: "From this standpoint, a faith in a personal God belongs to a less mature standpoint, where one still needs the sense of a personal relation to things; one is not yet ready to face the ultimate truth."[9]

And this ultimate truth, which is only for the mature, is that *we are alone*. Our own personal minds can hope for no divine mind in which to share. And to seek one is to be a pathetic child. Sasha allows her mind to embrace the scientific findings of the expanse of the universe. These findings make no direct assertion that because the universe is enormous, a personal order is impossible.[10] But the comprehensive social practice that accompanies the scientific findings whispers to Sasha, "Grow up and face the fact that you live in an impersonal order. If there is a God, you must at least be a grownup and not trust this God to do much more than give you individual comfort."

Martin contemplates the age of the earth and the waves of extinction. There's nothing in the scientific theories of evolution

8. This is the very conception that Michael Polanyi stands against in his book *Personal Knowledge: Towards a Post-Critical Philosophy* (Chicago: University of Chicago Press, 1974). Polanyi shows that it is always persons who discover anything, and that in the end there is no way to exorcise the scientist from their personhood. Nor should they want too, for he shows that most great breakthroughs actually come from such personal realities.

9. Taylor, *A Secular Age*, 363.

10. "Now this bent to impersonality was greatly reinforced by the new cosmic imaginary. The vast universe, in which one could easily feel no sense of a personal God or a benign purpose, seemed to be impersonal in the most forbidding sense, blind and indifferent to our fate. An account in terms of impersonal causal law seemed called for by the new depth sense of reality in the universe." *A Secular Age*, 363. We'll see in part 2 that the relationality of physics provides a way to see an echo of the personal bounding across this enormity of space.

that exclude a personal order.[11] Evolution as a scientific finding does not eliminate the cause of a personal God—divine action may indeed be found within evolution. But the comprehensive social practice of "science" has no time for this. In fact it laughs at such presumptions, sarcastically howling, "Well, if you're a little child, too scared to face facts, then fine, you pathetic baby,"[12] adding, "Isn't it just simpler not to have some divine being directing things? And, see, science is brave enough to always look for the simplest explanations. And it is courageous enough to hold to what it finds. Don't you want to be like that? Be an adult and integrate your beliefs with your practices."

So there is little conflict and great possibility for dialogue between scientific findings and faith. As we'll see, it is important for ministry that we wade into these conversations at some level. If we don't, then scientific findings are swallowed up by the comprehensive social practice of "science" and its *telos* of embracing an impersonal order and glorifying naturalism. To minister to Aly and Sasha demands that we engage these conversations.

But to wade into these conversations is to confront the sure conflict with the comprehensive social practice of "science" and its commitment to an impersonal order as being mature. Taylor explains this further: "An important part of the force which drove many people to see science and religion as incompatible, and to opt for the former, comes from this crucial difference in form. In other words, the success of [the social practice of] science built on, and helped to entrench in them, the sense that the Christian religion they were familiar with belonged to an earlier, more primitive or less mature form of understanding."[13]

The comprehensive social practice of "science" demands that we wade into dialogues between *scientific findings* and faith—this

11. Though, as we'll see below, a strict natural selection moves into a naturalism that opposes all personal conceptions of the unfolding of species in terms of biological explanation.

12. This is nearly the response of Daniel Dennett to Alvin Plantinga in their dialogue book *Science and Religion: Are They Compatible?* (London: Oxford University Press, 2011). Dennett keeps using the analogy of superman for Plantinga's position. The tone basically says, "If you're such a child to believe in super heroes, then, fine, I guess your theistic position makes sense. But, I've outgrown underoos!"

13. Taylor, *A Secular Age*, 363.

is the only way to oppose the assertions of the social practice of "science." It reveals that actually the social practice of "science" is not science at all. Only when we enter into these constructive dialogues with scientific findings can we show that the personal commitment of Israel's laws and the incarnation of Christ are not primitive fairy tales for the immature. Rather, they echo across the universe, providing an integration that connects our own personal mind with the mind of God. If we can't (or refuse to) do this, adolescents particularly will be drawn to the impersonal presumption of "science," because in attacking its elder sibling it has won the crown of maturity, and its iconoclastic banter, the robe of authenticity.

DO YOUNG PEOPLE HAVE
TO CHOOSE?

It is the comprehensive social practice of "science" that leads people to believe they must make a choice. Aly feels stupid when she comes back to church on Christmas Eve, a mix of immaturity and a sense of inconsistency. In Baby Brooklyn she planted her flag in the social practice of "science." She believed that she was opting for science over religion because it was more integrated and therefore mature. But here she was back at church, willing at some level to bear the feeling of stupidity. She can't admit this to herself, but the feeling of stupidity was less crushing than the heavy cold flatness of the impersonal order under which she now suffers. But nevertheless Aly feels stupid because she is running back to what she assumed was a lesser social practice because she believed it lacked the integration "science" promised. If the universe was indeed impersonal, then she was a stupid child for making believe it wasn't. She felt embarrassed for running back to personal fairy tales when she was too sad to face the harshness of an impersonal order where those we love are struck sick to death. Aly felt bad because in her own mind she was regressing. She was jumping back into a more immature social practice and worldview (but nevertheless, one that seemed to provide her more hope than "science").[14]

14. Aly's experience is described by Taylor: "A crucial feature of the malaise of

When "science" moves from findings and theories to a *comprehensive* social practice, it is just as demanding of loyalty as religion. And the social practice of "science" does this, because it is a learned way of life that claims all other perspectives are wrong—it is a comprehensive system or philosophy of life. Social practices ask for loyalty, "science" as much as faith.

But recognizing this, those of us in the church have too often taken a dangerous and unfortunate misstep, failing to see the distinction between scientific *findings* and the comprehensive social practice of "science." And this has had an adverse impact on the likes of Aly. When scientific *findings* are fused with "science," it is assumed that you have to choose one or the other. You can either be a person of faith or a person of "science." But not both.

While most young people are deeply uneasy with this distinction,[15] they nevertheless sense that this is the expectation of the church. It is assumed that if you're going to be a person of faith, then you have to deny scientific findings like a heliocentric solar system, stem cells, evolutionary adaptation, and string theory. But who can do this and actually live in our world? For instance, it's often (wrongly) assumed that to be a person of faith you have to deny the finding of evolutionary adaptation. But no one, not even the hard-core creationist, denies that the earth revolves around the sun.[16]

Yet, we should see that this strict either/or is only in place if we allow the findings of science to be swallowed by the comprehensive social practice of "science." People living the social practice of faith can and must engage scientific findings, even doing scientific theory construction (some are brilliant scientists). As we've seen above, very little in scientific findings actually

immanence is the sense that all these answers are fragile, or uncertain; that a moment may come, where we no longer feel that our chosen path is compelling, or cannot justify it to selves or others. There is a fragility of meaning, analogous to the existential fragility we always live with: that suddenly an accident, earthquake, flood, a fatal disease, some terrible betrayal, may jolt us off our path of life, definitively and without return. Only the fragility that I am talking about concerns the significance of it all; the path is still open, possible, supported by circumstances, the doubt concerns its worth." *A Secular Age*, 308.

15. We discovered this unease in a small research study. See white paper: http://scienceym.org/downloads/.

16. Actually there is a group who does. But they are so fringe that they need not be mentioned.

contradicts the core commitment of the social practice of faith, that there is a personal force acting in the universe. There is no either/or to face, and Aly doesn't have to feel stupid. People living out the social practice of faith are not inconsistent for engaging scientific findings; if not for the elder sibling of faith, the scientific approach would not have been. It is actually endemic to the social practice of faith itself to engage, wrestle with, and actually construct scientific findings and theories. It was the social practice of Christian faith that pushed Newton to construct his equations and experiments, not to mention others like Michael Faraday, James Clark Maxwell, Lord Kelvin, and Asa Gray.

Taylor argues that one of the reasons the "immature" label sticks to faith, and the comprehensive social practice of "science" wears the crown of maturity, is because many people have experienced nothing but bland and flat religious learning. Taylor explains: "What happens is that people are convinced that there is something more mature, more courageous . . . in the scientific stance. The superiority . . . is heavily influenced by the person's own sense of his/her own childhood faith, which may well have remained a childish one."[17] Without the depth of wisdom, and the direction into the many practices that draw us close to God, faith as a social practice *can* seem infantile and stale.

The caricature that faith is for babies is exactly that, a caricature. Aly can still sense that this social practice of faith has the depth and wisdom she needs. But she must now fight with the whispers that she is immature and stupid for still believing.

THE COMBATIVE EDGE
OF THEODICY

Recently, the caricature of faith has expanded, taking on a combative edge. The comprehensive social practice of "science" has ridiculed big brother faith not only for being immature, but for being *immoral*. These are twin critiques that Aly can't avoid, and most adolescents directly wrestle with—immaturity and

17. Taylor, *A Secular Age*, 365.

immorality. Adolescence is the culturally imposed development time when the young are asked to seek maturity and take responsibility, learning to judge the moral from the immoral. All social practices, because they provide a way of life, deliver an ethic, a deep sense of what is right and wrong, of what is allowed and what is restricted. "Science" asserts that the social practice of faith cannot be trusted because it is not only immature but also immoral.

If Neil deGrasse Tyson is a high priest and spokesman for the comprehensive social practice of "science," then Richard Dawkins is its supreme ethicist.[18] Dawkins, an Oxford zoologist and bestselling author, has not only made a strong case for the immaturity of faith, but has bombastically asserted that faith is *evil*. Dawkins believes the practice of faith is diseased. It is a mental illness that must be eradicated.

This is all just a smear campaign, no different from the commercials during an election year. But after 9/11 Dawkins had his case in point. Those deeply committed to a religious social practice had murdered thousands. And, in what was utterly illogical to the worldview of the comprehensive social practice of "science," the killers killed themselves as well.

"See," Dawkins could assert, "religion is a dangerous mental illness. It makes such little sense and drives people so nuts, that they will not only kill others, but also themselves. It is not only immature but dangerously illogical."

But this alleged murderous impulse of the social practices of faith was indeed a dirty trick of the younger sibling—as devious as Jacob's switcheroo on Esau. With a little perspective, we can spot how secularized governments, who laud the social practice of "science," have actually ruthlessly killed more people than any religious government.[19] This is all about perception, and the

---

18. "Science itself, of course, cannot demonstrate scientifically the acceptance of science as the sole arbiter of truth. That is not a scientific but a philosophical claim, though Dawkins's working assumption is that it is scientific. Science, specifically evolutionary biology, functions like a religion for Dawkins and those like him." Ernest L. Simmons, *The Entangled Trinity: Quantum Physics and Theology* (Minneapolis: Fortress Press, 2014), 21.

19. See David Bentley Hart, *The Atheist Delusion: The Christian Revolution and Its Fashionable Enemies* (New Haven: Yale University Press, 2009).

comprehensive social practice of "science" has done well to coat faith with a brush dripping of the paint of illogical immorality. And that's Dawkins's point! His aim is to show that faith is dangerously illogical. What makes faith an illogical mental illness, in Dawkins's mind, is that next to "science," it refuses to flatten all of reality to temporary puzzles, and recognizes—even delightfully embraces—mysteries.[20] The social practice of "science" in its drive toward progress, "recognizes no mysteries, only temporary puzzles"[21] that sooner or later will be solved. Because the world is impersonal and there is no mind behind it, everything is an object, and an object (absent personal mind) is only a puzzle that can be cracked.[22] This is pushed so far that it is assumed that one day we will unlock the very puzzle of love, mercy, and self-sacrifice. But, every attempt to do so seems oddly cold and reductive,[23] because it lacks the mysterious spirit of the personal—a personal order.

"But, still," High Priest Dawkins and his followers herald, "it is immorally illogical." And to make this case, the priests of the comprehensive social practice of "science" point to theodicy (why God would allow bad things to happen). Matt Dillahunty from *The Atheist Experience* even goes so far as to say, "I'm more moral than God, because I'd never *allow* a three-year-old to suffer and die." Theodicy becomes the unbreakable puzzle that proves that there is no personal order causing anything in the world.[24] It is illogical to believe that there is a loving and

20. "For example, Richard Dawkins' characterization of religion: 'Religion is about turning untested belief into unshakable truth through the power of institutions and the passage of time' is deliberately contrasted with a science that tells the truth about the universe—'Religions do make claims about the universe—the same kinds of claims that scientists make, except they're usually false'. This approach is highly problematic for many reasons, not the least of which is that, historically speaking, the claims that scientists make are also 'usually false'. Good science is arguably about being false in a constructive way that takes us nearer to truth, rather than capturing truth in some timeless way. Seen in the light of Einstein's relativity, Newton was 'wrong', but we do not discard his achievement for that reason." Tom McLeish, *Faith & Wisdom in Science* (London: Oxford University Press, 2014), 167.

21. Taylor, *A Secular Age*, 367.

22. This again is to echo Scruton's thesis.

23. See Barbara L. Fredrickson's book *Love 2.0: How Our Supreme Emotion Affects Everything We Feel, Think, Do, and Become* (New York: Hudson Street, 2013).

24. Ian A. McFarland points to how the changing of our place in the universe opens up big questions of theodicy: "Humans have existed for only a tiny fraction of

powerful person causing things in the universe. This person, the puzzle goes, would then allow children to get cancer and earthquakes to crush villages.

As long as human beings have existed, we've been assailed with questions of theodicy. Job wonders why he was struck with such afflictions. But only recently (really, since the eighteenth century) have these kinds of questions been seen as puzzles that need a solution. As a matter of fact, it has been only recently that we have given these kinds of questions the name "theodicy."[25] Only since the comprehensive social practice of "science" has given us an impersonal universe without the mystery of a personal mind, has theodicy been used against faith.[26]

But in many ways, to play the theodicy game is to play by rules that promise that faith will be mocked. The rules of the theodicy game presume that *everything* is a solvable puzzle and mysteries are nothing more than hidden contingencies yet to be discovered. For instance, we recognize that there are particles that make existence possible. And we've discovered some of them. But all the dots are far from connected. What these particles are and how they function are mysteries. But when we

the hundreds of millions of years during which multicellular organisms have populated the earth, and all the evidence indicates that the suffering and death produced by natural disasters (e.g., floods, landslides, volcanic eruptions, bolide impacts), predation, and disease have characterized terrestrial life from the beginning. Nor is there any reason to suppose that things would be different for life elsewhere in the universe. These facts raise serious problems for a defense of creation from nothing. How can it be that in a universe where all that exists depends for its existence at every moment and in every respect on the divine will, any state of affairs can come about that contradicts God's will for the flourishing of all creatures? Since the seventeenth century the attempt to answer this question has been described as theodicy, or the justification of God's ways with creatures." *From Nothing: A Theology of Creation* (Louisville: Westminster John Knox, 2014), 112.

25. Taylor points to how this argument might connect with adolescents: "The failure of theodicy can now more readily lead to rebellion, because of our heightened sense of ourselves as free agents. The connection here is not one of logical argument so much as of existential attitude." *A Secular Age*, 306.

26. "It is obvious that theodicy, while it is always a possibility within theistic modes of belief, can be less acute if we see ourselves as in an inscrutable world, at threat, but having God as our helper. Once we claim to understand the universe, and how it works; once we even try to explain how it works by invoking its being created for our benefit, then this explanation is open to clear challenge: we know how things go, and we know why they were set up, and we can judge whether the first meets the purpose defined in the second. In Lisbon 1755, it seems clearly not to have. So the immanent order ups the ante." *A Secular Age*, 306.

say "mystery," most often we mean the part of the puzzle yet to be disclosed. Right now, we're not sure what these particles are, but soon, or someday, we'll crack this code and solve the particle puzzle. Mystery is redefined as just the occurrence of *temporarily* unknown variables. But this is to radically redefine mystery, and to do so in a distinctly impersonal tone.

Mystery is the unimaginable depths of reality itself. Mystery is the confession that there are events, occurrences, and happenings in the universe that cannot be captured by the human mind, and yet these things encounter us. Mystery is to be encountered by the deepest experiences of being that cannot be explained. Not simply because they are challenging riddles, but because they are a form of being above or beyond any form of human logical understanding or technological knowhow.

When the comprehensive practice of "science" heralds a need for answers on the playing field of theodicy, the game is rigged. It asks faith to concede that reality is nothing more than impersonal material puzzles that can be cracked—so if God is all-powerful, and providence is real, and yet God is not able to keep babies from getting cancer (and even was stupid enough to create cancer in the first place) then how could there be a God? And if there were such a God, he would be an immoral bastard! The difference between what *is* and what *ought to be* seems such a complicated and impossible puzzle to solve that it can only lead to one logical conclusion: there is no God, and anyone who claims there is, is a stupid child, too ignorant or brain-dead to solve the simplest puzzle. They are so brain-dead, Dawkins would assert, that they are a risk to us all.[27]

We can't trust people of faith, because they refuse to flatten everything into an impersonal, material puzzle. And without making everything an impersonal puzzle, some things in the universe will escape logic and usefulness. The comprehensive

---

27. Taylor offers an important nuance that I don't have space to explore. "I want to emphasize that I am talking about our sense of things," he writes. "I'm not talking about what people believe. Many still hold that the universe is created by God, that in some sense it is governed by his Providence. What I am talking about is the way the universe is spontaneously imagined, and therefore experienced. It is no longer usual to sense the universe immediately and unproblematically as purposefully ordered, although reflection, meditation, spiritual development may lead one to see it this way." *A Secular Age*, 325.

social practice of "science" has tricked us into conceding that reality is impersonal and what is ethical or trustworthy is what is rationally logical and ultimately useful. The arrival of theodicy historically comes with the new societal wave of technological pursuit. Technological breakthroughs, bound to the social practice of "science," are really little more than deeply sophisticated puzzle solving.

STEVE JOBS LEAVES THE CHURCH

After Steve Jobs's biography came out, it was common to see blogs and articles relaying an anecdote: a junior high Jobs takes a *Time Magazine* with a cover photo of a starving children to his Lutheran pastor. Jobs, the budding technologist, asks his pastor, "Why would God allow these children to starve?" According to Jobs, the pastor had no good answer. Jobs never again entered a church. The blogs and articles push us to have better answers for young people like Jobs or they too, like the famous and talented Apple founder, will leave the church and never return.

This is too superficial. Young Jobs came to the pastor with a puzzle. He demanded that the pastor solve the puzzle. When the pastor couldn't, not necessarily because he lacked the skill but because the question itself evacuated the mystery of a personal order, Jobs left. It could be interpreted that what disgusted Jobs was that the pastor and the church believed that suffering had no usefulness, that there was no puzzle to be solved. Rather, the only thing suffering, joy, beauty, and pain reveal is that indeed we are persons, seeking to connect with and love each other. But next to a modern impulse to fix and solve (and, as we would find out, the young Jobs would grow to have an insatiable drive to solve puzzles, so insatiable that he justified intimidation, fear-mongering, and rageful attacks), the pastor's response seemed stupid and childish. But, even more, it seemed immoral and useless.

Jobs's pastor crosses a line that pushes him ethically out of bounds to the comprehensive social practice of "science." Dawkins can see such people as dangerous and evil because they refuse to see the universe as only an impersonal puzzle. They are willing to embrace the mystery of beauty, suffering, love, mercy, and even pain. Those of us who hold to the mystery of the personal claim that such realities are the tissue of personhood that continue to echo in the universe, calling us to seek connection with each other. Sometimes our actions bring us together with others for no usefulness other than joy, love, and sharing. The reason we suffer is a perplexing mystery, and we, like ancient Job, have no answer for the puzzle before us. But what we do have is a deeper experience that "science" keeps disparaging and minimizing. We have an experience of the very personhood of God coming to our brokenness, giving us, not answers to riddles, but the mystery of communion, love, and mercy. We may have no answers, and this makes little brother irate. But what we do have is a mystery of friendship. We claim encounter with a personal force that reminds us again and again that although the universe is massive and we are but dust, we are persons, and there is a personal being seeking to encounter us. This echoes out across the mass of time and space in a soft but sure experience of the mystery of our own personhood.

And while Dawkins may call this crazy, he is only partly right. It opposes the comprehensive social practice of "science" that lives from its own normative commitments to an impersonal universe, but there is nothing in scientific findings or theories that oppose faith's experience of the personal—and young people in our ministries need to see this.

In making this point, we shouldn't be naïve. Even the methods used for scientific findings attend to material realities, and most often engage *a particular phenomenon* as a puzzle. Most often they seek some form of progress (like an advance in the theory of quantum mechanics or a new medical vaccine). But where little brother is a trickster, is in taking this method and making it constitute the whole of reality.

Scientific findings and theory construction start with material or human realities, but the comprehensive social practice of "science" turns this into materialism.[28] Scientific findings attend to the natural world, but the social practice of "science" turns

28. See the introduction to Stephen Barr's *Modern Physics and Ancient Faith* (South Bend, IN: University of Notre Dame Press, 2003).

this into naturalism,[29] indeed into a new material religion.[30] The comprehensive social practice of "science" takes a method of discovery and twists it into a metaphysic (an underlying philosophy of existence). And when it becomes a metaphysic (opposing the personal order), it can belittle other social practices, like calling faith immature and immoral.[31]

This shows that there is a true tension between the comprehensive social practice of "science" and the social practice of faith. But this tension doesn't eliminate the social practice of faith engaging (and even constructing its own) scientific findings and theories.[32] As Barbour writes, "Theism, in short, is not inherently in conflict with science, but it does conflict with

29. Alvin Plantinga helps explain and define naturalism: "Now central to the great monotheistic religions—Christianity, Judaism, Islam—is the thought that there is such a person as God: a personal agent who has created the world and is all-powerful, all-knowing, and perfectly good. I take naturalism to be the thought that there is no such person as God, or anything like God. Naturalism is stronger than atheism: you can be an atheist without rising to the heights (sinking to the lowest depths?) of naturalism; but you can't be a naturalist without being an atheist." *Where the Conflict Really Lies: Science, Religion, & Naturalism* (London: Oxford University Press, 2011), ix.

30. "To be fair it is not clear that naturalism, as it stands, is a religion; there is enough vagueness around the edges of the concept of religion for it to be unclear whether naturalism does or doesn't belong there. But naturalism does serve one of the main functions of a religion: it offers a master narrative, it answers deep and important human questions." Dennett and Plantinga, *Science and Religion*, 104.

31. "This whole way of seeing things, which comes about through the joint effect of science and the new cosmic imaginary; helped along by a notion of maturity which they generate along with the buffered identity, has brought about modes of unbelief which are much more solid. They are more firmly anchored, both in our sense of our world, and in the scientific and technological practices by which we know it and deal with it. This is why for a whole milieu today materialism has become the obvious, the default position. It is no longer a wild, far-out theory, but creeps close to what is seen as common sense." Taylor, *A Secular Age*, 366.

32. "I suppose it isn't really necessary to argue that there is (at least) superficial concord between naturalism and science; the high priests of naturalism trumpet this loudly enough. Naturalists pledge allegiance to science; they nail their banner to the mast of science; they wrap themselves in the mantle of science like a politician in the flag. They confidently claim that naturalism is part of the 'scientific worldview,' and that the advent of modern science has exposed supernaturalism as a tissue of superstition—perhaps acceptable and perhaps even sensible in a prescientific age, but now superseded. A particularly charming phrase, here, is the obligatory 'as we now know'; we were previously wallowing in ignorance and superstition, but now, thanks to science, we finally know the truth." Plantinga, *Where the Conflict Really Lies*, 307.

a metaphysics of materialism."[33] Actually, as we'll see, it is the shape of the social practice of faith that births the very method of scientific findings and theory construction in the first place.

33. Ian Barbour, *Religion and Science: Historical and Contemporary Issues* (San Francisco: HarperSanFrancisco, 1997), 82. Elsewhere he says, "In addition, many forms of materialism express reductionism. Epistemological reductionism claims that the laws and theories of all the sciences are in principle reducible to the laws of physics and chemistry. Metaphysical reductionism claims that the component parts of any system constitute most fundamental reality. The materialist believes that all phenomena will eventually be explained in terms of the actions of material components, which are the only effective causes in the world. Analysis of the parts of any system has, of course, been immensely useful in science, but I will suggest that the study of higher organizational levels in larger wholes is also valuable." *Religion and Science*, 78.

7.

The Faith of the Child as the Welcoming of the Scientific

Jared felt too full to move. Between the large Christmas Day meal and the piles of cookies and candy, he'd overdone it. As he threw himself into the large living room chair for a quick respite, lying in the chair to keep his full belly elevated, he felt a sense of contentment. Recognizing it, he was surprised. It was like seeing a close friend he'd somehow forgotten. It had been a long time since Jared felt this, at least since the news late last spring that he would not be the committee's choice for the church plant in Baby Brooklyn. Sitting in the chair with the lights of the Christmas tree washing the room in a soft hue, Jared realized it was over. He finally felt healed from the disappointment. Contentment had arrived. Maybe it was because of all the Christmas hymns and carols, but this contentment seemed to sing a soft soothing song of rest. As Jared just sat and listened to his inner tune, he felt joy.

But like the skipping of a needle on an old record player, Jared's contentment was invaded with a dull sense of unease. At first, he couldn't put his finger on the origin of this small sliver that was lodging itself in the body of his contentment. As he stared deeply into the white lights of the Christmas tree, he searched for the origin of his unease. And then he saw her face, reliving those tears that fell from Aly's eyes. It was vivid. Jared couldn't quite remember Aly's words. If called to testify in a court of law, he wasn't sure he could sequentially and literally recall her statements. But her face . . . that he couldn't forget. And it was true that details like the huge tears, quivering lips, and eyes wide with sadness struck him. If asked what haunted him, it was the whole of her face. It wasn't the details that communicated something to him, but the very tangible experience with what felt like her spirit, revealed in her face at that moment.

All this Christmas contemplation was quickly interrupted. Jared's big chair lounge was only a brief respite, and soon enough tasks were beckoning, particularly Sam and Svea's bedtime. Jared made his way upstairs. Sam was already in bed reading the comics his grandpa had given to him in his stocking. Jared reminded him it was lights out in twenty minutes, as he tucked him in and kissed his head.

Svea was nowhere near her bed, fooling around with something right outside the bathroom. Jared reminded her that it was time to brush her teeth and get in bed. Slowly but surely she did. Svea was the harder of the two to get to sleep, and it always tested Jared's patience. As she made her last arrangements, shifting stuffed animals with a clear logical progression that Jared failed to decipher, she finally announced, "Ready now, Daddy."

With a tuck and a kiss, Jared said goodnight. But as if the tenderness of bedtime had unearthed something buried in her mind, a pensive disposition rose to her face.

"Daddy," she said, with a heaviness wrapped in compassion, "can we pray for your friend Aly? I'm sad that her sister is sick." Taken aback by the concern and wisdom of her request, Jared said, "Sure. What should we pray?"

Next, Svea closed her eyes and prayed, "Jesus, love Aly, make her sister okay, and kiss her sad face. And may Sam never get sick. And hug Aly, because she likes hugs. Amen."

Jared repeated, "Amen." With a smile so broad it felt like it might split his cheeks, Jared walked back down the stairs. He thought of Aly's statement about feeling stupid and childish. He remembered that Sasha and Martin had also, in their own ways, wanted to avoid being an immature child. And yet, this child under the pink comforter, surrounded by dozens of stuffed animals, had ministered to Aly with a hug of love. This child had no fear of Aly's pain, embracing her sadness with love, mercy, and empathy. This child sought Aly's face even in prayer, asking God to encounter this broken young woman. Now standing looking at his family's nativity scene, Jared realized that the face of God is a child who lies in the feed box of a beast, bringing hope into the world. Into this huge, old universe of mass extinctions, God comes, embracing mangled persons with love.

Stunning

This universe that at one level seems so faceless, and yet God comes, revealed in the face of a child, reaches out for us, igniting within us an experience that refuses to be objectified, reduced, or deconstructed. It is a love that ministers face-to-face with an other. The incarnation gives to this universe God's face, which beckons us all to come as children and receive the love and belonging we long for. "It has, too," Jared said to himself.

But as he did, he wondered if this was just some cognitive work-around program, this feeling of the mystery of the love and compassion of a child. Maybe it was just a simple evolutionary trick to keep our genes going and our species thriving. To have minds for persons, minds that grieve for sick sisters, seemed a cruel trick of natural selection—and maybe it was. Jared wondered whether there was a face to the universe. Is there a personhood beyond the order of things, or are we alone? Are we encountered again and again by a faceless void that makes our deepest yearnings for the face of love just a pathetic torture trick, making the longing and loving of a child, stupid, ignorant, and even immoral?

Jared was becoming aware that if his youth ministry was going to be able to help Martin and Sasha as they wrestle with scientific findings next to the claims of faith, he'd have to become clearer about Aly's predicament. Aly's concern about being immature, and yet her longing to connect to some personal reality she didn't know if she believed in, seemed to be key. So he sent her a Facebook message asking her if they could meet again. Within minutes Aly responded, suggesting The Rusty Spoon the day before New Year's Eve.

Like the first time, Jared arrived before Aly. But this time things felt different. The air was filled with the smell of roasted coffee, but the cracked green Spanish tiles and rusted ceiling lacked the charm of his first visit. Maybe it was because this time Jared was seeing clearly, eyes free from the cloud of his own ambition and the possibility of being the pastor of a new church in this hip neighborhood. Or maybe it was just winter. Regardless, this time the wear and tear that felt cozy in the fresh warm air of the bursting spring, just felt old and dirty in the stale dark days of winter.

Before Jared could find a seat, Aly arrived. Where last time she seemed present but hidden, this time she was at ease. It was clear that she was truly happy to see Jared. Unlike last time, Aly was happy to take Jared up on his offer of a drink. She told him she'd have a caramel latte. When Jared raised his eyebrows and gave a teasing look that communicated, "Really, you, the organic, anti-oxidant conscious young woman, are choosing the ultimate of indulgent drinks?!" Reading his face like a book, Aly smiled. "Come on, it's cheat season," she said; and then her face quickly shifted from light to heavy. "Plus, I've been drinking so much bad black coffee at the hospital, I think I need a little caramel balance."

Jared just nodded and ordered. When he returned with their drinks, he asked, even before sitting down, "So how are things with your sister?"

Aly gave him the technical update, explaining her sister's condition, medications, and prospects. But then, she told about sleeping in her sister's hospital room on Christmas Eve. Since she could remember, every Christmas Eve night she'd slept in the same bed as her sister. And she'd be damned if a hospital room would break that streak. So Aly borrowed a little camping pad and a sleeping bag from a friend and slept on the floor next to her little sister.

Those big tears came again, and she paused for a moment. "There I was lying on the floor, with my right arm extended and reaching for Gena's hand. We fell asleep, like so many years before, holding hands. The last thing I remember before we drifted off was rubbing the top of her hand with my thumb. I had this pattern of stroking her hand from one side and then back to the next. Every time my thumb brushed her hand I would get a rush of overwhelming love for her, and my mind would race to so many past moments. It was like this touch brought with it these deeply felt memories of our life together."

Wiping her cheeks with a napkin, she continued, now with a look of intensity, even anger. "But then my thumb would hit that f-ing plastic tube taped to the middle of her hand and the real possibility that I would lose her, that this might be the last Christmas Eve we share a bed, would stab me so deep I'd wonder if I was bleeding."

Aly paused, looked out the window to stare at the busy motion on the street, using its frenzy as a sedative to collect herself. She then smiled, and her body communicated she was ready to shift the conversation. "And you," she said, "what about you, Jared, how was your Christmas?"

Jared smiled back and nodded quickly in a rhythm of three or four. "It was very good, relaxing and fun. The kids were really into it. It was our first Christmas where having kids was actually more fun than work. It was wonderful."

Aly exhaled, as if she was taking in Jared's experience like secondhand smoke. But this smoke was so laced with joy, and even peace, that it was a pleasure to take deep into her lungs. It seemed to heal her.

This was all quite a shift from their first meeting at The Rusty Spoon, so much so that Aly needed to say something. "You know the last time we sat here," she said, "I felt like I'd punched you in the stomach when I told you I had moved past thinking God does stuff in the world. That it was actually much easier to trust in science than God."

"Oooh, yeah, I remember," Jared said with a sarcastic tone. "And where are you now?"

"Well," Aly said, "I was pretty cocky that day. But I'm not really sure I'm anywhere different. I mean, I guess you did see me at church."

"I did!"

"But, honestly, I still feel stupid about it. I can say, honestly, that there is something to it all."

"You mean faith?" Jared asked, looking for clarification.

"Yes," Aly said. "There's a mystery to it that I'm sure will call to me the rest of my life from time to time. I did really need it at that moment. But then it all seems so questionable to me again."

"What does?" Jared had the feeling he was always one car behind her train of thought.

"I just don't want to be the kind of person who is *against* science. I mean in a real way I've given my life to science. The technology that we're developing at my job is going to be amazing. I mean the findings of gene therapy and our tech could really change people's lives.

"It would have made a huge difference in my sister's situation," she added, her voice quavering. "I guess while faith will always have a mystery that calls to me, I just want to be part of solving things, of figuring things out and making the world better."

"And faith doesn't do that?"

"I don't really think so, or at least not as well as science does. I mean science actually solves problems. It just sometime feels like faith is against this or something. Or at least makes more problems."

"I don't think that's really true," said Jared. "I mean, most of the first scientists were people of faith, even pastors and priests. Wasn't there something about their faith that led them to these findings?"

"I don't know. Maybe. But it just appears that eventually they threw off faith so that they could really solve stuff and make the world better."

"Or worse, like creating the atom bomb."

"I suppose," Aly said. "But still, I'm someone who likes the solutions that science can achieve. And quite honestly, I'm kind of sick of feeling that being such a person means I'm not as committed to God. I mean, if that's the case, which is what I sense, then I'm—to be honest—willing to be a grownup and choose science over faith."

Immediately Jared thought of Martin and Sasha. Here were three kids, among many others through the years, that were these kinds of people. They, like Aly, were drawn to the sciences. Had youth ministry failed them?

But Jared wasn't willing to let Aly off the hook that easily.

"I hear that," Jared said. "I think you're right that there's this sense that faith and science are opposed to each other. But are they really? And while science does look to find solutions, so does faith. Actually, I think this desire to find or discover something in science actually comes from its birthplace in faith."

Aly jumped in. "This is a fight my dad and my uncle have all the time. My dad is an experimental chemist and my uncle a neuropsychologist. My dad will argue that faith and science actually have nothing to do with each other. They exist in their own domains, so he has no problem being a Christian and being a scientist. He'll say science tells us how things are, and faith tells us why things are. But my uncle doesn't buy it, telling my dad only a chemist could think this. My uncle argues that faith and science are opposed to each other, in a fight to the death. It's just that faith is fighting with sticks and stones and science with F-16s. He tells my dad that people like him are just like Japanese soldiers stuck on some Pacific island in the 1950s, still fighting a war that's been long over, worshiping a God that only makes sense in a cave."

"Wow, harsh!" Jared said with a laugh.

"Yep," Aly continued. "They have some epic arguments at Thanksgiving. It makes things interesting. But to be honest, I think I agree more with my uncle. I don't want to be someone who can't embrace science and its findings. I don't want to be a child and be too scared that we indeed are alone in a huge universe. I mean, I think I felt like that as a kid in high school, but couldn't quite articulate it yet."

"Did you?"

"Yes, I think I did."

Jared thought of Martin and Sasha. "So now that you feel like you can articulate it," he said, "what do you think really bothered you?" Turning it into a kind of joke, he added, "If I were paying you as a consultant, what would you say to me about kids like you?"

Aly smiled a playful look of importance and said, "Well . . . hmm . . ." with her finger patting her head.

Pausing to think more and move beyond flippancy, she finally said, "My guess is that those kids need to know if all scientific things they're learning in school, and even finding so interesting and inspiring, have any connection to the thing the church believes. How does evolution connect to faith? Or chaos theory?

Or particle physics? Or, to quote my uncle, if faith is just a way of crawling back into cave. I mean honestly, I would have never told anyone, but in high school I had already started wondering if you can really believe that God cares about you next to what science has found. I think kids like me want to know how those things go together."

Then Aly said, "Yeah, I guess I wondered, does anything that science discovers say anything, or even change the way we think, about God? I never saw how it did. Or worse, I never saw the church care to even see if it might.

"So yeah," she continued, "I guess I'm with my uncle: religion and faith are just for childish people."

There it was again, the fear of being a child. After Jared's experience with Svea on Christmas night, he wasn't willing to let it go. "Aly," Jared interrupted, "why are you so scared of being a child? Remember, it was a child who embraced you that night after church. She didn't try and fix your problem, but just hugged you. I know it would have been great if she had some technical solution to solve your problem, but she did something, I think, more beautiful. She saw you and shared in your pain. To be a child is to experience a deep reality of belonging; it points to something beyond us. Actually, my bet is that when you held Gena's hand in the hospital room, what you remembered was the mystery and beauty of being children together, of all the ways you loved each other and shared in each other's lives. I just don't get why being a child is bad."

Aly nodded her head in affirmation. "That hug was so important to me. Actually, I'm not sure if I would have even thought to spend the night with my sister if not for the hug. It was so powerful that it almost shook me awake."

Jared was now a little bit on a roll. "And weren't the best scientists, like the people that actually had the most profound breakthroughs in scientific findings, childlike? I mean, they say that what made Einstein so brilliant was that he refused to not think like a child. It was through his childish thinking that he discovered $E=MC^2$."

THE CHILDISH GENIUS

If there is a picture of the quintessential proprietor of the comprehensive social practice of "science," it is, as we've said, Richard Dawkins. But if there is a picture of the exemplary scientist (of someone testing findings and building theories) it is Albert Einstein. Einstein's name and image have become synonymous with brilliance. If you do something amazing, or completely senseless, someone will say, "Way to go, Einstein." "Einstein" has become a descriptor for brilliance or, in irony, deep stupidity.

But, if you ace a test or come up with an amazing solution, no one says, "Way to go, Dawkins!" or "Amazing work, Tyson!" (They may say the latter, but that's because you just bit someone's ear off or got a face tattoo and they're referring to a whole different guy.)

I have sought to make a clear distinction between scientific findings and theories and the social practice of "science." No one says, "Way to go, Dawkins," because what Dawkins is known for is not his scientific findings, but his apologetic for an all-encompassing social practice. We use "Einstein" as our descriptor of brilliance, because he is the standard for theory construction. This shows that deep down we can sense this difference between scientific findings and the social practice of "science." Our young people should feel some tension with the social practice of "science." But there is no reason for the pursuers of scientific findings to oppose the personal order that Christian faith claims.

But, as Aly says, we have failed to show young people how this is so, leaving us open to the bombastic assertions of the priest of the comprehensive social of practice of "science" that we are indeed stupid and childish. As we said above, this is more than just a below-the-belt strike, more than just a smear campaign. Rather, to call faith childish is to assert that it is a primitive position that lacks maturity, ignorantly seeking for invisible personhood. The social practice of "science" opposes the way of the child for the purpose of gaining esteem. But when we move beyond the propaganda of the social practice of "science" we see something interesting. Not only does faith affirm the disposition of the child (Matthew 19:14), but so too does the pursuit of scientific findings and theories. And not only do scientific findings and theories take on the disposition of a child,[1] but like faith, they do so in and through personhood.

EINSTEIN IS A REAL EINSTEIN

It doesn't take much looking into Einstein's past to see that his brilliance for scientific theory construction was embedded in his childishness. Einstein's brilliance was actually his ability to construct thought experiments that were fundamentally childish and full of fantasy. He would then test whether his imaginary games actually held any mathematical veracity. Like a child, Einstein loved the thought of light, his mind playing with it, asking questions of how it worked and moved. He refused to go to class or listen to lectures, because, like a child, all he wanted to do was think about light.

One of his great imaginary games that would lead to the volcanic theory of 1905 was the thought of what would happen if he could ride on a beam of light (he started thinking about this when he was sixteen). And if he were riding on this beam of light, he wondered, what would happen if he tried to look at himself in a mirror? He would be invisible! The light from his face wouldn't make it to the mirror to reflect back.

The speed of light seemed to take what appeared to be the constants of time and space and bend them. Only light and its speed were constants; everything else was relative to them. If not for a childish mind, the theory of relativity would have been impossible, as would $E=MC^2$ and the possibility of splitting an atom. The comprehensive social practice of "science," in its propaganda game, has made faith the childish position. But actually, when it comes to doing scientific theory construction, the childish mind is genius.

---

1. "Only the great theologians who were also childlike in spirit have been able to come up with the basic insights and fundamental ideas that have advanced theological understanding." Thomas F. Torrance, *Reality and Scientific Theology* (Eugene, OR: Wipf & Stock, 2001), 84.

PERSONAL KNOWLEDGE

What made Einstein a real Einstein was not only that he was willing to think like a child,[2] but also because he continued to think about the universe through his own personhood.[3] It was through placing his own person on the light beam that he could gain the vision to see the structures of the universe.

The social practice of "science" believes itself more mature by purporting to be objective. The reason that faith cannot be trusted is that in the end it is a subjective, personal experience, while science deals with only objective facts. The social practice of "science" is not only committed to an impersonal order, but because the universe is impersonal, it is through objective impersonal instruments that we discover the structures of existence and the way the world really is. But to say this is to ignore how scientific findings and theory construction are actually done. The Hungarian chemist and philosopher Michael Polanyi has shown that there is no scientific knowledge that isn't

2. Walter Isaacson discusses Einstein's high view of the child. He says, "His cocky contempt for authority led him to question received wisdom in ways that well-trained acolytes in the academy never contemplated. And as for his slow verbal development, he came to believe that it allowed him to observe with wonder the everyday phenomena that others took for granted. 'When I ask myself how it happened that I in particular discovered the relativity theory, it seemed to lie in the following circumstance,' Einstein once explained. 'The ordinary adult never bothers his head about the problems of space and time. These are things he has thought of as a child. But I developed so slowly that I began to wonder about space and time only when I was already grown up. Consequently, I probed more deeply into the problem than an ordinary child would have.'" *Einstein: His Life and Universe* (New York: Simon & Schuster, 2007), 9.

3. "The great awakenings that happen in childhood are usually lost to memory. But for Einstein, an experience occurred when he was four or five that would alter his life and be etched forever in his mind—and in the history of science. He was sick in bed one day, and his father brought him a compass. He later recalled being so excited as he examined its mysterious powers that he trembled and grew cold. The fact that the magnetic needle behaved as if influenced by some hidden force field, rather than through the more familiar mechanical method involving touch or contact, produced a sense of wonder that motivated him throughout his life. 'I can still remember—or at least I believe I can remember—that this experience made a deep and lasting impression on me,' he wrote on one of the many occasions he recounted the incident. 'Something deeply hidden had to be behind things.'" Isaacson, *Einstein: His Life and Universe*, 13.

personal, that indeed the work of discovering scientific findings, and the commitment to a personal order, go hand in hand.[4]

Polanyi explains that all experiments start with a person who has personal experiences of reality. The scientist has assumptions, feelings, desires that move her mind. There is no scientist who can stand outside of the universe. What she looks to explore, she stands within. There is no way any human mind can vacate its personal nature and operate solely on objectivity. Instead, scientific discovery is much more like a child who discovers that she lives in a world of gravity by experiencing it personally, dropping her sippy cup from her highchair over and over again. The child is profound, because she is seeking to personally make sense of her universe. The child accepts that she is not apart from the world but stands within it. Scientific discovery is never like observing monkeys at a zoo, objectively standing outside their world, seeing things from some safe, distant perch.

Einstein was so brilliant and his breakthroughs so profound because he not only refused to separate his own person from the world of observation, but childishly imagined himself deeply a part of it. He didn't stand on an objective perch watching the speed of light, but instead rode it like a bull. It is from this deep personal perspective inside reality that Einstein becomes "a real Einstein." Personal knowledge is what makes scientific findings and theories possible. And it is personal knowledge that makes faith possible.

When Einstein discovered that $E=MC^2$, he was not wrapped in a lab coat, objectively doing mathematics on a blackboard, cut off from the world. Instead, like a child, Einstein was watching a train. And watching it, he was hit with a realization: mass and energy are the same thing! He saw what he'd always known somewhere deep within his person, that the faster the train goes the more mass it actually takes on. Speed (energy) bends mass; motion and objects are indeed interconnected. This was not so much a discovery for Einstein as an unveiling. He saw something he had known all along, but suddenly had the

---

4. See Michael Polanyi, *Personal Knowledge: Toward a Post-Critical Philosophy* (Chicago: University of Chicago Press, 1962).

words—actually, the numbers—to articulate it. It was an amazing discovery born from within his own personhood.

While the comprehensive social practice of "science" might be for objective adults, scientific discovery is the personal experience of revelation. Einstein knew this all along, because he had experienced in his own person the very structures of the universe. His great breakthrough was not somehow creating these phenomena, but learning how to name what his person felt all along.[5] As Polanyi says, the scientist is a person who always knows more than they are able to prove. His search is to prove what he knows but can't quite yet explain, what his person senses are objective structures of reality.[6] The scientist enters

5. Underneath the larger argument of this project is my own commitment to critical realism. I've talked at length of the place of critical realism in the field of practical theology; see *Christopraxis* (Minneapolis: Fortress Press, 2014). Most of the best perspectives on faith and the scientific too build their perspective on critical realism. Padgett explains: "[C]ritical realism is the view that the subjects studied . . . exist independently of the investigator's experience of them." Alan Padgett, *Science and the Study of God: A Mutuality Model for Theology and Science* (Grand Rapids, MI: Eerdmans, 2003), 29. He continues: "Realists take it as a given that human beings are not God and that the way humans see things does not determine reality." *Science and the Study of God*, 33. John Polkinghorne explains further: "A critical realist cannot claim the attainment of absolute truth, but rather an increasing verisimilitude—the construction of better and better maps of physical reality." *Scientists as Theologians* (London: SPCK, 1996), 17. Barbour adds, "Critical realists affirm that the theories of science and the beliefs of theology both make claims about reality—and that at least some points these claims are related to each other." Ian Barbour, *Religion and Science: Historical and Contemporary Issues* (San Francisco: HarperSanFrancisco, 1997), 161. Arthur Peacocke directs us further into how this relates to faith and the scientific: "From a critical-realist perspective both science and theology are engaging with realities that may be referred to and pointed at, but which are both beyond the range of any completely literal description. Both employ metaphorical language and describe reality in terms of models, which may eventually be combined into higher conceptual schemes (theories or doctrines). Within such a perspective, it is therefore entirely appropriate to ask how the respective claimed cognitive contents of science and theology might, or should be, related." *Theology for a Scientific Age: Being and Becoming—Natural, Divine, and Human* (Minneapolis: Fortress Press, 1993), 19. Polkinghorne adds, "In both science and theology, I believe that we can affirm a stance of critical realism—called "critical because the method of enquiry is subtle, with a delicate intertwining of experience and interpretation, and called "realism" because the investigation has the character of a process of discovery, rather than that of human construction." John Polkinghorne, *One World: The Interaction of Science and Theology* (Philadelphia: Templeton Foundation Press, 2007), x.

6. Barbour explains Polanyi's position: "Polanyi's unifying theme is the personal participation of the knower in all knowledge. In science, the heart of discovery is creative imagination, which is a very personal act. Science requires skills that, like

the experiment like a child, sensing that there is something out there that she can sense but not yet name.

FAITH AS PERSONAL

This personal experience of the scientific is similar, even related, to the personal knowledge of faith. We claim faith not simply because we have some objective proof. If we did, then we couldn't call it "faith" at all. But our experience of faith isn't blind; it is always seeking understanding. We, like all scientists, are part of the universe. We claim faith not because we have reached some objective plane. Rather, we claim faith because we have had personal experiences that have revealed to us that indeed there is a personal mind in the universe.

The experience of faith, like a scientific finding or theory, is an event of encounter. Just as Einstein witnessed something in watching the train, we too have witnessed the coming of God, feeling God's personhood next to our own in lived experiences of ministry—in those moments like when Svea reaches out to embrace Aly, taking her person into a mystery where the huge universe seems to deliver an embrace to her broken person. Or in a moment of prayer, like when Svea prays for Aly with Jared before bed. Aly feels the very objective reality of God through the experience of encountering God's action in such moments. Aly's experience too has come as an unveiling, a revelation, just as it did to Einstein. And just as Einstein took this experience and sought to verify it with equations, so we seek to

---

riding a bicycle, cannot be formally specified but only learned by example and practice. In all knowledge we have to see patterns in wholes. In recognizing a friend's face or in making a medical diagnosis, we use many clues but cannot identify all the particulars on which our judgment of a total pattern relies. Polanyi holds that the assessment of evidence is always an act of discretionary personal judgment. No rules specify whether an unexplained discrepancy between theory and experiment should be set aside as an anomaly or taken to invalidate the theory. Participation in a community of inquiry is a safeguard against subjectivity, though it never removes the burden of individual responsibility. Polanyi holds that all these characteristics are even more important in religion. Here personal involvement is greater, but not to the exclusion of rationality and universal intent. Participation in the historical tradition and present experience of a religious community is essential." *Religion and Science*, 94.

verify the experience of God's presence with the discernment of a community and its tradition.

But we should be careful. To say the scientific finding and theories and faith are both personal experiences does not necessarily mean that the scientific findings are an advocate for faith. This would simply not be true. What it does show is that the commitment of the comprehensive social practice of "science" to an impersonal order is actually inconsistent with the fact that it is persons who do scientific work. In an odd way, to hold to the *telos* of the social practice of "science," we are forced to see our own deepest experience, our own mind that reaches for otherness, knowledge, and love as a lonely abnormality and *not* as an echo of the mystery of the universe itself.

To call those of faith "childish" is also unfair, for those engaging in scientific experiments often return to a childlikeness to explore the depth of the hidden shape of the universe. So the warning must be clear: while scientific findings don't necessarily oppose the commitments of faith, they also don't directly support faith. Therefore, we are left to ask, How do we actually go about relating faith and the scientific? And how can this relating help the young people we minister to?

8.

Relating Faith and the Scientific, Issue One: SCIENCE Doesn't Say Anything

It's become common for some people to say, "Well, that's just science!" or "Science tells us . . ." As a matter of fact, this is what Martin said when discussing the inevitability of mass extinctions. His pushback to the group was that some coming mass extinction was "just science." This is a well-used rhetorical move because "science" is cloaked in the robe of high esteem in our technological society. To utter these phrases is to lift yourself to high ground in the battle to win an argument. But while this statement is rhetorically useful, it isn't true. There is actually no such thing as *science*, at least in the sense of saying one clear, unified thing. There is, indeed, a comprehensive social practice called "science," but its objective is to provide a way of living toward a goal: that there is no personal being behind the universe.

To say "Science says . . ." or "It's just science," isn't an accurate statement. Sciences are loosely held patchworks of multiple findings and theories. The stitches that hold this patchwork together are foci on natural and human phenomena. But there is no single way to do scientific work. When someone says "Science says," they are using rhetorical sleight-of-hand, because only particular scientific findings and theories say anything. Science itself is a loose container for a disciplined operation of exploring natural phenomena in a systematic way. There then is no way that "science" could say *x* or *y*. What speaks are particular theories and findings.

This is one of the main reasons that it appears so hard to talk about science in the church. Because we imagine that we can't quite get our arms around it. While that's true, it's because science isn't *any particular thing*. To discuss science in the context of youth ministry is necessarily to discuss the impact of particular scientific theories themselves. It is to put these findings and theories in discussion with our understanding of humanity, sin, eternal-life, and more. And this is actually what young people want. Sasha doesn't want to discuss "religion and science," but how the findings of astrophysics and her own experience through these findings of the mass of the universe relate to her experience of God. Martin cares little about what is philosophically at stake in relating religion and science, but through the theories of evolution, he has been drawn into contemplation. He wonders what is humanity compared to the enormity of time, and how can God be loving and good if mass extinctions are the way things are.

So *science* doesn't say anything, but, for instance, the theory of neuroplasticity says a lot. Science is just a room filled with people having many discussions at once. To stand outside this room and try to relate it to faith is impossible. The only way for faith to interact with science is to enter the room and walk into an ongoing conversation, listening as physicists talk of quarks, or paleoanthropologists speak of Neanderthal burial practices, or cognitive ethologists discuss the compassion of elephants, or computer scientists talk about the mechanisms of moral consciousness. There is no way for Jared to actually have a *conversation between religion and science* in his youth group. If Jared is to follow Aly's advice and help young people relate scientific findings and faith, he must engage *particular* theories and perspectives with particular understandings and practices of faith.

NO RELIGION

In a similar way there is *no such thing as religion*. Religion too is a loose categorical descriptor. To say *religion* is to refer to a generic patchwork held together by beliefs in something more than what is physical (i.e., the metaphysical). No one is really generically *religious*. Rather, certain people practice and believe particular things. If Jared were to try to have a retreat on "religion and science," he not only would struggle with how to enter the conversation, but in the end it would be a good bet that it would be boring. It would be working broad categories that have little impact on us personally. Only the deeply philosophical young person would be interested.

But to invite a conversation on prayer and the findings of neuropsychology might indeed be of interest. To explore with young people how prayer has affected medical recovery might take us into new ways of seeing the world, for instance.

To get drawn into seeing things as *either* religion *or* science is to be duped by the comprehensive social practice of "science." The social practice of "science" likes to boldly frame things as either "science" or "religion," telling us that they are distinct entities, locked in their own rooms. But this is to falsely claim that "religion" is just a set of rational (or irrational) judgments, and not a way of life that is bound up with our very experiences of reality. If science is just a loose categorical space where many conversations are happening at once, then "religion" is similar.[1] Part of what makes someone like Dawkins disingenuous is that he stands outside the room and supposes that because he can hear the commotion inside he understands it. If he were to walk into this hypothetical room, he would find not one single thing called "religion," but many at times oppositional practices, all seeking to encounter reality, not altogether different than the scientific.

What makes Dawkins disingenuous is that he stands outside the room and takes potshots—ironically doing something very

1. Peter Harrison explains: "Between Thomas [Aquinas's] time and our own, *religio* has been transformed from a human virtue into a generic something typically constituted by sets of beliefs and practices. *Scientia* has followed a similar course, for although it had always referred both to a form of knowledge and a habit of mind, the interior dimension has now almost entirely disappeared. During the sixteenth and seventeenth centuries, both religion and science were literally turned inside out." *The Territories of Science and Religion* (Chicago: University of Chicago Press, 2015), 16.

*un*scientific—refusing to enter the room and join the practices themselves. Dawkins does something Einstein refused to do: keeping his own self out of the process.[2] If Dawkins were to be truly scientific, he could only call faith a mental illness after he'd prayed with brothers and sisters who love him and sought to minister to him.

This assumption that there are two rooms, one for science and one for religion, is the legacy of the story of big and little brother, as stated above. It is now time that we return to the drama. Peter Harrison has told a convincing version of this story in his Gifford Lectures, showing how this artificial setup of religion vs. science came to be. While I can't rehearse his story in full, a few highlights are necessary to help Jared as he considers Aly's advice.

BACK TO LITTLE BROTHER

When the little brother of the comprehensive social practice of "science" tells his story, it is often paraphrased like this: *Back in the days of the Greek philosophers, science was born from the genius of people like Plato and Aristotle, Archimedes and Thales. But then medieval Christianity smothered it—those indeed were some dark days when the beliefs of the church restricted the noble work of science. Then the Enlightenment rediscovered science, and for the first time gave us truly logical, rational, and useful things to "believe in."*[3]

This little (and offensively reductive) history is nowhere near true, but it serves the purpose of allowing certain categories to be redefined, permitting little brother to reset the playing field for his own gain.

2. Or maybe it is there in a hidden way he refuses to admit. Maybe his own story is really about how faith or the church hurt him.

3. Harrison explains further: "In Brian Bunch's recent survey of the history of science and technology we are again informed that Western science began with Thales of Miletus. He and his successors 'were the first to believe that the universe could be understood using reason alone rather than through mythology or religion.' As a consequence of these ideas, the ancient Greeks established institutions in which individuals 'pursued science in somewhat the way the universities do today.' The advent of Christianity in late antiquity brought an end to these institutions, but science was revived during the scientific revolution." *The Territories of Science and Religion*, 24.

Ultimately what the stunt of this false history does is to redefine what "believe in" actually means. This redefinition is how little brother science pulls his trick on big brother faith. Little brother does something that Archimedes would have never assumed; he makes "believe in" refer solely to *theoretical judgments*. Once big brother is tricked into accepting this redefinition, little brother has won his independence, and in turn has changed the perception of big brother (meaning scientific activity is no longer part of the way of life of faith as it was originally. Christian faith as a way of life that seeks understanding of God in and through our embodied lives made it possible for some to study scripture and creeds—philosophers of texts—and other to be natural philosophers studying the structure of the universe as a way of faith. Christianity didn't smother science, but helped created it!).[4]

When little brother wins his independence, he in turn transforms the perception of big brother. Big brother is no longer faith as a way of life bound in our personal experience and commitments, but is recast as "religion," a self-enclosed field of its own theoretical judgments, relocated in a single room. Harrison has shown how the category of "religion" only really functions after the Enlightenment when "science," the little brother, pushes away from big brother and claims his own space. And of course, once big brother is redefined as religion, he has lost his ability to speak of anything that is not labeled the property of religion. Like an eight-year-old to an eleven-year-old, little brother now has the strength and confidence to yell at the older

4. "Modern Western empirical science originated and flourished in the bosom of Christian theism and originated nowhere else. Some have found this anomalous. Bertrand Russell, for example, thought of the Christian church as repressing and inhibiting the growth of science. He was therefore disappointed to note that science did not emerge in China, even though, as he said, the spread of scientific knowledge there encountered no such obstacles as he thought the Church put in its way in Europe. But the fact is, it was Christian Europe that fostered, promoted, and nourished modern science. It arose nowhere else. All of the great names of early Western science, furthermore—Nicholas Copernicus, Galileo Galilee, Isaac Newton, Robert Boyle, John Wilkins, Roger Cotes, and many others—all were serious believers in God. Indeed, the important twentieth-century physicist C. F. von Weizsäcker goes so far as to say, 'In this sense, I call modern science a legacy of Christianity.'" Alvin Plantinga, *Where the Conflict Really Lies: Science, Religion, & Naturalism* (London: Oxford University Press, 2011), 266.

brother to mind his own business. Soon big brother is convinced that he must keep his "beliefs" (his theoretical judgments)
between himself and his other religious friends.

Little brother has shifted our understanding of what we com-
mit to. He tells us that what matters is not seeking the flowing
river of our personal commitments as a whole, but rather to separate commitments into self-contained rooms that we choose to
believe in. The comprehensive social practice of "science" is so
powerful next to the experience of adolescence because it frames
the tension with faith, in theoretical judgments around what you
"believe in."[5] It avoids conversations about the mystery of meaning, and focuses on what can be logically judged as plausible. So,
focusing only on theoretical judgments, it asks young people,
"Will you really be the kind of immature baby that 'believes in'
things like water walking, snake talking, and sea parting? Come
on, think about this; it makes no sense. These beliefs should be
denied or locked in their own (padded) room."

"Science" doesn't ask young people to consider their life
within a deep stream of others who have lived and died praying,
worshiping, and experiencing the personal encounter of God.
Instead it tells us: just make rational judgments about the believ-
ability of what is not necessarily central (like whether the earth
was created in six twenty-four-hour days). It says: forget your
grandmother's prayers; forget the experience of feeding the
hungry; forget about embracing your friend in sorrow. That's
all pointless! What matters is whether it is theoretically plausible
to believe that water can be turned into wine. "It isn't!" little
brother says, so keep any nostalgia for that story in the room

5. "The contraction of the scope of 'I believe,' and the assumption of its more
familiar modern meaning—"to believe in the actual existence of some person or
thing"—begins in the seventeenth century. 'Believe in,' from this time onward, is
less a personal commitment than a theoretical judgment. It becomes a matter of disinterested intellectual assent to putative facts and, increasingly from the nineteenth
century, to doubtful or false claims. It is no coincidence that these transitions are
accompanied by the growth of the ideal of scientific objectivity and the gradual disappearance of moral and formative elements from natural philosophical discourse.
For the moment, however, my suggestion is that 'belief' is not a historically stable
concept in the West, and thus it provides a poor foundation for a notion like 'religion,' for which is claimed both transhistorical and cross-cultural applicability." Harrison, *The Territories of Science and Religion*, 49.

labeled "religion." And you should be pretty embarrassed to use it outside that room.

Aristotle and Archimedes, not to mention Newton or Kepler, would never have seen their work as a separate theoretical judgment. They would not have chosen to believe in "science" over faith, moving from one room to the next. For Galileo the pursuit of natural philosophy was searching for the meaning of God's act in nature.[6] Galileo, Copernicus, Newton, and Kepler searched for the movement of the earth, and its place within the universe, because of the same personal commitment that led them to take the Eucharist at mass.[7] They were seeking to know God by discovering the shape and movements of God's created realm. Just as you can know something about a painter from his work, so you can know something of God from God's creation, they assumed.[8] They so clearly thought beyond the

6. "Discussions of the relationship between 'science' and 'religion' originated in the early nineteenth century, when students of nature first began referring to their work as science rather than as natural philosophy (or natural history). Before that time there were occasional expressions of concern about the tension between faith and reason, but no one pitted religion against science or vice versa. By the 1820s, however, books and articles featuring the phrase 'science and religion' in their titles were starting to appear. One of the first, if not the first, English language books with the words in their titles came out in 1823: Thomas Dick's popular *The Christian Philosopher; or, The Connection of Science and Philosophy with Religion*. By midcentury 'science and religion' was becoming a literary trope, and during the 1850s and 1860s several American colleges and seminaries established professorships devoted to demonstrating (and preserving) the harmony of science and revealed religion." Ronald Numbers, "Introduction," in *Galileo Goes to Jail: And Other Myths About Science and Religion* (Cambridge, MA: Harvard University Press, 2009), 3.

7. "Science first achieved a recognizably modern form in the seventeenth century. Those concerned in its early development were, almost all, people who took seriously the existence of a religious dimension to life. Many of the first Fellows of the Royal Society were of a puritan persuasion. Indeed, it has been suggested that the Christian doctrine of creation, with its emphasis on the Creator's rationality (so that his world was intelligible) and freedom (so that its nature had a contingent character which could be discovered only by investigation, rather than by speculation) provided an essential matrix for the coming into being of the scientific enterprise." John Polkinghorne, *One World: The Interaction of Science and Theology* (Philadelphia: Templeton Foundation Press, 2007), 4.

8. Of course, anyone with a Barthian disposition will shiver to the bone when reading this line. But what is important to see is that the major reason Barth opposes natural theology is because of the ways that little brother has distorted the situation. Once religion and science are put into two categories, to allow for a natural philosophy is to lose transcendence, divine action, and the Word that judges and brings to life. Barth's opposition is so heavy against science because he is prophetically trying

distinct rooms of "religion" and "science" that they didn't even call themselves scientists, but instead "natural philosophers"—and to say "natural" was to presume engagement with God. They explored the natural as a way of faith, seeking the shape of God's creation as the way of faithfulness. Scientific findings and theory construction was born from and for the purpose of faith. There were no separate rooms.

And this is where "science's" history is just flat-out wrong. Attention to the natural world wasn't a separate theoretical sphere to "believe in." Copernicus never asked, "Okay, now, do I believe in science or religion?" or even "Am I now doing science, using its theoretical judgments, or am I using religion?" Rather, for him, mathematics was a language of worship; it was connected to his very way of life. But once little brother convinces us that "to believe" is a theoretical judgment, we are playing by his rules.

RELATING THIS TO YOUTH MINISTRY

If Jared is to follow Aly's advice and help the young people in his ministry engage in a dialogue with the scientific, he must do so by avoiding the trap of theoretical judgment and the temptation to compartmentalize. Jared needs to avoid the tricks of little brother, meaning he needs to avoid both seeing "believe" as solely a "theoretical judgment" and "religion" and "science" as completely separate self-enclosed worlds. If Jared can't avoid this, he'll think to himself, "I now need to make myself qualified to enter the room of science with an apologetic for religion. I need to enter into science so I can show my young people that religion is just as logical a theoretical judgment as science!" But as we've seen, this is to concede the rules of the game to the social practice of "science" and, I believe, in the end, not helpful to young people.

Rather, what Jared needs to do is continue to call his young people into the personal commitment of the experience of faith. He is a pastor after all! Jared doesn't need to make his young

to free theology and faith from being subjugated in religion. See for example *Church Dogmatics* III/2.

people into budding little scientists (some of them already are). Rather what Jared needs to do is show how the personal commitment of faith means the *seeking of understanding*. And this *seeking*, particularly in our age, suggests an exploration of specific scientific findings and theories, like cosmology, evolution, and neurocognition.

But what opens the door for Jared is that even a singular focus on these particular theories is not really what young people want or need. Rather, even a budding scientist like Sasha is interested in the scientific findings and theories because of what they do to her personal experience. She wonders what the lived experiences of prayer, confession, and the hope of salvation could possibly mean if there were aliens. Sasha must now wrestle with the experience of hearing that NASA's Kepler space mission has discovered 11 billion planets in what they call "the Goldilocks zone." Through her experience she is drawn into contemplations between her faith and scientific findings and theories. In a similar way, Martin hears that there are actually scientific findings and theories that heed the plausibility of events of mass extinction seen in shows like *The Walking Dead*. Martin wonders how we can say that we are made in the image of God, and even that every hair on our head is counted by God (Luke 12:7), and yet we human beings exist for mere seconds on the timeline of cosmic history.

Jared needs to enter into direct conversation with scientific findings, because the objective is not to defend religion next to the comprehensive social practice of "science," but to explore what disciplined and reasoned studies of our world might tell us about our lifetime, our yearning, and our personal experience.

So for Jared to follow Aly's advice and try to help his young people relate faith and the scientific, he must recognize that what is being related is not faith as a theoretical judgment (religion), but faith as a personal experience. He'll need to do this relating through the personal experience of ministry—like prayer, mercy, love, and service. These experiences must be the very starting place for the relating to occur.

And in turn, Jared must remember that faith as a personal experience is being related not to "science" as a social practice

or even as a contained field, but to particular findings and theories that affect our experiences. Sasha and Martin don't necessarily care about the philosophical presumptions of science as a
field, nor do they really care about certain findings and theories
(unless they'll be on the exam!). What they deeply care about
is how scientific findings and theories affect their lived experience. They care deeply about how the particular interpretation
of our existence of evolving from apes, or being only one of
many other hominid creatures, affects our lived experience of a
personal God who comes to our own person in the ministry of
love.

9.

Relating Faith and the Scientific, Issue Two: How This Relating Is Done

After the winter morning at The Rusty Spoon, Jared was resolved to follow Aly's advice. He needed to help his young people relate faith and scientific findings and theories. But he had no idea how he was going to do this, or even how to think about it.

Resolve has a way of weakening under the pressure of a full schedule. And as the new year dawned, all but the next task was dust under Jared's pace. Not only was he behind on getting things ready for the January high school ski trip, but the denomination's youth worker training event was only days away. Jared was honored, but a little overwhelmed, to be the host and emcee of the event, as well as leading a workshop.

Jared titled his workshop session, "From Dull to Dynamic Small Groups." There hadn't been much time to prepare as the event neared, so Jared went into it with only very broad notes but a clear sense of his larger point. He punctuated the need for small groups to be a place to ask difficult questions. He shared how he organized and trained his adult volunteers to be ready to engage young people's questions and how this had affected his ministry. He traced the transformation back to last summer's mission trip. "It was then that we decided to embrace a ministry of sharing in each other's humanity." Jared told how in the past he'd seen his small groups as a strategy for program building, rather than communities of shared life.

As Jared spoke, he felt exhilarated; the workshop seemed to be humming. For a moment he felt like he was standing outside himself, watching himself talk, and noticing that, indeed, it was all going well. Yet, underneath those pulses of excitement, he had another feeling that rushed him back into his body. Like waves, small pinched pangs of panic would crash into Jared chest as his subconscious reminded him that he didn't *really* know what he was talking about. To keep these pinched pangs of panic from growing, Jared just talked faster. It seemed to help . . . until the Q&A.

As Jared invited questions, the pain was acute as he anticipated the first response. The first few questions were logistical, giving Jared every opportunity to speak from his own experience. He told how many young people he had per group and how he trained the leaders. Jared noticed how much people liked it when he threw in a few stories to illustrate his answers. So he decided he'd keep this strategy going. But soon Jared's confidence was crumbling, and the pinched pain throbbed as the questions became pointed. Sarah, a youth worker Jared had seen around but never spoken with, asked, "How do you prepare your leaders for the really difficult stuff?"

"What do you mean?" Jared asked.

"I don't know," Sarah continued. "I guess I mean how do you prepare your leaders to talk with high schoolers about hooking up, or how do you deal with their questions around evolution?"

"Oh, no," someone jokingly added from the back of the room. "Sex and science, the two big no-no's in the church—watch out!"

Everyone laughed, giving Jared a second to race into every corner of his brain, activating every neuron cluster for an intelligible word. He stood as still as he could, searching for some hidden content to connect to and cure him from the state of blankness. Jared still needed more time, so he asked, "What do you mean? Can you give us an example?"

Sarah had been around the denominational youth ministry

conversation for years, but mainly stayed on the fringes. It wasn't until last year that she moved from part-time to full-time. But this move gave Sarah the confidence to inject herself deeper into the youth ministry conversations. She felt like she actually belonged. In response to Jared's call for clarification, she laughed and said, "Okay." She paused to put her thoughts together. The group sat in silence for a few beats, which felt like minutes to Jared.

"Well," she said, "for instance, almost all my ninth-graders are taking Earth Science, and I know in late October they're going to get to the evolution sections of the class. Right about then the questions start coming in our small groups. I personally feel like I can handle them; I tend to tell kids that evolution and faith really have nothing to do with each other, that they're really just two different perspectives that don't really talk to each other. They're like two different operating systems, I guess, like trying to run an Android app on an iPhone. So let's move on. But, I have parents and other adult leaders who don't feel this way. I have one leader, Lynn, who tries to show how evolution and the Bible go together, which seems tricky, and maybe dangerous, to me. And I even have a parent, Cal, who has brought in pamphlets from Ken Hamm, showing how evolution is a lie—I've put a stop to that now. But still I'm not sure how to prepare adult leaders, or parents for that matter, for these more difficult topics of discussion."

Jared had no direct answer, so he went to his ace strategy and told a story, sharing how over the last nine months he too had been hit with questions about science from young people and their parents. He shared a little bit about Sasha and Trent. But then he recounted in more detail his experience with Aly. Jared told particularly about the Thanksgiving dinner debates between her dad and uncle. People all laughed as he described the scene. He painted quite a picture of Aly's uncle accusing her dad of being an ignorant cave-dweller, chasing an invisible person. Jared did his best to say that he felt a little differently than either Aly's dad or uncle, that he believed there were real ways that scientific findings overlapped with faith.

He then held his breath and prayed that no one would ask him how.

ROUTES TO RELATING

It was a child's experience in China that would eventually provide us with the clearest map for the ways of relating faith and science—the echoes of which we can hear in Sarah's comments above. The young Ian Barbour was born to American nationals teaching at Yenching University in 1920s China. Ian's mother was a scholar in religious education, and his father was a geologist. As a child, Ian and his family became close friends with the French paleontologist Pierre Teilhard de Chardin. Teilhard was ingeniously relating evolutionary findings with the practice of faith. While he was on a dig in China, the Barbours and Teilhard became close.

Teilhard saw himself as a "scientist-theologian." Within decades, following the footsteps of his boyhood hero, Ian Barbour, too, became a "scientist-theologian" himself. But unlike the paleontologist Teilhard, he chose physics.

These dreams of following Teilhard's footsteps all but disappeared under the grind of studying cosmic rays. But in the 1950s a Ford Foundation Fellowship took Barbour back to his boyhood. The fellowship allowed the young Kalamazoo College professor to spend a year at Yale Divinity School studying theology and ethics. Now the trajectory of the rest of Barbour's career was set; his vocation, like his boyhood hero, was to relate science with religion.

In his 1997 book *Religion and Science*, Barbour presented a fourfold model for this relationship, and his map has become paradigmatic. Barbour explained that there are four options in relating faith and science: 1) conflict, 2) independence, 3) dialogue, or 4) integration.

Like a married couple, religion and science may relate through fighting and argument. They might yell their perspectives at each other, the resentment of misunderstanding drawing them together, but with the bitterness of *conflict*.

Or religion and science may have decided that the time for talking is over; they are just two different people with different desires and hopes. One stays in the house and the other moves across town. It is best if they live *independent* lives. Of course, at moments they'll have to be together for a graduation or funeral. But when they are, they'll make no eye contact, striving to avoid each other. If they never talk, the peace is kept.

Or maybe faith and science are a couple where all the romance has disappeared, but in its absence they have found a friendship. They are different people, but now that there is no pressure to be in love this difference is welcomed. They've freed themselves from the guilt of the past, and now they enjoy long *dialogues* on the porch over coffee. With all the defensiveness and jealousy gone, these conversations are rich. There remains a few sore subjects between them, but at this stage, what counts is the places of connection.

Or, finally, faith and science might be a couple that at times publicly fights at a restaurant, or ignores each other for a full weekend, but these are just signs of an electricity between them. These tensions are just building to an explosion of *integration*—boom-chick-a-wow. In these moments the two become one.

THE FLATNESS OF THE MAP

Barbour's map provides clear paths for relating faith and science, and it is helpful. But while this map is genius in its directionality, it is weak in its topology—that is, it's too flat. Barbour presumes that the issues between faith and science, between our married couple, are contained only between the two. In his map Barbour assumes that there are only two entities relating. But this is not the case, as we've seen above. When we move closer to the ground, reality becomes more complicated, and the map is less helpful. We see that there is not just a couple needing to relate, but a whole constellation of figures.

The flatness and absence of this constellation in Barbour's map can be seen in the title of his book *Religion and Science*. Barbour makes no distinction between "religion" as a set of theoretical judgments, and the practices of personal encounter with divine action—which is the pursuit of faith. It is one thing to relate "religion" as theoretical (metaphysical) judgments to science, and quite another thing to relate "faith" as the lived experience of encountering the personhood of God.

One of the reasons that Dawkins can be so bombastic in his critique is that he fails to clearly state *what* he is relating to "science." Dawkins sees violent conflict as the only option for relating because he chooses to see only "religion." He can poke fun at faith by laminating it to "religion." Dawkins thinks that faith is absurd because it makes no theoretical sense in our material world. But judging faith by a cut-off external standard is no way to relate to it. If Dawkins wants to relate to faith through conflict, the only way to do so is to take on faith's own methodologies (this would be truly scientific) and use its practices of personal encounter to seek the action of God. Only after doing this could he contend that there is outright conflict between faith and "science."

So while Barbour's map is helpful, it lacks detail. For example, Barbour's map fails to make important distinctions between the social practice of "science," and the scientific as particular findings and theories.

Mikael Stenmark has spotted these problems. Although appreciative of Barbour's work, he has jiggled its parts enough to shift the map, adding nuance and texture. Stenmark reminds us that when discussing forms of relating, and seeking to map them, we need to have an eye for goals (*telos*). To get beyond the surface of our married couple and truly understand their ways of relating, we have to get underneath their strategies of conflict, independence, dialogue, or integration, and seek to understand their goals, their deepest pursuits.

It is when we focus on the *telos* that our vision shifts, and we see not just a couple but also the presence of others. We recognize that we must be clear about what we are seeking to relate. For instance, the goal of the comprehensive social practice of "science," as perpetuated by Tyson and Dawkins, is to convince us that the universe is an impersonal place, and to ridicule anyone who is too weak and immature to face this fact. To relate the social practice of "science" with religion or faith will change the terrain of the paths Barbour laid out.

It will be a bumpy road to try and find *dialogue* between faith and the comprehensive social practice of "science." And the path of *integration* will be impossibly treacherous—filled with steep sharp cliffs, alligators, and lava streams. These paths are treacherous because the *telos* of each is diametrically opposed. The social practice of "science" seeks to convince us that the universe is an impersonal place, while faith seeks again and again to both encounter and understand a personal universe given to us by a personal God. If the hope is to relate the social practice of "science" and faith, the paths available are only conflict or independence. Each perspective's *telos* is too distinct to allow for either dialogue or integration.

But if we decide that what we seek to relate is faith with scientific findings and theories, then the terrain changes. The *telos* of scientific findings and theories is to understand the very shape of material reality itself. So now the path to dialogue is open, for the *telos* between faith and scientific findings and theories are not diametrically opposed (though they are not exactly linked). But now this dialogue changes. It doesn't depend anymore on some obscure thing called "science," but on the specific methods and findings of, say, particle physics or paleontology. What Stenmark shows is that we are not just generically relating religion and science. We must deal with the *telos* of multiple perspectives.

BACK TO SARAH
THE YOUTH WORKER

Sarah, the youth worker at Jared's workshop, has chosen the path of independence. She has allowed the social practice of "science" to claim evolution for its own pursuits. The social practice of "science" uses evolution as a point in its goal to persuade us that indeed we live in only an impersonal world, not caring that evolution's methodology (its research methods and findings) doesn't actually prove this. The comprehensive social practice of "science" turns evolutionary findings into some kind of conclusive statement about our existence, like "Evolution proves that all we are is animal." Darwin shows us that there is a link between living organisms through natural selection, but the social practice of "science" takes that to mean that any design in the world is merely accidental, for its quest is to prove that the world is an impersonal place.

Intuitively, Sarah recognizes this and refuses to follow the path of conflict—she doesn't want to be a closed-minded, antiintellectual person. The best she can do, then, is the path of independence; her only option is to keep faith and evolution apart. She decides to avoid discussing evolution at church, or does so only vaguely, telling young people not to sweat it, because evolution is Android and faith is iOS. This can only be true if we squeeze faith into some theoretical judgment and close our eyes to how the social practice of "science" uses evolution for it own goals.

The parent in Sarah's ministry, Cal with the Ken Hamm tracts, operates from a similar perspective but takes a different tack, seeing evolution as a weapon of the social practice of "science." Sarah and Cal are in a death match of difference, but in actuality their struggle is intense because of their similarity. They have both conceded that the relating will be done between religion and the social practice of "science." Their only difference is that Cal, unlike Sarah, is not willing to follow the path of independence and chooses instead the road of conflict. But they are both being led by the same map. Cal uses Ken Hamm pamphlets as a weapon. Sarah seems more reasonable than Cal, but actually they have both conceded that the fight is between religion and the comprehensive social practice of "science."

The adult leader, Lynn, that Sarah mentioned to Jared tries the more difficult and seemly dangerous thing, to find a place of dialogue, to explore if there are actual points of overlap. This seems dangerous because it can be misunderstood as a desire to find intersection between the presumed categories of religion and the social practice of "science." But this not what she is after. Rather, Lynn sees connections between the *findings* of evolution and the experience of faith. Lynn recognizes that this is not a perfect link. The path of dialogue is not paved and remains rocky. But at the methodological level, evolution's findings of radical human uniqueness seem to her to open up conversations about spirituality and divine encounter. The very fact that the earliest artifacts we have of *homo sapiens* are cave paintings suggesting worship seems to deliver an opportunity for dialogue. What Lynn seeks, which is so important to notice, is to relate faith (as pursuing the encounter with a personal God) with scientific findings (methodological pursuits for the verified shape of material reality). When we make the distinction between what we are actually seeking to relate, these paths of conflict, independence, dialogue, and integration are shifted.

WAIT!

But we must be careful. It is clear that the comprehensive social practice of "science" and scientific findings and theories are different—they have different pursuits and goals. But just because they are different doesn't mean these distinct pursuits might not simultaneously affect a single person. For instance, a scientist like Trent (Sasha's dad) feels the weight of the comprehensive social practice of "science" when he constructs scientific theory.[1] He sees how a finding of physics might indeed point to a personal force in the universe, realizing that a deeply finetuned universe indeed seems to have personal mind. Trent is uneasy sharing this at a physics conference, fearing that the goal of the comprehensive social practice of "science" will punish him for these very scientific findings. Trent says, "Unfortunately, you can't get promoted and get tenure in a state university for saying you see God in our finely tuned carbon universe."

But this also shows that the goals for the social practice of "science" and scientific findings and theories are different. When Trent creates an experiment to test the concept of a theoretical physicist, his goals are methodological (as opposed to epistemological). He is seeking what is empirically verifiable through multiple repetitions. If he has an epistemological goal (a

---

1. When Trent does his scientific work, of course, he is engaging in a social practice. Physics has its own social practices (its own history, tradition, and goals), but these social practices are open and discursive; they don't claim to be a life philosophy as I'm describing Dawkins's comprehensive social practice of "science."

way of seeking to know), it is to discover the shape of reality as it is delivered to him through the methodology of the experiment. So Trent doesn't necessarily share the goal of the comprehensive social practice of "science." He isn't trying to show that there is *no* personal mind in the universe. His goal is to describe the way the world is. But this goal isn't completely isolated from the pressure of the social practice of "science." Trent has to worry that if indeed his scientific findings oppose the goal of the social practice of "science," his whole methodology will be ridiculed as immature and immoral.[2]

So to decide which path on Barbour's map to follow, we must first be clear about what we hope to relate. When Sarah's small group asks questions, they are *not* asking how theoretical judgments of religion relate to *either* the comprehensive social practice of "science" or the methods of scientific discovery. Rather, what the small groups of high school students want to explore is how faith, as an encounter with a personal God who acts in the universe, can be related to a certain scientific finding/theory called evolution. And they are asking this, as we saw in the last chapter, because of their experience. They are asking, Do the findings of evolution conflict or connect in any way with my (or my family's) experience of a personal God? If I've been told reading the Bible is a practice of faith that takes me into an encounter with a personal God, how am I to understand the very different story of evolution?

2. Throughout I've been drawing a strong distinction between scientific findings and theories and the social practice of "science." I stand by that division and think it is helpful in regards to ministry. But that said, Trent's experience here reflects that my division is not as clear as I've made it appear. Stenmark points further to these muddy waters: "Science may be regarded as merely a set of theories and religion as only a collection of beliefs. Clearly science and religion include these aspects! But science should not be identified with its theories or religion with its beliefs. Moreover, we do not grasp enough of the character and function of scientific theories and religious beliefs if we abstract them from the processes in which they are generated, that is, from their social and historical context; scientific theories are one product of scientific practice and religious beliefs are one output of religious practice." Mikael Stenmark, *How to Relate Science and Religion* (Grand Rapids, MI: Eerdmans, 2004), 16.

SHIFTING THE MAP

When we seek to relate faith with scientific findings and theories, we discover that Barbour's map shifts. The paths of conflict, independence, dialogue, and integration are redrawn. The original broad shape can still be spotted. But like comparing maps of North America from the seventeenth and twentieth centuries, the detail becomes more fine and the pathways more accurate. It is the focus on *telos* (goals) that is the lens that pulls things into sharper detail.[3] We are not only pushed to be clearer about what we are actually relating, but also to recognize that any relating worth its name will have either overlap, openness, or refusal at levels of its deepest pursuits. So it isn't enough to ask, Do faith and scientific findings conflict? Rather, we must first recognize the *telos*, or goal of each, and then push deeper, and ask, are there indeed places of intersection? And what does this intersection say about our existence? From Stenmark's perspective there are three options of relating that allow us to account for the distinct *telos* of our multiple players. Taking this into account, Stenmark shifts Barbour's map, redrawing its lines.

OPTION ONE

Option one is to see no overlap between faith and scientific findings and theories. This is the view of Aly's dad (the "cave-dweller"). The good news is that because there is no overlap between them, there is no need for conflict. They are two totally different domains that have little to do with each other. Steven Jay Gould, and more recently Michael Ruse, have proposed a position called NOMA, which stands for "non-overlapping

3. "I suggest that we analyze the kind of job that science and Christian faith (or religion more generally speaking) do in terms of the purpose or the goals of these two practices and the means that their practitioners have developed to achieve these goals. Once we have a good grip on this we are in a position to assess whether the two compete for the same job (the competition view), or do completely different jobs (the independent view), or do jobs that overlap to some extent (the contact view)." Stenmark, "How to Relate Christian Faith and Science," in J. B. Stump and Alan Padgett, *The Blackwell Companion to Science and Christianity* (London: Wiley-Blackwell, 2012), 63.

magisteria." The idea is fairly simple: faith and scientific findings exist in two non-overlapping domains. Aly's dad can keep his faith in one part of his life and his scientific pursuits in another. But NOMA ignores that human beings have an insatiable impulse to give loyalty and authority to some entity. To just "keep 'em separated" doesn't work, and that's why this non-overlapping is itself a magisterium. A king only has the majestic authority to rule in his own domain. Once he steps outside it, he may deserve respect, but he is no longer bestowed with authority. It is the same way with faith and science.[4]

From within option one, Sarah is right; faith and evolution have nothing to do with each other. In church, evolution has no authority to speak about origins, and in school, faith is mute. What gives them their authority is their expertise. Scientific findings work in the domain of material facts. Faith rules in the realm of meaning. These two different attentions, to facts and to meaning, allow faith and scientific findings to live behind their separate fences. And fences make for nice neighbors.

But the problem with option one is that when young people ask Sarah about evolution, they are asking from within the social practice of faith—not necessarily the theoretical judgments of religion. And social practices seek coherence across our lives. Aly's dad can put religious theoretical judgments and scientific findings in different zones, separating them in his life. But this separation is only possible if he has turned faith into religion. Faith as a social practice will resist this. For instance, when Gena is sick he forcefully feels these two domains crashing through the other's fence, as he prays by her bedside, asking God to act and heal her while the plastic tubes pump meds into her body.

4. Here is an example from Michael Ruse. He connects his position to the fathers and reformers, and clearly he has a point here. He could have also added those with Radical Orthodox leanings. While I understand this point and have been drawn to it, in the end I go a different route because of the call of ministry itself. Ruse says, "If you follow the route marked out by Augustine and Aquinas, by Luther and Calvin, then the answer is very different. The basic, most important claims of the Christian religion lie beyond the scope of science. They do not and could not conflict with science, for they live in realms where science does not go. In this sense, we can think of Christianity and science as being independent, and we can see that those theologians who have insisted on the different realms were right in their view of the science-religion relationship." *Science and Spirituality: Making Room for Faith in the Age of Science* (London: Cambridge University Press, 2010), 234.

No one, Jesus says, can serve two kings (two masters—Matthew 6:24). Faith is not the religion of theoretical judgments, but a way of life.

So complete separation of faith and scientific findings and theories, stuck in their own domains, doesn't seem possible. Aly's dad wonders when Gena is sick whether it is time to trust faith or science. It feels like this is the job of the scientific, and yet he can't help but pray. If in youth ministry we desire for young people to actually *live* the faith, something like NOMA won't do.[5] Sarah's ministry will never be able to engage young people's deepest questions—those times where the fences bust apart—if she continues to contend that faith and science are separate domains with no overlap.

OPTION TWO

Recognizing that this won't do, the temptation is to move into Stenmark's second option—union. This perspective holds that the goals of faith and scientific findings can be brought into harmony. Assuming this, Aly's uncle can state that being a person of faith is like being a Japanese solider in 1950, lost on some Pacific island, not realizing that WWII is over. He uses this analogy because he assumes a shared union between faith and scientific findings. This shared union is to thrive and progress toward solutions. He thinks faith is backward and old, because he can't see how it could move toward answers better than scientific work. With Gena, he's sure that the scientific findings that produce modern medicine are far better than prayers, fasting, and incense, just as penicillin is better than leeches. Aly's uncle can't

---

5. Richard Coleman adds, "There are two primary assumptions behind NOMA. First, the domains of science and religion are equally worthwhile in explaining the totality of human life. Second, they should remain logically distinct and fully separate in their style of inquiry. Gould would like to see insights from both styles of inquiry integrated in order 'to build the rich and full view of life traditionally designated as wisdom.' The philosophy behind two magisteria leaves us wondering how is it possible to integrate truths that are logically distinct and functionally so different. What banishment to separate domains does accomplish is barring the door to interdisciplinary inquiries when overlaps arise naturally and exploring them is intriguing." *State of Affairs: The Science-Theology Controversy* (Eugene, OR: Cascade, 2014), 219.

see why faith is needed at all. It's no match next to the technological outcomes of the scientific.

But he can assume this because he wrongly believes faith and
the scientific share the same pursuits. But this is not the case.
There is not union between faith and the scientific in their deepest objectives. The union that Christian faith seeks is with the
act and being of a personal God in both life and death (Stenmark
calls this faith's "soteriological goal"). The methodological goal
of the scientific is to solve problems, diagnosing and then functionally overcoming constraints.[6] The goal of the scientific is to
empirically deliver results, solutions, and answers.

But faith has little of this as its pursuit. Faith reaches not
for results, solutions, and clear answers, but for encounter with
a transcendent personal reality that remains always shrouded
in mystery.[7] Both faith and the scientific seek epistemological
experiences of reality—they want to discover the way the world
is (hence they are not completely separate domains). Nevertheless, their methods for discovering this reality are distinct.
They're not just distinct in that the scientific uses verification
and empirical observation, and faith uses ministerial actions of
care, prayer, mediation, and confession. It's more than that.
These distinct methods provide unique commitments to the
shape of reality itself. The health sciences see Gena mainly as her
illness, and see her illness as the problem of low white blood cells.
But faith sees Gena as a person who must be ministered to. The
goal for the scientific in relation to Gena is to functionally over-
come her sickness (something Jared, Aly, and her family yearn
for). But faith, on the other hand, asks, Who is Gena, and how
does she live and participate in this personal world? What kind
of life and death upholds her personhood in love and mercy?
And in life and death, how might we help her commune with
this personal God and those she loves? These are quite different
aims.[8]

6. See Atul Gawande, *Being Mortal* (New York: Metropolitan Books, 2014) for a
discussion of this from within medicine.
7. All Christian traditions have a place for apophatic theology, of course some
more than others.
8. Stenmark says something very similar, "We do not have to satisfy merely material needs to be alive and well, however. We also have to give attention to spiritual
and existential needs. Our well-being thus also depends upon our ability to deal with

OPTION THREE

The third option, and the one Stenmark finds the most promising, is overlap or contact. There are significant ways that faith and scientific findings and theories overlap and make contact with each other. But faith and the scientific also remain distinct, with different goals.[9] "We can say that science operates with the presumption that there are causes to things, religion with the presumption that there are meanings to things. Meanings and causes have in common a concept of order, but the type of order differs."[10]

When we focus on goals, we can see that indeed faith and the scientific have places of overlap, but there are also important points of divergence. With Gena's illness or the ability to land a rover on Mars, the scientific has a technological goal, "and we value [the scientific] because it is useful and . . . helps us control, predict, and alter the world."[11] A major goal of the scientific

our experiences of suffering, death, guilt, or meaninglessness. In dealing with these phenomena, religion has proved to be of great value. It enables us to make sense out of these existential experiences, to diagnose them, and find a way through the barriers to our well-being. We might say that religion aims to make the world existentially intelligible." Mikael Stenmark, *How to Relate Science and Religion* (Grand Rapids, MI: Eerdmans, 2004), 29.

9. Once we realize this, two of Barbour's paths are no longer pass-able. Just as in the sixteenth century there was assumed to be some Northwest Passage connecting the Atlantic with the Pacific oceans, only to discover ice and lakes, our maps also change, eliminating two of Barbour's paths. Once we become clear about what we are relating (faith and the scientific, not religion and the social practice of "science"), and spend some time examining faith and the scientific findings' distinct *teleologies*, we discover that there is no passing on the route of independence and integration. As we'll see, only conflict and dialogue are open in a contact/overlap perspective. Because of their distinct goals and pursuits, it would be impossible to ever imagine an integration between faith and the scientific that would not lead to some *tertium quid*—some mixing that would swallow one perspective into the other (this would be to fall into the trap of Stenmark's second option). But in the same way, it would be hard to imagine following the path of independence. If we were relating religion (theoretical judgments) with scientific findings, it might indeed be possible to get them separated, allowing only one kind of theoretical judgment to speak in one fenced-in zone. But once our relating is between *faith* and *scientific findings and theories*, this clean demarcation isn't possible. Our lived experience with ill Gena and suffering Aly will not allow for any clean lines between them.

10. Stenmark is quoting Rolston (Rolston 1987: 22). *How to Relate Science and Religion*, 29.

11. Throughout this project I have added to the scientific "findings" and "theo-

is to drive toward findings that might be useful in controlling and manipulating our material universe. And of course, there is a good to this. Aly and her family put great hope in the technological operations of scientific findings and theories. They're quite happy, and rightly so, that the oncologists, pharmacists, and surgeons possess the know-how to help Gena.

But, this technological goal is not necessarily shared by faith. Most often, faith has no overlap with the technological goal of the scientific (though faith has deeply practical dimensions that impact our lifestyles and communities). People of faith enjoy Wi-Fi and air travel as much as anyone, thinking little about it as they line up for the next release from Apple. This technological goal diverges from (as opposed to overlapping with) faith. They are different, with two different pursuits. Most often faith doesn't begrudge these technological goals.

But faith must also recognize in this divergence that the technological goal of the scientific leads into interpretations and actions that are different than faith. For instance, the technological goal is to alter Gena's condition, controlling her immune system and predicting the impact on it of a particular drug. But this technological goal tends to morph Gena into her diagnoses, making her a problem to solve. Faith's commitment to her personhood will celebrate the ways the technological alters our world, but not if it opposes or crushes personhood and the environments in which people live.

This shows that faith has its own goals. Faith has a *moral goal* that seeks to uphold a personal order wherein human life is livable and life is valued. Persons are more than their diagnoses; they cannot be totalized into problems to solve. Persons have value that transcends their function. Therefore, persons must be able to eat, breathe, love, and laugh. The divergent realities of faith and science are pulled together like magnets when the technological goal overlaps (chafing against) the moral goal of faith. When the technological goals of the scientific produce weapons for murder, devices of antisocial behavior, and

---

ries." Both of these are important because both signal the scientific's two goals: findings connect to its technological goal and theories point to its epistemic goal.

ecological crises, there is an overlap between faith and the scientific. And this overlap is contentious.[12]

But most often faith is happy to leave the scientific to its technological goals, because faith has it own goals to pursue, quite distinct from the scientific. The ultimate goal of faith is what Stenmark calls "the soteriological goal." Faith seeks communion with the personhood of God (salvation).[13] Faith pursues its soteriological goal by articulating a story that explores what is broken with existence, how existence is healed, and the ways to live in this healed state. The goal of faith is the transformation into new life through encounter with the person of God who comes to our broken world to minister to us. If Jared is to help his young people relate faith and the scientific, he must not give up the distinct pastoral pursuit of encountering the presence of God through the acts of ministry person to person.[14] As we've said above, he must hold onto his pastoral impulses and allow faith and the scientific to be distinct.

But because Jared is committed to seeking a personal God *in*

12. Though not always. For instance, interesting interdisciplinary conversations are happening between technologists and theologians on the impact of social media on young people. Yet, what draws them together is not the goal of the scientific but articulations of faith (or some pseudo-faith that has a moral goal). We wonder if all these screens are good for our young people.

13. "Hence it seems as if Christianity, and not only science, has an epistemic goal, that is, it attempts to say something true about reality. If so, a religious practice like Christianity is meant to tell us something true about who God is, what God's intentions are, what God has done, what God values, and how we fit in when it comes to these intentions, actions, and values." Stenmark, "How to Relate Christian Faith and Science," 65. Stenmark continues, "I would like to stress that this epistemic goal is subordinated to the soteriological goal. The soteriological goal shapes the epistemic goal of Christianity. This is true, at least, in the sense that many Christians do not merely affirm the truth of beliefs such as that there is a God, that God is love, or that God created the world. Instead their primary aim is to have God in their lives. Many Christians believe that God's revelation, although it is incomplete, gives knowledge that is adequate for believers' needs. For them it is sufficient to know what is necessary for them to live the life they must in relation to God. These believers aim at significant or important truths, truths that are useful for them in their relation to God." Stenmark, "How to Relate Christian Faith and Science," 65.

14. When I talk about divine action taking the shape of ministry, I mean that God acts in the world not as an interventionist force, but interacts with the world in love, in participation. Polkinghorne explains that this move from intervention to interaction is shared by Peacocke, Barbour, and himself. He says, "We all refuse the word 'intervention', and accept the word 'interaction', as the way to speak about divine acts." *Scientists as Theologians* (London: SPCK, 1996), 41.

the world (in time and space) there is an epistemic goal embedded within the soteriological goal. There is a goal to know and understand the world we live within. This epistemic (knowledge and understanding) goal is necessary at the very least to test and explore if the shape of the world (of our experiences of time and space) fits the soteriological story of brokenness, redemption, and communion in and through personhood. The incarnational center to Christian faith means the world and its order matter to us.

TO THE OVERLAP

This is where we see an overlap and contact between faith and the scientific that is open to dialogue—at the level of epistemic goals.[15] While the scientific is mobilized by technological goals, its most primary drive is toward the epistemic. It seeks to construct theories from within its findings that articulate the shape of our world. Sarah tries to keep young people's questions about evolution in one domain and questions of faith in another. But this isn't possible next to the soteriological (salvation) goal of faith. The young people in her ministry aren't seeking to know intricate scientific debates about evolution, but they are deeply seeking to know if the story of faith (bound in the soteriological goal) is plausible next to theories of evolution. How do they make sense of these distinct stories? Do these perspectives conflict, or are there points of dialogue? Can humanity be loved through its brokenness if we're just the accidental results of natural selection?

What Sarah and Jared seek to relate are the epistemic findings

15. Stenmark explain his connection to van Huyssteen's transversal method, which I lean on in my work *Christopraxis* (Minneapolis: Fortress Press, 2014); see chapter 10. Stenmark says, "Van Huyssteen and I have both instead suggested that there could be an overlap between the rationality of science, theology, and religion (the idea of transversal rationality), but we have rejected the ideas of a universal rationality (Dawkins and Wilson) and of a contextual rationality (Gould and Brümmer). By accepting the idea of transversal rationality, one thereby endorses the idea of rationality not only as person-related but also as practice-related. That is to say, to know whether a person is rational in believing or doing something we need to know not merely who he or she is but also what kind of practice he or she participates in." *How to Relate Science and Religion*, 121.

and theories of the scientific with the lived story of faith. They are engaging the overlap when they put scientific theories in discussion with the story of faith. Jared recognized in his conversation with Aly, that if he is to be committed to the soteriological goal of faith, then he must engage with the scientific. He must seek ways to help his young people recognize how the findings of the scientific connect with the story of faith.

As Jared reflected on his conversations with Sasha and Martin, he recognized that each was asking how the scientific findings of astrophysics, evolution, and cognitive science connected to faith's commitment to a personal God who creates a world of ministering love. But they were asking him these questions not because they were confused and somehow thought he was a genius philosopher, knowing everything about science and religion. Rather, they asked Jared because he was their pastor, helping them practice a life of faith that moved them toward the soteriological goal of experiencing a personal God.[16]

And it was next to this soteriological goal that they wanted to know how faith could deal with the findings that indeed aliens might exist, and mass extinctions happen. Jared wasn't asked to defend faith, necessarily, or to find a way to correlate religion with science. But he *was* being asked to think alongside young people about how our world is shaped, and our unique personhood within it. Sasha wanted to know how the story of redemption could work if there are other worlds with other intelligent beings. Martin wondered, If everything dies, then how could the soteriological story of resurrection and eternal life work?[17]

16. Padgett says, "We cannot, however, live by science alone. The natural and social sciences are limited. They are unable to answer our deepest needs for meaning, values, and purpose, needs which are theological or philosophical in nature. So science is important but not all important. Science cannot save us. It is itself based upon important assumptions and values that it cannot justify in its own terms but must assume from other disciplines." Alan Padgett, *Science and the Study of God: A Mutuality Model for Theology and Science* (Grand Rapids, MI: Eerdmans, 2003), 20. We cannot live by epistemological exploration only. Rather, we need the experience of ministry. And this is the only real reason for a pastor or youth worker to enter into this conversation.

17. Stenmark adds to this point: "What is at stake in religious matters is not only whether some beliefs are true or what conclusions we should draw regarding certain arguments, but how we actually should live our lives. It is not just a matter of making up one's mind: it is also a matter of choosing or denying a way of living. This

THE DARK NEWS OF GENA

Jared dropped the phone from his ear to the desk. Everything felt stale and the room seemed drab and distant as his eyes raced across his office. His shoulders felt too heavy to hold up and he slouched down into his chair under their weight. All his senses were dulled, but smell. He felt overwhelmed by the smell. The candle on his desk mixing with the pastes, inks, and papers of the supply room next door made his eyes water. If not for the toxic smell, he'd wonder if this moment was actually happening. For a few seconds he felt nothingness, as if life was too flat and gray to call it real, like he was seeing through its thinness. But then with the velocity of a piano dropped from an airplane it hit him with startling shock. He thought of Aly, lying on the hospital floor Christmas Eve holding Gena's hand, and the tears streamed uncontrollably. Grief flooded him. Aly's words from the day before New Year's Eve pounded in Jared's mind like a drum; he could hear it as if she was now whispering it in his ear. "I just don't want to lose my little sister," it repeated over and again. But now she was lost. Gena was dead.

choice cannot be postponed for real human beings. We must live right now, one way or another. Hence, real people are rationally justified in taking risks, because of their predicament, that the 'religious believer' in much scientific and religious literature would not be justified in taking. So what it is rational for such a being to believe about religious matters cannot help us, since we are in a radically different situation."
How to Relate Science and Religion, 112.

10.

Finding Personhood: The Face

"I can't believe she's gone," Aly said as she leaned in to hug Jared, her tears wetting his shirt. She was gone. As Jared's eye met Aly's, he wasn't sure if he could do this. To be asked to do Gena's funeral was such an honor that it took his breath away. But his own grief was so heavy. He had known Gena since she was little. This was the first time someone from Jared's youth ministry had died; the first time he'd been asked to do a funeral. And the experiences with Aly the last year just made this all the more difficult. At the same time, Jared felt this quiet confidence that indeed this was his calling.

Walking into his senior pastor's office, Jared felt all these emotions swirling inside him. Tanisha, the senior pastor, sat quietly in the corner, waiting as people slowly entered her office. The point of their gathering was to plan the service. But Tanisha had done enough of these to know that they all started with pastoral care. As everyone took their seat in a misshapen circle, Jared noticed the swollenness of their faces. He actually couldn't take his eyes off their faces. They beckoned to him in a way he couldn't quite put his finger on.

"Well," Tanisha began in a low reverent voice, "we're here, really, to be together. And together we're going to plan a worship service. This is a service where we stand with Gena's body, rehearsing again the story of the life, death, and resurrection of Jesus' own body—trusting this beautiful sister, daughter, niece,

and friend to God. That's why we're here." The room remained
silent for a minute, then Tanisha spoke again. "Jared will be
leading the service."

"We're so happy for that," Aly's mom quickly interjected.
"Gena really loved youth group, and you've meant so much to
both the girls." She then paused and added with tears, "I am
going to miss her so much."

"I am so sorry," Jared said. Aly's dad began to cry hard, throw-
ing his face into the crook of his elbow. Through the sob-
bing, the words flowed. "It's been such a long, long journey
with her and this damn illness, so much hope and so much
despair. She was, she really was getting better, but then bam!
The stupid, damn pneumonia took her. The chemo had obliter-
ated her immune system. They promised us that they had some
new drug that would stabilize it, giving them the options to go
aggressive at the cancer. But it ripped her apart. I regret it, I
damn well regret it; I watched her waste away before my eyes. I
keep thinking that maybe, maybe she could have lived a happy
six months more if we hadn't gone so aggressive. But I couldn't
surrender to that fate; I couldn't face the fact that I would lose
her. But she's gone. And I can't stand the thought that I'll never
again look into her eyes. That never again, will I lie feet to feet
with my little Gena on the couch and ask her 'What's on your
mind, my little pea?'"

"I remember that," Aly added through her tears. "You'd
always tell her you could read her mind."

"I could!" Aly's dad said, wiping his red eyes. "Her face told
everything. I just had this connection to her; I could just almost
see her thoughts all over her face." His voice dropped low.

Then, full of sadness laced with rage, he shouted, "I'm just
so mad she's gone! I will never see that sweet face again!" He
dropped his head onto his knees, and Aly threw her arms around
him.

Uncle Leon, the neuropsychologist and antagonist of the
Thanksgiving debate, sat as still as a statue, back straight against
his wooden chair. His only movement for the first few minutes
was to repeatedly lift his right hand deliberately to his right eye
and wipe the tears that gathered at the top of his cheekbone with
his index finger.

Jared found himself watching Uncle Leon. This was the first time Jared had met him. But it didn't feel that way, particularly because somehow Uncle Leon looked just as Jared had imagined he would: tall, slim, and balding, with an aura of intellectual importance, even haughtiness. It was an eerie feeling of recognition and fascination accompanying Jared's grief.

As Aly threw her arms around her dad and the tears fell, Uncle Leon, who so far had remained silent, looked out the window and said, as if to himself, but loud enough for room to hear, "Faces are a mystery. They haunt us. How do our minds grasp onto faces? They make little scientific sense."

THE FACE IN SPACETIME

Uncle Leon had contended that science was superior to faith because of its technological goals—it solved problems and gave us useful solutions, getting us a better world, with clean water and heated buildings. The more he held to the superiority of this technological goal, the more Uncle Leon was susceptible to taking on the comprehensive social practice of "science," and calling faith immature and immoral. But now, in the crater of Gena's death, his confidence in these technological pursuits was shaken. This moved him more into the epistemic (understanding) goal, and this epistemic attention gave him openness. He wondered why science couldn't tell us more about how our minds grasp faces. He wondered why all the theories seemed insipid next to the mystical chasm of the loss he felt with the disappearance of Gena.

The funeral liturgy that Jared used was flush with language of the mystery of the giving of God's face. Faith is the experience, the epistemic discovery, of encountering the face of God.[1] The

1. Scruton adds, "The lamentation in Psalm 13 is expressed thus: 'How long wilt thou forget me, O Lord? Forever? How long wilt thou hide thy face from me?' In Psalm 17 we read 'As for me I will behold thy face in righteousness; I shall be satisfied, when I awake, with thy likeness.' The fourth psalm implores God to lift up 'the light of your countenance upon us'. Clearly we have moved a long way from the Torah. The hope of a face-to-face encounter fills the Psalms from beginning to end, and the hope is turned to a promise by the Apostle Paul, who tells us that now we see through a glass darkly, 'but then face to face.' God's face, which Moses was forbidden to see, is now at the centre of faith and hope, and the way to it, Paul says, is agape,

liturgy held together face and mind, because in the experience of faith, God comes not to rational calculators of thought, but to embodied persons. God comes to human beings with faces that reveal their depth and draw them to each other, and minds that contemplate the mystery of the universe. The experience of salvation is not the pure rational knowledge that your sins are forgiven, but the encounter with the divine mystery that promises you life, communion, and love through a human face that sees you for the sake of ministering to you. Faith is driven by a soteriological goal; it seeks only the face of Christ and him crucified (1 Corinthians 2:2). But because this God comes with a face—a name to Israel and in the body of Jesus Christ—this soteriological experience draws us into seeking epistemic understanding. Because Jesus (salvation) comes into time and space, to take the journey of faith is to ask epistemic questions of the reality God enters.[2]

Christianity is not unique in having a soteriological goal. Other religions, philosophies, and cultures also seek nirvana, enlightenment, paradise. Yet what makes Christianity different, and the unique proprietor of the scientific, is that this soteriological goal is inextricable from the epistemic.[3] For us to encounter

the New Testament word for neighbor love, translated as caritas in the Vulgate and described by Kant as the 'love to which we are commanded.'" Roger Scruton, *The Face of God* (London: Bloomsbury, 2012), 73.

2. Torrance says it like this: "Since Christian theology is pursued not in terms of a God-man relationship, but in terms of a God-man-world [sic], or God-world-man relationship, theological knowledge is bound to be closely related to the knowledge of the universe as the created medium of space and time through which God makes himself known to us, if only because God by his creation has placed man [sic] within the universe as that constituent element in it whereby the universe comes to know itself, as it were, and thus unfolds its latent structures and intelligibilities under the process of human inquiry and interaction with the universe." Thomas F. Torrance, *Transformation & Convergence in the Frame of Knowledge: Explorations in the Interrelations of Scientific and Theological Enterprise* (Grand Rapids, MI: Eerdmans, 1984), 249.

3. "The way Christians think about creation (and the same is true for Jews and Muslims) has four significant consequences. The first is that we expect the world to be orderly because its Creator is rational and consistent, yet God is also free to create a universe whichever way God chooses. Therefore, we can't figure it out just by thinking what the order of nature ought to be; we'll have to take a look and see. In other words, observation and experiment are indispensable. That's the bit the Greeks missed. They thought you could do it all just by cogitating. Third, because the world is God's creation, it's worthy of study. That, perhaps, was a point that the Chinese missed as they concentrated their attention on the world of humanity at the expense

the living God who seeks to save us, we must do so in the space-time of this world. Our experiences of transcendence are bound within encounters through our bodies in time and space, with a God who enters spacetime, through the face of Jesus Christ.[4] T. F. Torrance says it this way: "Thus the [incarnation and] ascension means that we cannot know God by transcending space and time, by leaping beyond the limits of our place on earth, but only by encountering God and his saving work within space and time, within our actual physical existence."[5]

And because God comes to us in the revelation of the embodied face of Jesus Christ, faith asks questions like: What is reality? What is this world that God enters? Transcendence, in Christian faith, is experienced through the face of Jesus Christ who ministers to us *in the world*, calling us deeper into the world to minister to our neighbor.[6] This means that because God enters spacetime in the incarnation, the epistemic goal is closely connected to its soteriological aims in faith.

The overlap between faith and the scientific happens at this epistemic level.[7] It was indeed the epistemic drive, born from their faith, that led Galileo, Faraday, and Maxwell to passionately

of the world of nature. Fourth, because the creation is not itself divine, we can prod it and investigate it without impiety. Put all these features together, and you have the intellectual setting in which science can get going." John Polkinghorne, *Quarks, Chaos & Christianity: Questions to Science and Religion* (London: Crossroad, 2005), 29.

4. "In the risen Christ, in whom hypostatic union between God and Man is carried through to its *telos*, there is involved an hypostatic union between eternity and time, eternity and redeemed and sanctified time, and therefore between eternity and new time. The resurrection of the man Jesus, and his exaltation to the right hand of the Father, mean the taking up of human time into God." Thomas F. Torrance, *Space, Time and Resurrection* (Edinburgh: T&T Clark, 1998), 98.

5. Torrance, *Space, Time and Resurrection*, 134. "The doctrine of Incarnation, with the idea of God becoming a human being, also implicitly fostered a novel understanding of the universe. Torrance holds that ontologically the doctrine of Incarnation confirmed what the doctrine of creation had earlier laid a basis for. These are the 'three masterful ideas,' as Torrance calls them: rationality, freedom, and contingency of the universe." Tapio Luoma, "Thomas F. Torrance," in J. B. Stump and Alan Padgett, *The Blackwell Companion to Science and Christianity* (London: Wiley-Blackwell, 2012), 586.

6. This has been the thread running through all of my work. And it is embedded in the work of Bonhoeffer, Levinas, and others.

7. We could also call it a transversal moment, using van Huyssteen's position—though van Huyssteen sees this transversality most often happening through a shared rationality. I affirm this; see *Christopraxis* (Minneapolis: Fortress Press, 2014).

seek the shape of reality. And it is the similar epistemic questions about aliens and cosmology and mass extinctions and evolution that drive Sasha and Martin. This attention to spacetime and the drive for an understanding of reality is what allows for this overlap or contact between faith and the scientific. It will be this overlap that will move Jared into these discussions in his youth ministry.

But as the liturgy unfolds, on this sad day of Gena's funeral, the words from Uncle Leon back in Tanisha's office still ring in Jared ears—"faces and minds are a mystery that haunt the scientific." It was becoming clear to Jared that while faith and the scientific overlap in their epistemic goals (in their pursuit to say something true about reality), Christian faith also seeks something different, something it appeared the scientific was unable or unwilling to search for (particularly once it cuts itself off from faith). Faith seeks the face, the deep and beautiful mind, of God and neighbor.

Like a lightning bolt that hit Jared in an instant, he realized both that he needed to help his young people relate to faith and science, and also that he would need to keep the soteriological goal central, remembering that in the end he was a pastor. He would need to go in through the lens of their personhood, connected with God and each other, witnessed to in the mystery of unique and revealing faces. This pastoral concern that would move Jared to relate faith and science has a very old antecedent. The Christian breakthroughs of the fourth century were pastoral, giving us a way of thinking about the world that scientific work would depend on more than a thousand years later.

THE CHRISTIAN BREAKTHROUGH

In 325 a young man accompanied his mentor and hero to Nicaea. This was a great opportunity for the young man. Not only would he learn from his elder, but he would participate in defending the experience of his church back home.

The church in Alexandria that Alexander led held that Jesus was *begotten but not made, true God of true God.* But a local academic named Arius was promoting a different idea. He was saying that Jesus was a special fellow, but was a creature made, and therefore subordinate to and ranking under, God the Father. To Arius it was a clear philosophical and logical argument: fathers are greater than their sons, and so Jesus ranks lower than the Father. Special, sure, but not true God of true God. Of course, it was a little cleverer than that, but this was essentially Arius's point.

While Alexander and his young assistant, Athanasius, were no simpletons, their argument rested somewhere other than pure academic logic. The reason that Alexander held so strongly to his position was because he was a pastor. And as pastor he had experienced the work of this living Jesus, ministering new life to his people. At Nicaea they'd claim Jesus was the fullness of God entering into time and space.[8]

This Nicene commitment (and its creed which would follow) brought with it a whole new philosophy—a new way of seeing the world. Athanasius spent the rest of his life fleshing out this Nicene position,[9] showing that we live in an open system, in which God comes to us as the revelation (the discovery) that Jesus is indeed true God of true God, ministering life out of our death. But this discovery happens in time and space. Time and space are created by God, the Father; but the Son, who is true God of true God, begotten but not made, is found in time and space as revelation (the discovery) of God's very act and being—of God's own mind.

From Nicaea, faith has a deeply epistemic goal to articulate the

8. My return to these patristic thoughts are both to draw from the depth of the tradition, but also to affirm that they may have seen truths and we don't. Polkinghorne explains that theology is like music; twenty-first-century music is not assumed to be better than nineteenth-century music. They are just different. Here Polkinghorne says more about the importance of these theological thoughts. "Despite the need for engagement with contemporary thought, I think that theologically we also need to benefit from the insights of preceding generations: The theologian of the twentieth century enjoys no presumptive superiority over the theologians of the fourth or sixteenth centuries. Indeed, those earlier centuries may well have had access to spiritual experiences and insights which have been attenuated, or even lost, in our time." John Polkinghorne, *Scientists as Theologians* (London: SPCK, 1996), 84.

9. "Thus Athanasius contends that the Arians have invented for themselves a God without any 'works,' distinct from the biblical God who is immediately present to and evident from his works." Khaled Anatolios, *Athanasius: The Coherence of His Thought* (London: Routledge, 1998), 115.

shape of time and space, because its soteriological commitments are encountered through the time and space of Jesus coming to us. It was this shift to the encounters of revelation in an open system through empirical attention that allowed modern scientific findings to be pursued. The legacy of Nicene Christianity in the fourth and fifth centuries (and then through the sponsorship of Western Christianity in the sixteenth and seventeenth centuries) laid the groundwork for the modern scientific pursuits.

When the scientific is done in the legacy of its earliest work in Nicene Christianity, it seeks to articulate the shape of the reality of time and space in and through our *personal* experience of it. Not only are faith and the scientific related through Nicene Christianity, but the line of communication between them is connected as both seek to describe our world of time and space. The overlap, or contact, happens in the shared epistemic goal born from the creativity and struggle of Alexander and Athanasius.

A MODERN SCOTTISH TWIST

T. F. Torrance, a twentieth-century Scottish theologian who studied under Karl Barth, has made these points about Nicaea—that it is an open system that calls for understanding time and space as central. Karl Barth is known for his disdain for natural theology, and many (wrongly in my opinion[10]) have in turn seen Barth as opposed to dialogues between theology and science. Yet, the story goes that the young Torrance told the elderly Barth, just before Barth's death, that he saw a link between Barth's work and the new physics that redefined space/time. Torrance explained that just as the new physics—that is, Einstein—would no longer allow space/time to be disconnected from experience, so you, Torrance said, are opposed to any dualism between nature and our experience of God. Barth's response was, "I must have been a blind hen not to see that."

Torrance believed that faith and the scientific could be related because of the impact of two individuals we've already met in

10. See Paul D. La Montagne, *Barth and Rationality: Critical Realism in Theology* (Eugene, OR: Cascade, 2012).

this book: Maxwell and Einstein. A fellow Scotsman and deeply devout Christian, James Clerk Maxwell[11] had asserted that it was his commitment to Nicene Christianity and its creed that gave him the imaginative picture to think about electricity as a field (creating field theory).[12] And it was how this field theory described light that would infatuate Einstein like a twelve-year-old boy with a new video game.[13] The young Einstein wanted only to think about light, forgetting classes and commitments. And it was Maxwell's book that he devoured as he did so. Thinking about light alongside Maxwell and his Nicene commitments gave Einstein a new picture of the cosmos.[14] He discovered that

11. "It is notable that Michael Faraday and James Clerk Maxwell, both devout Christians, made use of physical reasoning analogous to perichoretic understanding in developing the notion of a classical field. Colin Gunton points out the possible perichoretic origins of Michael Faraday's work on electricity and the nature of matter. Faraday broke away from the mechanistic notion of charged particles acting upon one another at a distance; he suggested that, instead, charged particles represent concentrated regions of 'lines of force' where the force lines fill the space between the particles, thereby creating an electromagnetic field. James Clerk Maxwell then provided a mathematical formulation for Faraday's notion of spatially interpenetrating 'lines of force' interrelating charged particles to each other, these field lines being part of what particles actually are. Faraday's and Clerk Maxwell's work thus anticipated, and remains a central component of, modern quantum field theory as it attempts to represent the mass-energy interactions of elementary particles." James Loder and Jim W. Neidhardt, *The Knight's Move* (Colorado Springs, CO: Helmers & Howard, 1992), 203.
12. "This abandonment of the mechanistic for the sake of the dynamic and the relational is what led Lord Kelvin to say Clerk Maxwell had lapsed into 'mysticism.' However, it was precisely this 'mysticism' that eventually allowed Maxwell to arrive at his famous four equations describing an electromagnetic field and laying the theoretical foundations for relativity theory." Loder and Neidhardt, *The Knight's Move*, 208.
13. Michael Polanyi explains this passion of Einstein, coupling it with Kepler: "So we see that both Kepler and Einstein approached nature with intellectual passions and with beliefs inherent in these passions, which led them to their triumphs and misguided them to their errors. These passions and beliefs were theirs, personally, even though they held them in the conviction that they were valid, universally. I believe that they were competent to follow these impulses, even though they risked being misled by them. And again, what I accept of their work as true today, I accept personally, guided by passions and beliefs similar to theirs, holding in my turn that my impulses are valid, universally, even though I must admit the possibility that they may be mistaken." *Personal Knowledge: Toward a Post-Critical Philosophy* (Chicago: University of Chicago Press, 1962), 145.
14. Elmer Colyer explains this further: "There are other incidents of what Torrance calls 'cross-fertilization' or 'hidden-traffic' in which ideas taken from theological science have positively and decisively influenced natural science. Torrance

the universe was an open system, echoing Athanasius. It was a system that responded (was relative) to the speed of light, as opposed to being closed in frozen laws. And it was Maxwell who had calculated the speed of light at 186,282 miles per second. In Torrance's mind, the impact of Einstein's new physics is almost beyond measure. But maybe its greatest impact for faith is how it upends Newton's closed system and allows for a picture where the strangeness of encounter and revelation is still possible. It claims that the truth of existence is found in the oddity of paradox (of course the Copenhagen school of quantum physics, inspired from Einstein's findings, would show this even more so).

Newton (but mainly those that followed him) had frozen the universe into a closed system of laws, wiping away the inner logic of paradox that Nicene Christianity upheld as the structure of existence. Torrance never tired of reminding us that not only was this closed system in opposition to the breakthrough of Nicaea, but also Newton was a fan boy of old Arius. Newton's work, while clearly amazing in one way, was corrupted in another by following Arius's logic. Newton even called himself (secretly to his friends) an Arian Christian, with no sympathy for the doctrine of the Trinity. It would be Einstein, with a hand from Maxwell, who would not only reveal Newton's error, but also produce a physics that was an open system filled with inner realities of logical paradoxes.[15] While Einstein didn't intend it, Torrance shows that this was indeed a return to the logic of Nicaea.[16] Torrance spent the rest of his career showing

contends that James Clerk Maxwell utilized an onto-relational concept of 'person' drawn from theology in developing his dynamical field theory, a theory that Torrance regards as the most significant breakthrough in modern physical science between Newton and Einstein." *How to Read T. F. Torrance: Understanding His Trinitarian & Scientific Theology* (Downers Grove, IL: IVP, 2001), 186. Colyer continues: "In addition, Torrance sees the new Einsteinian science playing a crucial role in 'liberating theology from the tyranny of false ideas' such as a closed mechanistic and deterministic universe or a receptacle notion of space, both of which have created many serious difficulties for theology. It is difficult to make sense of the incarnation, miracles or the resurrection within the Newtonian cosmology other than as a breach or suspension of natural law." *How to Read T. F. Torrance*, 188.

15. We should be careful in calling it Newton's error. Of course, there is much about Newton's theories that remain.

16. Einstein's God was not personal. He had a deep love for Spinoza's God. See

how Nicene Christianity could be in dialogue with modern scientific pursuits and Einstein's new physics.[17]

Torrance believed this because of how Nicene Christianity shaped the epistemic goals of scientific findings and theories. "Modern science rests on certain ultimate beliefs (like the contingence, intelligibility and freedom of creation) that it did not generate on its own."[18] What Torrance means is that "the universe [is] endowed with an astonishing reliability and constancy, but also a kind of spontaneity and freedom that takes us by surprise and repeatedly defies what we anticipate or can articulate."[19] And this reliability and yet open surprise is exactly the world that Nicene Christianity proposes. "Torrance contends, that this is what we should expect of a creation called into being and sustained by the sovereign Creator revealed in Jesus Christ, for in Jesus Christ we discern this same astonishing combination of freedom and constancy, of spontaneity and reliability, of unpredictability and order."[20]

But this moves us back to the story of Athanasius, and its ramifications for Jared, as he grappled with the impact of Uncle Leon's words.

Matthew Stanley's "That Einstein Believed in a Personal God," in Ronald Numbers, *Galileo Goes to Jail: And Other Myths About Science and Religion* (Cambridge, MA: Harvard University Press, 2009).

17. "Torrance . . . sees Einstein's work as transcending and qualifying Newtonian physics and its deterministic and mechanical conceptualization of the universe. The universe revealed by the new science is not understood 'as a closed deterministic system, but as a continuous and open system of contingent realities and events with an inherent unifying order . . . a finite but unbounded universe with open, dynamic structures.' It is a finite, unbounded universe open to the activity of God and compatible with the interactionist God-world relation that Torrance embraces and finds arising out of classic Nicene theology." Colyer, *How to Read T. F. Torrance*, 188.

18. Colyer, *How to Read T. F. Torrance*, 31.

19. Colyer, *How to Read T. F. Torrance*, 173. Torrance says further, "For theology the radicalization of contingence implies that in creating the universe out of nothing God gave it a nature and order of its own which we are obliged to respect. There is theological warrant, therefore, for the independent empirical investigation of the universe by natural science—indeed such an investigation is a duty toward God laid upon us by his work of creation." Thomas F. Torrance, *Divine and Contingent Order* (Edinburgh: T&T Clark, 1998), 72.

20. Colyer, *How to Read T. F. Torrance*, 173.

118 EXPLODING STARS, DEAD DINOSAURS, AND ZOMBIES

A PROBLEM STILL TO FACE

Soon enough Athanasius became an elder himself, aged by the battles with Arius and his followers. The Council at Nicaea had affirmed that Jesus was indeed of the same substance as God the Father. The essential importance of this paradox stretched out in Nicaea would be honed further in the Council at Constantinople (381). But sadly, Athanasius would not live long enough to participate.

The Council of Constantinople highlighted the other side of the paradox—that Jesus was no hologram or God in human disguise, but truly and fully a human person. Athanasius may not have lived long enough to make it to the Council at Constantinople, but his legacy was in attendance.

Between Nicaea and Constantinople, the back-and-forth of conflict and controversy around these paradoxes was intense. This paradox of the divinity and humanity in the embodied Jesus remains a point of much discussion. And Athanasius was at the center, showing how deep these paradoxes stretched, linking things like freedom and constancy, spontaneity and reliability, unpredictability and order.[21] As Torrance has shown, these paradoxes, seen through the divinity/humanity of Jesus, would be essential presumptions for the creation of the scientific.

But there remained a deep tension that Athanasius couldn't seem to solve. He had shown through the experience of ministry (through the soteriological) that these paradoxes existed (and the scientific has more fully shown them in the universe). But how all these paradoxes could be held together remained a point of tension for the Nicene supporters. And until they figured this out, the Arians would not rest. How was it possible,

21. "Jesus reveals that God is not primarily something, nor some action, but someone. Indeed Athanasius, in his dispute with the Arians, noted that when Philip asked Jesus to 'Show us the Father,' 'He said not, 'Behold the creation,' but, 'He that hath seen Me, hath seen the Father,' Zizioulas' contentions that personhood is fundamental to the nature of God, and that his image is revealed clearly in creation in human beings, are credible in light of the incarnation. The incarnate divine person Jesus Christ establishes an irrevocable bond between human personhood and God's personhood. Human personhood is therefore of infinite worth. People are not things (cf. Rev 18:13)." Christopher L. Fisher, *Human Significance in Theology and the Natural Sciences* (Eugene, OR: Pickwick, 2010), 182.

even intelligible, to claim that Jesus was both fully divine and fully human, that God was one, but also three—Father, Son, and Holy Spirit?

Just as the young Athanasius was invaluable to the elderly Alexander, the baton was passed again, and a group of young, creative, friends came to Athanasius's aid. This team of three did for Athanasius what he couldn't do, pointing to the very coherence of these paradoxes, while upholding them as paradoxes.

THE TEAM OF THREE

This team of three from the hill country of Cappadocia may have been the most creative and important minds of the first thousand years of Christian history.[22] They had a unique teacher who inspired within them both the intellectual creativity they would need, and the attention to concrete experience of Jesus in time and space that Athanasius drew from. This teacher was no philosophical man, no wrinkled and blinded sage, squinting from a multitude of hours staring at scrolls in the candlelight. Rather, the great teacher of the team of three was a woman, Macrina.

Macrina's parents and grandparents had directly experienced persecution in the days of Emperor Galerius, when Christianity was perceived as having no place in the empire. But despite the persecution, her father had become a successful lawyer, finding a way for his eldest daughter to be betrothed. But as Macrina awaited her wedding day, her fiancé tragically died. From this misfortune she heard a new call, to give herself to Jesus and a life of prayer and learning. Her first objective would be to teach her siblings the way of prayer and Christian thought.

For her devotion she was sainted, and three of her brothers would also come to be remembered as saints (as well as her mother, who spoke of her daughter Macrina's impact on her own spiritual life). Two of our team of three were Macrina's brothers. Basil of Caesarea, and the younger, Gregory of Nyssa. The third was Gregory Nazianzus. Basil met Gregory Nazianzus

22. Of course, in that list you'd have to include Augustine, who was living and writing around the same time in North Africa.

in Athens, as Basil built his learning on the foundation that Macrina had given him. Basil and Gregory Nazianzus became fast friends, both deeply devoted to the commitments of Nicaea, and as smart and creative as the day was long. The church would remember this team of three as the Cappadocian fathers.

SOME HYPOSTASIS

As the church struggled to keep these paradoxes of Nicaea from flying apart in the battles with the Arians, the team of three would find a profound solution. Athanasius had spoken beautifully of participation, stating how God in the incarnation participates so deeply in creation, so that creation, in turn, might participate in God. And Athanasius could affirm this because Jesus the Son was of the same *ousia* (*homoousios*) as the Father. Upholding this shared *ousia* was necessary because of the experience of ministry. Jesus encountered the personhood of others, face to face, bringing life out of death. Athanasius held to the shared *ousia* because of the soteriological. But the problem remained: How could we have this deep union and also differentiation? How could Jesus be true God of true God, sharing the same *ousia* (substance/being) as the Father, yet also be truly and fully human? How could Jesus be God and therefore able to save us? This Jesus who is one *ousia* with God, must also then be fully and totally human, sharing our humanity completely—meeting us face to face. For only that which is subsumed is saved, only that which is borne is healed.

Basil and his brother Gregory had experienced the ministry of Jesus through the prayers and visions of their sister. And Gregory Nazianzus, too, had experienced the ministering Jesus in a shipwreck. They had experienced Jesus save them. From within these soteriological experiences of ministry they redefined a common concept. Just as Einstein redefined time and space as spacetime, taking us into a deeper inner reality of a common conception, so too did the team of three redefine the humanity/divinity of Christ.[23]

23. "Torrance is in favor of the relational notion. Behind this there are two reasons. First of all, Torrance makes the claim that the Nicene theologians had to think

Before the Cappadocians got a hold of it, *hypostasis* and *ousia* were synonymous terms, both meaning *being* (that's how Aristotle meant it). But, the team of three saw something deeper in this concept that touched their experience. While *ousia* generically meant *being*, they redefined *hypostasis* as a unique form of being, born from within relations. The Cappadocian Fathers asserted that *ousia* had a sense of self-constitution, but *hypostasis* asserts a kind of being that *is* through its relations. *Ousia* is static being, period, but *hypostasis* is a form of being born from within a pattern of relationships. Amazingly, some fifteen hundred year later, Einstein discovered something very similar. Mass, space, and even time were not static elements of being (unchanging substances), but were deeply shaped by their relations. Space and time, what before Einstein we thought of as the most unchanging things, were changed in their *relation* to the speed of light. Both the epistemic pursuits of faith, and the scientific, contend that to discover the being (the reality) of existence, a personal mind (of a minister or scientist) must indwell reality enough to intuit a pattern of relationships.[24] Both faith and the scientific contend that reality is contingent on relationship.[25]

The Cappadocians did something more. They did not just spot the depth of relationship in reality, but found a way to allow for that depth to create connection and particularity.

of the relationship between God the Father and God the Son and their identical being (*homoousion*) strictly in relational terms, so that the idea of space and time was itself affected. This further anticipated the rise of relational notions of space and time in later physics, especially in the theories of relativity of Albert Einstein. This feature is an example of Torrance's idea of how theology has made a substantial contribution to science, or, as Torrance says, 'far from theology being based on natural science, the opposite, if anything, is nearer the truth' (Torrance 1980, 44)." Luoma, "Thomas F. Torrance," 582.

24. Here I'm leaning heavily on Polanyi and essentially echoing the project of Torrance, which is to place Polanyi and the patristics in conversation.

25. "Thus it came about that in seeking to articulate its understanding of God's activity in creation and Incarnation, patristic theology rejected a notion of space as that which receives and contains material bodies, and developed instead a notion of space as the seat of relations or the place of meeting and activity in the interaction between God and the world. It was brought to its sharpest focus in Jesus Christ as the place where God has made room for Himself in the midst of our human existence and as the place where man on earth and in history may meet and have communion with the heavenly Father." Thomas F. Torrance, *Space, Time and Incarnation* (Edinburgh: T&T Clark, 1997), 24.

They redefined hypostasis to mean something like person-hood—a form of particularity born out of relation.[26] For instance, human persons are constituted not in and through their individual wants, but through the relationships that make them. You are a particular brother, a sister, a friend, or mother because there is a relation with another person that bestows upon you the shape of your own being. But in so doing, it gives you the gift of unique particularity[27]—"you are you're mother's only one" (to quote a Bon Iver song).[28] You are hypostatic because you share

26. Peacocke, one of the scientist-theologians, moves in this direction of person-hood. I cannot follow his thesis through, so this longer quote will have to suffice. But within it are a number of important points and directions. He says, "So we can-not help asking what kind of universe is it, if it can generate such entities as per-sons? As I have put it elsewhere, if the stuff of the world, the primeval concourse of protons, neutrinos, photons, etc. has, as a matter of fact and not conjecture, become persons—human beings who possess 'inner' self-conscious lives in relation to other human beings—then how are we properly to interpret the cosmological develop-ment (or the development of the ensemble of universes) if, after aeons of time, these fundamental particles and energy have evidenced that quality of existence we call 'personal', with its distinctive self-awareness and new kind of agency in the world? Does not the very intimacy of our relation to the fundamental features of the phys-ical world, the 'anthropic' features, together with the distinctiveness of personhood, point us in the direction of looking for a 'best explanation' of all-that-is (both non-personal and personal) in terms of some kind of causality that could include the per-sonal in its consequences? . . . Since the personal is, for the reasons given above, the highest category of entity we can name in the order of created beings, and since 'God' is the name we give to this 'X', we therefore have good reason for saying that God is (at least) 'personal', or 'supra-personal' and for predicating personal qualities of God as less misleading and more appropriate than impersonal ones—even while recognizing, as always, that such predications must remain ultimately inadequate to that to which they refer, namely, God." Arthur Peacocke, *Theology for a Scientific Age: Being and Becoming—Natural, Divine, and Human* (Minneapolis: Fortress Press, 1993), 112.

27. "The authentic human being is not egocentric but exocentric. I am only truly human, truly personal, insofar as I greet others as persons. It is relationship that changes me from an individual, a unit—what the Greeks call *atomon*—into a person, what the Greeks call *prosopon*, a countenance or face. As an icon of the Trinity, I become truly myself only if I face others, looking into their eyes and allowing them to look into mine." Metropolitan Kallistos Ware, "The Holy Trinity: Model for Per-sonhood-in-Relation," in John Polkinghorne, *The Trinity and an Entangled World: Relationality in Physical Science and Theology* (Grand Rapids, MI: Eerdmans, 2010), 126.

28. Scruton adds, "Persons are the kind of thing that can recognize others as per-sons and be recognized in turn as persons. Persons are accountable to others, and see themselves as others in the eyes of others. They enter the world of objects as 'things to be judged', and are therefore encumbered by duties and gifted with rights." Scru-ton, *The Face of God*, 61.

in the life of another, and in that ministry of sharing, you are you, a unique face, unable to be denied for your own beauty and wonder.[29] *Hypostasis or personhood asserts that our particularities emerge from within our relations.* And just as the engine for the hypostatic union of Jesus' own person, and the Trinity itself, is for the sake of ministry, so we too are most fully human when our particularities (distinct personhood) emerge from within relational actions of ministry.

The team of three had done it. They had found a way to hold together the paradoxes central to Nicaea. It was through hypostasis. This is the amazing breakthrough that made the Cappadocian Fathers the most creative minds of the first millennium of church history. As a way to affirm their hero Athanasius, they showed that God is a relation of three *hypostases* in one *ousia*, three persons in one being. And in Jesus' own person is a *hypostatic* union, where the divine and the human form a relation that leads to the single particularity of the one Lord. This union-through-relationship allows Jesus to be fully divine and fully human without division, confusion, or separation. Personhood, or *hypostasis*, allows for a coherence of freedom and constancy, spontaneity and reliability, unpredictability and order. Persons act this way all the time, as does the universe. We can build a trustworthy and meaningful life with others because they are dependable and at the same time surprisingly spontaneous. They are reliable yet unpredictable enough to make us laugh, ordered enough to find and be shared in, but shockingly *other* than us.

---

29. Torrance and Scruton would affirm this. Scruton says, "Modern moral philosophy recognizes that personhood is a central category, and also that personhood is a relational idea: you are a person to the extent that you can participate in a network of inter-personal relationships." *The Face of God*, 157. Torrance continues: "Nevertheless a person is what he is only through relations with other persons. Thus the incommunicable existence represents the fact that a person is really objective to what is other than he and that this objectivity of one person to another is a constitutive ingredient in personal being." Thomas F. Torrance, *Reality and Scientific Theology* (Eugene, OR: Wipf & Stock, 2001), 176.

THE HYPOSTATIC IN THE SCIENTIFIC

This was indeed a genius move by the team of three, and one that would not only put the Arians to rest, but impact our conception of the scientific. We've already shown this connection with Einstein's new physics. But what ultimately this *hypostatic* perspective delivered to the scientific is the almost unthought commitment that the universe behaves like a person. It assumes that the *hypostasis* is the hidden, but sure shape of all forms of existence. The order we live in is a personal one—it is *hypostatic*.

But we should be careful here; it is the commitment to a personal order that the comprehensive social practice of "science" refuses, and in turn, the scientific does not affirm. But ultimately what is denied by the scientific is not *hypostasis*. Rather, the scientific actually holds to this logic of particularity through relations (patterns through interconnection). What the scientific doesn't affirm is that there is a center of consciousness, a mind, resting at the center of the universe. Faith may, from within its soteriological *telos*, believe this, but the scientific doesn't. It can be a *tertium quid* (a kind of monstrous Frankenstein) that leads to only a God of gaps to make the scientific bend to this center of conscious commitment.

But avoiding this doesn't mean we have to duck claiming that the universe operates as a person, through *hypostasis*, affirming that we indeed live in a personal order. Eastern Orthodox theologian John Zizioulas says it this way: "The universe behaves *like a person*, not in the prevailing Augustinian and modern Western sense of 'center of consciousness,' but . . . namely as *particularities emerging from relations.* There is an interpenetration between nature and relation, causality and indeterminacy, chaos and stability or structure, making predictability difficult, or even impossible, not because our knowledge of natural laws is imperfect but because there is in reality no such thing as nature 'in the nude' . . . without . . . a modifying relationality. And this is exactly what we find in personhood."[30]

30. "Relational Ontology: Insights from Patristic Thought," in John Polkinghorne, *The Trinity and an Entangled World: Relationality in Physical Science and Theology* (Grand Rapids, MI: Eerdmans, 2010), 154. Torrance here highlights further the

Zizioulas names that there is a relationality that echoes across the universe that is indeed *hypostasis*.[31] This makes our own personhood beautifully in step with the mystery of the universe. The Hungarian chemist and philosopher Michael Polanyi is right: we know more than we can say (we have tacit knowledge of the universe) because the same personal relationality in our own being is analogous to the relationality that holds the universe together. There is a witness to a deeply personal order in our existence that too often the scientific does not acknowledge, but nevertheless assumes, asserting that indeed all the universe is bound in the contingency of relationship.[32]

mistake of Augustine, in a different way supporting Zizioulas's point: "The concept of the person and of personal relations in God and in ourselves demands of us fuller consideration than we have given it hitherto. If God's personal self-communication strikes into the innermost centre of human being, personalizing it, then it is through an apprehension of that modification of personal being that we may be able to think more intelligibly of God who is transcendently in himself what he is in his personal relations with us, and as such is the one personalizing Person who is the creative source of all our personal relations with him and among ourselves. This is the line of thought that St. Augustine did not take, which is understandable in view of the habit he had of interiorizing his thought so that it became turned in upon itself thereby damaging its transcendental structure in relation to the triune God. St. Augustine's rather psychological, interiorizing approach to the truth, by looking for it within the depths of his own spiritual being, meant that he had to fall back upon some sort of ontologistic participation by the light of the human mind in the Light of God, the theory of illumination which evoked the critical reaction of St. Thomas." *Reality and Scientific Theology*, 174.

31. Jürgen Moltmann holds to something similar: "Orthodox theology, on the other hand, adhered firmly to the patristic church's concept of hypostasis: in the human being, nature coalesces into its hypostasis, so that physical human existence comprehends in itself all stages of the anorganic and the organic." "The Spirit in Creation and New Creation," in Michael Welker, *The Spirit in Creation and New Creation: Science and Theology in Western and Orthodox Realms* (Grand Rapids, MI: Eerdmans, 2012), 71.

32. "An . . . idea important to the emergence of modern science is the contingent rationality of the universe, a rationality (including the human mind) created by God out of nothing and utterly different from God, a rationality that is neither necessary, nor arbitrary, and might have been different than it is. Torrance argues that contingent rationality means that we cannot deduce the order or intelligibility of the universe from what we know about God, nor can we regard that order as an embodiment of eternal, a priori or antecedent forms, ideas or formal causes that can be known and developed apart from actually investigating nature (Euclidean geometry, for example). Contingent order or rationality has to be investigated by empirical contact with nature and by experiments in order to be discovered and known. Thus Torrance sees the idea of contingent order as absolutely essential to the genesis of modern empirical/theoretical science." Colyer, *How to Read T. F. Torrance*, 185.

Nothing stands alone. Just as no person is an island, so too is no particle!

BUT, THE FACE

At the level of *particularities emerging from relations* we see faith and science's clearest overlap or contact. It is here that we can claim that faith and science can be in dialogue. They overlap in a shared commitment to this hypostatic composition of reality. In different ways, and using different names, faith and science seek something like the *hypostatic* in their epistemic pursuits. They are both seeking to discover how particularities emerge from relations. For instance, science asks, What happens when particular particles collide? Or, how does a bacterium penetrate a certain organic host? Faith asks, How does prayer connect us to the compassion of God? In what ways does God come near to children? Faith and science find a generative overlap, leading to exciting dialogue, because their epistemic goals (to articulate reality) are moving on the same network (to use a computer analogy). This shared network is *hypostatic*; it is the personal experience of patterns of relationship in space/time.

But how this hypostatic personal reality is embraced is different, as the questions above show. The methodologies of scientific findings and theories depend on the *hypostatic*, but these very methodologies see the universe as functioning like a person (bound in relationality), *but without a face.* The scientific cannot see how particularities emerging from relations lead ultimately to the face of God and those made in this God's image. It cannot even see how experiences of ministry—sharing in the depth of each other's person—is transformational.[33] Without the mystery

Ian Barbour explains further Torrance's view of contingency: "Thomas Torrance has written extensively on the theme of 'contingent order.' He stresses God's freedom in creating as an act of voluntary choice. God alone is infinitely free, and both the existence and the structure of the world are contingent in the sense that they might not have been. The world might have been differently ordered. We can discover its order only by observation. Moreover, the world can be studied on its own because in being created it has its own independent reality, distinct from the transcendent God." *Religion and Science: Historical and Contemporary Issues* (San Francisco: Harper-SanFrancisco, 1997), 210.

33. Scruton gives some texture to what I mean by ministry. I mean ministry as a

of face, the scientific will seek to reduce and deconstruct our deepest experiences like love, mercy, and compassion as just selfish genes (or something else). The methods of the scientific reduce the mystery that there are faces in the world with minds so deeply subjective and mysterious that only the soteriological can make sense of them.

This is exactly what Uncle Leon meant when he said faces and minds are things science cannot explain. The logic of the *hypostatic* doesn't (without face) take the scientific to the mystery and wonder of ministry—that there is a relationship so deep that it makes the broken whole, what is dead alive. The hypostatic reality of particularities in relation is only revealed in its utter profundity when it is seen through the face of Jesus Christ, who is the relation of the divine and human for the sake of ministry. Without face, the scientific can never in itself get to this level. And sitting in Tanisha's office, grieving the loss of Gena, Uncle Leon knows it. The scientific may have its technology, but it has no answer for the beauty and pain of the embrace and loss of a face of one who is deeply connected to you.[34]

So if faith and the scientific have their overlap at the place of hypostasis and the search for relationships in spacetime, they have their distinction at the location of face. Faith seeks through relationship for the face of one another in love. Faith sees the hypostatic leading to the ultimacy of transformation of death into life through ministry. The scientific sees this hypostatic reality as leading to knowledge of the material. Faith seeks the

distinct form of action (and being in the world) that takes us into personhood, to the face, and the logic discussed here. Scruton says, "I shall argue that we can reconcile the God of the philosophers with the God who is worshipped and prayed to by the ordinary believer, provided we see that this God is understood not through metaphysical speculations concerning the ground of being, but through communion with our fellow humans. The religious community adapts the view from nowhere that is God's to the view from somewhere that is ours. We can justify this, I maintain, by exploring more fully the meaning of three critical words: 'I', 'you' and 'why?' And in exploring those words I shall be constructing a general theory of the face: the face of the person, the face of the world, and the face of God." *The Face of God*, 21.

34. I have no space for a deep conversation of causality in divine action. But if I did, what I'd seek to explore is how divine action is a hypostatic reality and therefore is bound within the universe, ordering the universe, but the distinction of divine action happens in the shape of ministry to faces as hypostatic. I've discussed this more in depth in *Christopraxis*, chapter 7.

face of God in mystery (this is its soteriological goal). The scientific uses the underpinning of the hypostatic to speak of material conditions and causes.

The scientific has no word for Aly's dad, no real answer for why the face of Gena affected him so deeply and why the pain of her absence throbs. It can only offer faceless answers, speaking of natural selection and genetic conditioning.[35] It has no answer for the infinite mysteries of our yearning for faces to love and persons to minister to, of why Aly's dad would rather, in a heartbeat, die in the stead of Gena.[36]

THE FUNERAL OF FACES

Her face was everywhere. Not only was it piercing the mind of Aly and her family, but also because it actually *was*; they had filled the narthex and sanctuary with her picture. There was a photo from Gena's graduation on the bulletin, three large 2 × 4 posters on easels as you entered the sanctuary, and propped on the casket a half-dozen pictures of Gena at different youth group activities. When Jared saw one with Gena and him making a goofy face, the tears came without control.

---

35. Alexei Nesteruk points to the facelessness of science. He says, "Science is a useful tool of biological and physical survival. But its justification and its foundation must be clarified as ever. There is something in human life that cannot be described scientifically but which has an infinite value for human beings as persons. Science is good but it is not sufficient to enable one to understand what it means to be a human person. The warmth of human relationship and the transmission of grace through generations make humanity unique and special among other types of 'existence', which are described scientifically as existences of impersonal, that is, effectively 'non-living' bodies." *The Universe as Communion: Toward a Neo-Patristic Synthesis of Theology and Science* (New York: T&T Clark), 199.

36. Scruton makes a beautiful statement here I'm trying to echo throughout this chapter. He says, "You can situate human beings entirely in the world of objects. In doing so you will in all probability reduce them to animals whose behavior is to be explained by some combination of evolutionary psychology and neuroscience. But then you will find yourself describing a world from which human action, intention, responsibility, freedom and emotion have been wiped away: it will be a world without a face. The face shines in the world of objects with a light that is not of this world—the light of subjectivity. You can look for freedom in the world of objects and you will not find it: not because it is not there, but because it is bound up with the first person perspective, and with the view from somewhere of the creature who can say 'I.'" *The Face of God*, 49.

It was a hard day, maybe the hardest in Jared's life and surely of his ministry. But through it all there was beauty and wonder as well. The service was moving and the privilege of leading it was humbling. But after, at the small reception, Jared felt particularly stirred. All those faces that ministered to him, all those faces he was privileged to ministry to. The tears and togetherness came with a tangible feeling Jared couldn't quite name—and didn't want to. There was a quiet assurance in the midst of deep suffering. There is something about a funeral. People come with naked faces, needing other faces to be with and minister to. It was a terrible, but beautiful experience. And Jared was deeply moved by it.

As the reception wound down, Jared was conscious that he couldn't leave, but he couldn't remember why. Almost all the people had filed out and the exhaustion of the whole experience landed in Jared's chest, making his throat raspy and rough. But just when he was about to give up on the riddle and head for home, Sasha and two other young people from the youth group walked in. Noticing their sweats and T-shirts, it clicked. Jared had arranged for them to help clean up and tear down the room. He now wished he hadn't, but it was too late for second thoughts.

So together the four of them moved tables and washed the counters. Jared figured they could get it all done in twenty minutes. It was about all the energy he had left. The three kids were mostly quiet. The reverence of the day was still somehow soaked into the concrete and wood of the church building. They felt it. And Jared was happy for it. He didn't have the energy to do much more, especially to be the excited youth pastor.

But just as they were about done, Jared and Sasha were moving a table together to the storage closet, when she asked, "So how was it?"

As if shaken from a trance, Jared felt jerked by Sasha's direct question. "You mean the funeral?" Jared asked.

"Yeah. Was it sad?"

Jared breathed deeply and said, "Yeah, it was really sad. I mean, the pictures were haunting and made me miss her. I think I'll see her face every time I close my eyes for a week." They stood in silence for a few seconds.

"That's what I just don't get," Sasha added.

"What?" Jared asked.

"I mean, like the universe is so big and our planet is so small and our life is so short and yet it hurts so bad when someone dies. I mean it is almost unbelievable for me to think that it could have been me."

"Oh, it will be, someday!" Jared said, cringing as he heard himself say it.

"Yeah," Sasha said. "Yeah, so what is this thing? This life? This planet?"

Then Jared had an epiphany. Aly's challenge to relate faith and scientific findings had haunted him for almost a year, but he couldn't find a way to do so. Yet, just then he saw how. He realized that he didn't need to somehow become a scientist or even a religious apologist. Sasha wasn't asking him to understand everything about theoretical physics or cosmology. She wasn't really even asking if the theories of the scientific were true. For the most part she held that they were. What she wanted to know, what she wanted help in exploring, is whether there was a place for faces within these theories. Could real people, real relationships, be part of it all? Sasha wanted to know what we would do with aliens not because she needed faith to defend some worldview, but because she wanted to know if there is a place for these deep experiences of life, death, love, and suffering within a universe so big? She wanted to know if the human face was particular, the human experience valuable and unique, and what it would mean if we discovered other faces, other experiences, other beings, in the mass of the universe?[37]

Jared realized that this was Martin's question, too. He was essentially saying that he believed in the theory of evolution. But standing alone, evolution had no face—no concrete experience.

---

37. This explanation of Torrance's perspective is essentially what I contend young people are wanting and I have put in the mouth of Sasha. Colyer explains: "In other words, in scientific inquiry we are faced not only with an astonishing intelligibility, but also with the question of why there is a contingent intelligible universe. But it is a question that science cannot answer. And so, Torrance contends, this contingent and intelligible universe cries out mutely for a sufficient reason, and in so doing points beyond itself. The universe as a whole, as it has come into view in modern science, has a kind of subtle referential character beyond itself in the form of a question." *How to Read T. F. Torrance*, 202.

It had no concept of even his own face—it didn't touch his life. It assumed that at some future date all the faces would be drowned in the waters of mass extinction. Martin was asking, is there a way to hold to uniqueness of face, to the depth and beauty of the human condition, and still affirm evolution?[38]

Right there, exhausted, Jared realized that what he needed to do was help his young people look for overlaps, for open spaces where the spiritual wonder of face, of the personal, might connect with the scientific findings and theories they wrestled with. Was there a place for personhood in the findings and theories of physics, evolution, and cognitive science?[39] Although the comprehensive social practice of "science" had made a strong pitch for an impersonal universe, was it possible to see echoes of hypostatic personhood in the theories of the scientific? Is it possible that the scientific might have something to say to the personal?

How Jared would answer this, he wasn't sure . . .

38. By searching for the face, I mean something like Coleman is presenting here. The search for the face is the search for a transcendent reality that is embedded in space/time of an incarnate logic. Coleman says, "An experience of transcendence and a search for ultimate meaning have always been part of the human experience, and to dismiss this phenomenon is tantamount to diminishing what it is to be human." Richard Coleman, *State of Affairs: The Science-Theology Controversy* (Eugene, OR: Cascade, 2014), 214.

39. Jared's breakthrough is to try exactly what Coleman asks here: "What if theology's role in the public square is not primarily to 'explain' the data in competition with science, but to re-describe a world already provisionally described and partially explained by science?" *State of Affairs*, 257.

PART II

(Part Sasha)

11.

Sasha and Big and Small Infinity

The thrill was intoxicating. From the fear of defeat to the jubilant celebration of victory was a dazzling rush. Jared screamed and jumped as if he'd finally seen his beloved Detroit Lions win a Super Bowl—or a playoff game for that matter. But his cheering had nothing to do with first downs or post patterns. Jared was screaming like a mad man because of math!

On the stage of a small school theater six high school students from Ridge West High were jumping up and down, draped in T-shirts that read "Team Kepler of RWH." And the student in the middle of the gawky celebration was Sasha. She had just answered the deciding question that gave her team the state mathlete championship. Jared couldn't believe it. Not only was she a state champion, but the MVP. He was thrilled, but his exuberance was nothing compared to Trent's, who was pumping his fist and jumping so high that Jared wasn't sure what would give first, the floor or his knees. The howling celebration of Trent cracked Jared up, shaking him enough from the moment to recognize that he was going wild about math. Just a few hours earlier, Jared had dreaded the thought of the hours at this competition, reminding himself it was his job. He'd wished for any other event than a mathlete competition. But now he was more than a fan. He was a fanatic.

The next thing Jared knew, he was sitting with the mathlete team at their pizza celebration. They filled two tables with the team and parents. Jared felt honored to be invited, but Trent actually had insisted on it. The pitchers of Pepsi and the pepperoni slices went down easily as the celebratory chatter filled the pizzeria with a buzz. As the meal shifted to dessert, the volume dropped, but the joy was still palpable. As it did, Jared pointed to Sasha's team T-shirt, asking, "Why does it say 'Team Kepler RWH'?"

Lily, Sasha's teammate and close friend, interjected. "For the planet-hunter, dude!"

"Planet-hunter?" Jared asked, racking his mind for the reference, assuming it referred to some Sci-Fi movie. Jared loved the genre, so not being able to place the reference disturbed him. *Star Wars*, *Battlestar Galactica*, and *Interstellar* came to mind, but there was no connection.

So, owning his ignorance (something he'd learned to do in the last year) he said, "Where is that from? I don't think I know that reference. Is it *Star Trek*?" (Jared had never gotten into that classic. He actually hated it.)

Lily, Sasha, and Derek, a senior teammate sitting next to Lily, laughed, which made Jared only feel slightly bad. What was worse was that Trent too rolled out a deep chuckle when Jared voiced his ignorance.

"Man," Derek said, "the planet-hunter is NASA's Kepler spacecraft that has discovered thousands of new planets and just recently found hundreds more that might have the conditions to support life."

"Aliens, Dude!" Lily added. "It's hunting for aliens. That's freaking cool. Why not name ourselves after that? It's rock-n-roll." Lily was about the coolest mathlete Jared could imagine. With her red-streaked hair and orange-rimmed glasses, she looked like she should be working a shift at The Rusty Spoon.

"Wow!" Jared said, trying to recover some dignity, but by now Jared was used to being behind on things like this. "Cool," he responded, to continue the conversation. "Sasha and I have actually talked a little about the possibilities of aliens."

"It's not a possibility," Derek interrupted, "it's completely probable. It's just a matter of time. I mean, the math is clear. The probability is overwhelming when you think of the mass of the universe. It is almost a mathematical certainty." He proclaimed this with a mixed tone of scientist, math nerd, and preacher.

Trent, actually in another conversation, turned and added, "It might be a mathematical probability and seems logical from a mathematical perspective, but there are some big cosmological and biological hurdles to get past." Just as quickly, Trent returned to his other conversation.

But Sasha wouldn't let her dad have a flyby rebuttal without a response, rehearsing a conversation Jared assumed had happened over and again at home. "But the math is clear, Dad, and math is the most beautiful language of nature; it must be respected." Trent waved his hand at her dismissively, as if to say, "Yeah, yeah, I've heard you say that before."

But Jared was still interested in this Kepler thing. "But if it is a planet-hunter why is it named Kepler?" he asked. "Is that the guy who built it?"

Jared figured they should know this if they named their team "Kepler." But this wasn't the case. As if his confidence was melting away in front of Jared, Derek said with a long pause and a disconcerted look on his face, "I don't know." But Sasha had a slight clue, getting Derek off the hook: "I think he's an old scientist, I think one of the first or something."

"Yeah," said Lily. "That's right! He was like a guy who helped Galileo or something. I think when Galileo was being like totally oppressed by your people," she said with a sneer.

"My people?" asked Jared.

"Yeah," Lily said with more bravado. "When you church people put chains on Galileo and locked him in a cell because he said the earth moved."

"Okay," Jared said with skeptical incredulity. "I'm not sure that was *my* people."

"Well," said Sasha, "it was the church. It just feels like the church has always been scared of a big infinite universe. Like I told you before, Galileo shows that the church isn't really big on science."

"Yeah," Lily added, bouncing in her chair like a fighter in his corner awaiting the bell. And then she threw her first jab. "Why have you church people always been afraid of aliens? I mean it seems like you need such a small world with the earth at the center, so you torture poor Galileo just so you're not spooked by extraterrestrials."

Lily shook her head playfully, yet with an air of seriousness as she adjusted her glasses. "Lame, man, real lame."

12.

Galileo and Alien Life: The Story of Galileo Galilei

It appears a devastating fact of history that the church took poor
Galileo into a Vatican jail and beat him by ten for every public comment he'd made that the earth moved around the sun.
It is such a devastating fact that every young person seems to
know the tale like they know about Santa Claus. They're not
sure when or who told them the story; it's just something they've
always known. The problem is that just like Santa Claus, the
tale of Galileo's jailing and torture is make-believe. Galileo was
never jailed, and not once beaten. He did find himself in some
tense moments, and was indeed pushing the church into a new
way of seeing the heavens above.[1] But never did Galileo see
himself as anything other than a committed Catholic philoso-

---

1. Ian Barbour discusses the origins of this myth: "Such instances of the conflict
between science and religion were the theme of two influential historical accounts
written in the aftermath of the Darwinian controversy, J. W. Draper's *History of the
Conflict between Religion and Science* [1874] and A. D. White's *A History of the Warfare
of Science with Theology in Christendom* [1896]. Both of them portrayed a protracted
'warfare' in which the conservative forces of theological dogmatism opposed the
progressive forces of scientific rationality and were defeated in successive engage-
ments. Both studies gave the Galileo affair as a prime example." *Religion and Science:
Historical and Contemporary Issues* (San Francisco: HarperSanFrancisco, 1997), 25.

pher.[2] As a matter of fact, he gave one of his daughters to the church as a nun, and she devoted her life to prayer—particularly for her father.

Becoming a natural philosopher and arguably the first modern scientist was never the goal for young Galileo. His father was a music teacher and Galileo himself a skilled musician. His father had actually written a book about musical theory. Recently, studies have shown a connection between musical aptitude and skills in math. There seems to be some connection between the mysterious structure of music and the mathematical order of nature.[3] So looking back, it is not surprising that one of the greatest mathematical minds of the seventeenth century was the son of a musical theorist.

For Galileo's family, money was an issue. When it became

2. David Wooton in his biography *Galileo: Watcher of the Skies* argues that Galileo was much less than a devoted Catholic. Yet, Wooton's argument seems to rest on absence, explaining what's not seen in Galileo's correspondence (though he knows that much of Galileo's writing was lost after his death). For instance, Wooton contrasts Galileo with Castelli, saying, "But Galileo is not Castelli. Galileo never praises preachers, prays to saints or purchases indulgences, and only rarely does he ask that others pray for him (never, to the best of my knowledge, before he loses his sight). Now and again there is a glimpse of him going to church, even listening to a sermon—but his thoughts are elsewhere. All this, you may say, is argument from silence. I agree. It would be wrong to base any conclusion on a profoundly cynical letter sent to Galileo describing a girl who had the stigmata. Equally, no conclusions can be drawn from the fact that Galileo once visited Loreto, where there was a famous shrine: he was following in the footsteps of Cosimo II, who had made the pilgrimage fashionable. But in the end Galileo's silence becomes so remarkable that we simply cannot ignore it. For 'Galileo never spoke of Jesus. There is simply no direct testimony to what he thought of Christ.'" (New Haven: Yale University Press, 2010), 141. This is a classic argument from silence. I personally acknowledge Wooton's point and recognize he could be right. But in this short story I'm following more the likes of Shea who says, "Galileo may not have been a conventionally devout Catholic, but he was deeply convinced that God had singled him out to make not only some but all the new celestial discoveries." William Shea and Marino Artigas, *Galileo in Rome: The Rise and Fall of a Troublesome Genius* (London: Oxford University Press, 2003), 32.

3. Einstein's own mathematical mind was honed around music, just as Galileo's was. Isaacson said, "What Einstein appreciated in Mozart and Bach was the clear architectural structure that made their music seem 'deterministic' and, like his own favorite scientific theories, plucked from the universe rather than composed. 'Beethoven created his music,' Einstein once said, but 'Mozart's music is so pure it seems to have been ever-present in the universe.'" Walter Isaacson, *Einstein: His Life and Universe* (New York: Simon & Schuster, 2007), 38.

clear that the boy had an aptitude for numbers, he was encouraged to become a doctor. But like Luther, who just seventy-six years earlier had turned Europe on its head when he denied his father and became a monk instead of a lawyer, Galileo would deny his own father's wishes and chose philosophy over medicine.

Galileo ended up both studying and teaching at the university in Pisa, the place where the tower leans. The story is that Galileo would climb that tower to drop things from it, intrigued by the speed of their descent. This is probably part of the fairy tale. It is true that Galileo thought a lot about dropping things from heights, and about motion more generally, but it was probably more of a thought experiment, like Einstein's riding on a light beam, than an actual occurrence.[4]

Nevertheless, Galileo was out to show that the revered philosopher Aristotle was wrong. Poor Aristotle had not fared well of late. He had been rediscovered in the twelfth and thirteenth centuries, and with the help of Thomas Aquinas, his thought became the foundation of late-medieval theology. To be a Western Christian, in no small part, was to be in dialogue with Aristotle. Since the days of Aquinas, Aristotle was a rock star, but by the early 1500s his scientific brilliance was being questioned.

Luther, that crass monk in Germany, had already taken his shots at Aristotle, landing devastating blows using Paul's epistles and justification by faith alone. But now one of the Catholic Church's own was questioning Aristotle's assertion that heavier items fall faster to earth because material always returns to its source. So because a rock is more densely bound to the ground than a feather, it will more quickly return to its source.

---

4. J. L. Heilbron explains, "We have it on Viviani's authority that Galileo dropped different weights of the same material from Pisa's Leaning Tower to show, 'to the dismay of the philosophers,' that, contrary to Aristotle, they all fell at the same speed. And he did it not once, or secretly, but 'with repeated trials . . . in the presence of other teachers and philosophers, and the whole assembly of students.' Iconoclasts have thrown doubt on this vignette although the tower's tilt made it a perfect platform for the experiment. They objected that no one among the literate throng supposedly present, not even the peripatetic philosophers of motion who went away grinding their teeth, recorded the event." *Galileo* (Oxford: Oxford University Press, 2010), 59.

Yet, Galileo realized that this wasn't accurate. A cannonball and feather actually drop at the same rate, his experiments showed; the pull to the earth affects them equally. The only difference, Galileo showed, was wind resistance. The pull of gravity was equally universal—and equations could prove it. Galileo's point was that if a feather and cannonball were dropped in a vacuum they would fall at the same rate.[5] In a spooky symmetry of history, the very year Galileo died, a baby in England was born who would crack this code, showing the universal constant law of gravity. That baby was Isaac Newton.

THE SUN AT THE CENTER

Truth be told, Galileo never really liked Pisa, so when a chance came to move to the Republic of Venice and teach in the university at Padua, he jumped at the opportunity. It was not only a bigger and better university, but, more importantly to Galileo, it offered more money. His father had died, and Galileo's only inheritance was debt. Padua promised more money and time to work on his calculations. But it also provided more freedom. As a republic it had its distance from the Vatican and the impositions of the pope. In Padua, Galileo could take his swings at Aristotle without much fear of repercussion.

Aristotle had asserted that the earth, and the heaven it sat in, were eternal. The earth was at the center and the stars, moon,

5. Wooton summarizes Aristotle's position and Galileo moving beyond it. He says, "According to Aristotle there are two types of movement: natural movement, which is directed towards an end, and halts when an object arrives at its natural resting place; and forced movement, which continues only for so long as there is a mover acting on the moving object. As others had done before him, Galileo modifies the account of forced movement to include the idea of an impressed force. But he also invents a quite new type of movement, which he calls intermediate movement. Imagine a perfectly round ball standing on a perfectly smooth sheet of ice. The slightest touch will start it moving, and it will continue to move indefinitely. If this seems too much like an impractical abstraction, think of a river: it flows constantly, and yet the gradient is often minute. It seems that flowing water has almost no resistance to movement; otherwise one would be able to identify a slope that was not steep enough for a river to run down it. Aristotle held that the natural condition of all sublunary things is to be stationary, and that all movement naturally ends in the cessation of movement; Galileo was now suggesting that movement (if it is neither upwards nor downwards but sideways) might have no natural end." *Galileo*, 43.

and sun moved around it. To Galileo's contemporaries, this seemed not only logical but also biblical. But a devout Christian from Poland named Nicolaus Copernicus followed Augustine, and he recognized that the scriptures must not be confused for a treatise on the natural world. The Bible speaks the truth with certainty about who God is and how God acts, but it is no cosmological textbook, and says little about the actual movements of the heavenly bodies. So this devoted Christian theorized that it was the sun, not the earth, that rested at the center of the universe.[6] That meant it is the earth that moves around the sun, and not the other way around—which Aristotle had believed.

After reading Copernicus's book years after his death, Galileo was convinced, mainly because it fit so well with his own experiments and equations on motion. But it wasn't actually Copernicus's math that convinced Galileo; it was the person on Sasha's T-shirt: Johannes Kepler, the same guy after whom NASA named the planet-hunter. He'd written his own book providing the mathematical backing for Copernicus's theory. Kepler, a pious Lutheran, was teaching at a seminary when he wrote his book.[7] And when Galileo read it he was convinced that the earth was in orbit around the sun—and not in the circles that Copernicus had assumed, but in an oval-like movement.[8] This was

6. "The great Copernicus (1473–1543) was an ecclesiastic, being a canon of Frauenberg Cathedral. He was probably an ordained priest at the time of his death." Stephen Barr, *Modern Physics and Ancient Faith* (South Bend, IN: University of Notre Dame Press, 2003), 9.

7. "Kepler, a German Lutheran and deeply spiritual Christian who once had to interrupt his research to defend his mother against charges of witchcraft, showed that the planets did not move in the perfect circles long assigned to them. Their orbits were ellipses. And they sped up when they got closer to the sun and slowed down when they were farther away, puzzling behavior for heavenly bodies not allowed to change in any way." Karl Giberson, *The Wonder of the Universe: Hints of God in Our Fine-Tuned World* (Downers Grove, IL: IVP, 2012), 30.

8. Annibale Fantoli explains that Kepler's book and Galileo's observation actually followed each other, coming together to make clear that the earth moved: "For two reasons the year 1609 marks a decisive turn of events in the history of astronomy. The first consists in the publication of the *Astronomia Nova* of Kepler. The second is the beginning of observational astronomy with Galileo's use of the telescope. These two events, completely independent from one another, will be of fundamental importance for eliminating the world view of the world." *Galileo: For Copernicanism and for the Church* (Vatican: Vatican Obervatory Foundation, 1996), 107.

just the conclusion of speculative equations until Galileo got his hands on a child's toy.

ITALY'S STEVE JOBS

The same year that Kepler's book came out, Galileo got ahold of his first telescope. His first thoughts were not necessarily scientific. Rather, Galileo had "his mind on his money and his money on his mind." Like a hip-hop artist, Galileo was a genius on the hustle. He was always looking for a way to up his salary and win more freedom for himself. In a republic like Venice, quick financial gain was possible, and Galileo had already sampled it when he had found a rudimentary way to calculate longitude. The implications for trade and defense were enough for this rich port city to pay. So when Galileo held a telescope for the first time, he saw possibilities no one else had before—both for proving Copernicus's theory, but also, importantly, for making some quick cash.

Just as Steve Jobs didn't create the personal computer but exponentially improved it, so Galileo didn't invent the telescope but turned it into an important instrument. For about three hundred years before Galileo, people all over Europe had been making lenses for spectacles. But only recently had a Dutch lens maker put them into a tube. He imagined it as a plaything for children, a way to make a few coins at carnivals. But Galileo was not only an imaginative businessman with concern for design, use, and capital (Steve Jobs), but also a hands-on, dirty, technical engineer (Steve Wozniak).[9] Galileo realized that he could radically improve this tube, upping its magnification by twenty times, by grinding his own lenses. Soon enough he was standing on top of a building with all Venice's important men, showing

9. "We live in a world where manufacturers are constantly offering us improved versions of products, so if you or I had been shown a primitive telescope we would have asked immediately what scope there was for improvement. Galileo's world was not like this. Even new technologies—guns, printing presses, compasses—were improved slowly and over very long periods of time. By the summer of 1609 there were thousands of people—many of them mathematicians, scientists, engineers—who had seen and used the new telescopes. But Galileo was the only person who immediately saw in the telescope a challenge: how could one improve it?" Wooton, *Galileo*, 90.

them boats at a distance that would need hours of travel before becoming visible to the naked eye. The military defense use was so clear that Galileo was now a secure man with an agreement to take a very high salary from the Republic for the rest of his life.

THE SPACE TRAVELER

Galileo also had his own ideas of what to do with this tube, so one night he turned it on the moon and was the first human being to see it magnified.[10] There was so much more to see! Soon Galileo had discovered satellites (moons) around Jupiter. This observation, as well as others, along with more accurate calculations, proved that Copernicus was right. Galileo's next move was to publish a book.

With literary flare, *The Starry Messenger* positioned Galileo as a space traveler, beaming himself across the heavens, describing his discoveries. Unlike Han Solo in the *Millennium Falcon*, Galileo's vehicle of transportation was the telescope. Galileo was the first person to see himself as spaceman![11]

The book made Galileo's name one of the greatest in all of Italy. Princes and bishops now called him a treasure. But, of course, at the same time that it intrigued people, it disturbed them. For instance, it had been assumed that the moon was a perfect sphere, flat and smooth like a marble. But when Galileo discovered its surface was rocky and pocked, people where thrown into cognitive dissonance. Many assumed that if there were mountains on the moon like here on earth, then surely it was logical to assume that there were moonmen—aliens![12]

10. "He pointed the telescope to the heavens in November 1609, and, for the first time in history, the human eye had a close-up view of the Moon." Shea and Artigas, *Galileo in Rome*, 21.

11. "In his final choice of title, Galileo presented himself as a traveller returning from a voyage through the heavens with strange and wonderful things to report. If the book was the message about the stars, then Galileo was the messenger who had come from the stars. He was, thanks to the telescope, the first spaceman—indeed this is how Viviani describes him on the monument he erected to record his achievements." Wooton, *Galileo*, 99.

12. David Wooton explains how the thought of life on other planets goes back to Bruno. He discusses this through Donne. He says, mentioning Galileo and Kepler,

Like Sasha, they wondered what the life, death, and resurrection of Jesus (and the taking of the Eucharist) would mean if the moon were inhabited. What makes the Christian imagination able to produce scientific findings and geniuses like Copernicus, Kepler, and Galileo is also what makes it susceptible to aliens. Because it is within creation, at a particular place in spacetime that God encounters us in Jesus Christ, we're forced to ask, What happens if this location is relativized by the expanse of space? And if God comes to us in human form, what happens if intelligent life comes in many forms, like Tatooine's Mos Eisley Cantina? At one level this makes sense; if the fullness of God takes on human form, then what does this have to do with aliens? But the particularity of the incarnation means that there is always identification and differentiation. Jesus lives as a Jewish man in the first century, so what does this have to do with a woman in Africa in the twenty-first? I'm not sure that alien encounters would undercut the Christian imagination of a personal universe, but

"Donne would have learnt from Hill about the possibility of life on other planets, and of planets circling other stars; he would also have learnt that these strange ideas derived from Giordano Bruno. If he read Galileo's *Starry Messenger*, with its account of the moon as having mountains and valleys, Donne would surely have responded exactly as the great German astronomer Johannes Kepler did that spring when he read one of the first copies to arrive in Germany—he saw a remarkable vindication of Bruno's perverse theory that there might be life elsewhere in the universe. If Donne read Kepler's *Conversation* he would have found the link with Bruno spelled out." *The Invention of Science: A New History of the Scientific Revolution* (New York: Harper, 2015), 9. "Thus Bruno imagined an infinite universe, with numberless stars and planets, all possibly inhabited by extraterrestrial life forms. Since Bruno did not believe that Christ was the savior of mankind (he was a sort of pantheist), he did not have to worry about how the Christian drama of sin and salvation was played out in this infinity of worlds." *The Invention of Science*, 147. He continues: "Bruno was not the first to imagine an infinite universe with extraterrestrial life. Nicholas of Cusa, in his *On Learned Ignorance* (1440), had argued that only an infinite universe was appropriate for an infinite God. Nicholas thought the earth was a heavenly body which from a distance would shine like a star, an idea which caught Montaigne's attention. But Nicholas assumed that the earth and the sun were similar bodies. A habitable world was, Nicholas thought, hidden behind the shining visible surface of the sun; as for the earth, it, like the sun, was surrounded by a fiery mantle which was invisible to us, and which you would see only if you viewed the earth from outer space. Thus Nicholas made the earth into a heavenly body, but simultaneously he made the sun into a terrestrial one. Bruno, by contrast, was the first to distinguish stars and planets as we do now, making the sun a star and the planets, including the Earth, dark bodies shining by reflected light." *The Invention of Science*, 148.

rather, could witness to it. But we'll have to explore this more below.

ALIENS AND A PERSONAL EXISTENCE

What seems clear, both today and in Galileo's time, is that the possibility of life elsewhere is slim. Most of the infinite space beyond us is absent of, and even opposed to, life. Galileo saw it that way, telling his anxious readers, first, that he saw no clouds or water on the moon, therefore organic life was impossible. Plus, to add to the impossibility, the divergent temperatures were too great to support life. It was too hot when the sun hit it and far too cold when dark. Galileo was already pointing to a fact we'll explore in the next chapter. Life is a tricky riddle that needs the most precise conditions to be sustained.[13]

This is exactly what the Kepler planet-hunter is searching for. It is looking for those odd planets that just may be at the right temperature to have water for life—and these planets are out there, making intelligent alien life possible. But as Trent had mentioned, there is a biological timing issue that makes it anything but a certainty. Not only do we need very finely tuned conditions for life, but also we need huge amounts of time to create the kind of intelligent life that could fashion civilizations, and invent communication technologies, and hyper-speed drives. It has taken our planet 4 billion years to do so, and only in

13. Shea explains further: "Our source is a letter that he wrote on 28 February to Carlo Muti, the nephew of Cardinal Tiberio Muti, in whose house Galileo had debated the nature of the moon with someone who claimed that if it resembled the Earth because it had mountains, then it should also have living creatures like those we find on Earth. The argument may appear innocuous, but it opened a Pandora's box: If human beings are found on the moon how can they descend from Adam? And if they do not, what about original sin and the significance of the Incarnation of Jesus Christ? It is in order to avoid having these questions raised that Galileo promptly put down his reply on paper. There can be no organic life on the moon because there is no water there. This he inferred from the absence of clouds, but even if it were granted that water occurs on the moon, Galileo points out that this could not be used as an argument that there is life there. The reason is that the variation in temperature is too great, since a lunar day or a lunar night lasts fifteen of our terrestrial days or nights. This means that the surface of the moon is scorched for 360 hours and subjected to incredibly low temperatures during the next 360 hours. Galileo did not have to say more to feel confident that he had scalded or frozen a potentially dangerous implication of lunar mountains." Shea and Artigas, *Galileo in Rome*, 92.

the last 100,000 years (which is just a drop in the ocean of time on this planet) has there been intelligent life (and only 10,000 years of that has had civilization). Only in the last hundred years have we had the ability to send signals into space.[14] Not only would another planet need to have these very fine-tuned conditions to get life, but in turn, its evolving would have to match our own with enough harmony that we could make contact.

To play out the scenario, it is possible that on another planet intelligent life is now just creating basic writing, and by the time they're ready for radio-wave communication (not to mention a spacecraft able to travel a million light-years), our civilization would have imploded as we face a mass extinction and ecological disaster. Or they could be ahead of us, and if not already extinct themselves, would have to be enlightened enough to avoid moral corruption or self-destruction and seek contact with other intelligent life in the universe as aggressively as we are. So, oddly, Martin's concern for mass extinctions and Sasha's questions about aliens are linked, most directly in their opposition (this shows that again science is no unified thing, but a loose container).[15] So, while the size of the universe and sheer numbers of planets moving around stars make it seem logical that just *one* other planet has intelligent life on it, the necessities of time and contact make this seem a very thin possibility.

Nevertheless, through Galileo's telescope our vision was for the first time expanded to show the size of the universe and

14. Giberson has some skepticism about aliens. "All this fussing and fretting about aliens might lead one to believe that some sort of signal had been received—an unmistakably intelligent message like what Jodie Foster's character, astronomer Ellie Arroway, deciphered in the movie *Contact*. The great distance to the planet rules out the possibility of actual alien Zarminians being among us, but a mere twenty light years is no barrier to radio transmission. If the Zarminians started twenty years ago broadcasting messages to earth, or even generically in all directions, we would be receiving them by now. Radio waves have, in fact, been emanating from earth in all directions for almost a century and could be detected by any extraterrestrial civilization with the appropriate technology. But we are receiving no radio messages from 581g or any other planet in the universe. So why all the excitement about the Zarminians?" Giberson, *The Wonder of the Universe*, 88.

15. Of course, there is more hope for life if the aliens are actually advanced beyond us. Maybe they evolved to extended consciousness and communication thousands of years before us, and even found ways of protecting themselves from mass extinctions. But this all gets into Sci-Fi.

open to imagine aliens.[16] What shook Galileo's readers, and shakes Sasha too, is how the existence of aliens would challenge the soteriological goal of faith. How would the incarnation, Eucharist, and forgiveness of sins work with extraterrestrials? Would it make faith's soteriological goal meaningless? Yet, from within the epistemic goal of faith, the existence of aliens may give witness to how deep the personal (and even *hypostatic*) nature of the universe might be. If these aliens were the kind of personal beings who gave and received ministry (and the evolutionary theory of our species seems to assume that they would have to be to get the kind of shared-mind innovation necessary for advancement—these are what some theorists call the "ratchet effect"), then they too could reflect the image of the personal ministering God that is revealed in the face of Jesus Christ. To encounter aliens with personal faces, then, would point to the depth of a personal order, upending the assumption that our personal being is just an improbable oddity in a cold, impersonal existence.

And this is where Sasha is stuck. She is pulled in both directions. If there are aliens, she questions faith's soteriological goal. But even if Jared or Trent can help her reconcile this, if she's honest, her deeper issue is the divergent epistemic assertions of faith when it comes to space. She wonders if our personal minds are just a mishap of the universe (maybe even more so if there *isn't* alien life). In other words, she wonders if it is possible that faith's assertion that the universe is personal is only an illusion of our subjectivity. The more Jared talks with Sasha the more he realizes that Sasha's issue isn't really whether there are aliens, but how it is possible to see the mind of God and the importance of personhood in a universe where there are not only big infinites (galaxies, massive black holes, and supernovas) but also the smallest infinity (Higgs particles, dark matter, and quarks).

The myth of Galileo's jailing seems believable because the ramifications of his telescope were profound. After Galileo, we are no longer at the center of the universe, and therefore we can

---

16. Copernicus actually started this, and it was Bruno who, drawn to Copernicus's theory, asserted that ours was just one of many worlds. Bruno was burnt at the stake in part (but only part) for this assertion. He had made a number of other heretical assertions that doomed him.

question whether we are the center of attention at all. Galileo's discoveries show that indeed space is massively larger than could be imagined. This profoundly starts us on the path of contemplating the actuality that these big and small infinites do indeed exist. And we are led to wrestle with how they witness (or not) to a personal God.

THE TROUBLE

As Galileo's star was rising in Italy, so was his trouble. The leaders of Venice realized that Galileo had not been completely truthful about the telescope—the hustler was exposed—but don't hate the player, hate the game! Galileo had assured leaders of the Republic that he alone possessed the ability to make magnified lenses for the telescope. But soon others were figuring out his engineering trick. The cushy lifetime salary was stripped from him. With hurt feelings, Galileo decided to depart the Republic of Venice for his hometown of Florence. Many wondered why, and in retrospect, it may have been a bad decision.[17] The money and free time in Florence wasn't much greater, and the freedom was much less. Venice was mostly free of papal power, but not Florence; it was deeply entrenched in Vatican oversight. However, the prince of Florence admired Galileo so deeply that an opportunity to head home as a court mathematician was too good to pass up.

As time passed, appreciation for Galileo only increased. He was invited on trips to Rome, to private audiences with the pope, toting along his telescope. But rumblings were starting. They came first within the Florence court itself, some wondering how this assumption that earth moved around the sun could fit with scripture. The book of Joshua says the sun, not the earth,

17. Wooton adds, "Why leave Venice? In order to be welcomed not just in Florence, but more importantly in Rome. . . . When we think of Venice we think of a bustling port, a cosmopolitan city—the most cosmopolitan city in Europe, just as Padua was the most cosmopolitan university. Galileo saw things differently. Venice was on the periphery, its only allies the far distant English, the French and the German Protestants. If you wanted to convince the people who counted, if you wanted to be heard throughout the educated world, it was to Rome that you must go. Why on earth did he think this? In the end there is perhaps only one answer: because he was a Florentine, and that is how Florentines thought." *Galileo*, 115.

stood still (Joshua 10). Maybe overestimating his own abilities, Galileo responded, committing himself to scripture on all matters but cosmological.

For most, this made sense. But the fracture that tore the Western church in two was still throbbing after the Protestant Reformation. Not only were many looking to protect the church from any new heresies, but they'd also taken it on the chin for not upholding the truth of scripture. So some, particularly the Dominicans, would be damned if they would allow a genius mathematician to speak about scripture and put the church further at risk.[18]

The heat was turned up on Galileo—it wasn't just zealous Dominicans now, but also fellow philosophers. Galileo's radical support for Copernicus, as we said above, opposed Aristotle. And there are few creatures more vindictive than scholars whose theories have been opposed. So when Galileo took on Aristotle, he was, in turn, taking on the philosophical establishment (and it would be his fellow philosophers, even more than clergy, that would make sure Galileo was silenced).[19] Historian John

18. "The popular conception of Galileo as a martyr for freedom of thought is an oversimplification. That his views were different from those of the majority of the academic establishment did not make him a liberal. He cherished the hope that the Church would endorse his opinions and, with many of his contemporaries, looked to an enlightened papacy as an effective instrument of scientific progress. But what Galileo does not seem to have understood is that the Catholic Church, attacked by Protestants for neglecting the Bible, found itself compelled, in self-defense, to harden its position. Whatever appeared to contradict Holy Writ had to be treated with the utmost caution." Shea and Artigas, *Galileo in Rome*, 51.

19. Peter Harrison adds more texture, taking this point deeper: "There is no doubt, for instance, that Galileo was tried by the Inquisition and forced to recant the Copernican hypothesis. But to cite this as an instance of science-religion conflict is to misconstrue the context. For a start, the Catholic Church endorsed the scientific consensus of the period, which, on the basis of the available evidence, held that the earth was stationary in the middle of the cosmos. To this extent it might be better to characterize the episode as a conflict within science (or, more strictly, within astronomy and natural philosophy) rather than between science and religion. Second, the first use of the Galileo affair for propaganda purposes was by Protestants seeking to discredit Catholics, so that it was initially given a role in conflicts within religion. Related to this is the fact that the Copernican hypothesis had first been postulated some eighty years before the trial of Galileo, and hence the context of the Protestant Reformation is a key to understanding why the papacy took steps at this particular time. Finally, even if it could be constructed as a science-religion conflict, the condemnation of Galileo was not typical of the Catholic Church's attitude toward the study of nature, since at the time the church was the single most prominent sup-

Hedley Brooke says it this way: "Galileo seems to have felt that his difficulties with the Catholic Church had their origin in the resentment of academic philosophers who had put pressure on ecclesiastical authorities to denounce him."[20] These, particularly Jesuit, philosophers were not willing to stand by and let Aristotle be disparaged. And it is they who Galileo attacked (again, in retrospect, probably not a good move).[21]

But Galileo's hubris may have been spurred forward by what he saw as a serendipitous occurrence. A bishop from Florence who admired and supported Galileo had been named pope.[22] It now seemed time for Galileo to publish his book in support of Copernicanism and silence those opposing philosophers. But what Galileo didn't realize is that Pope Urban's mantle of authority was now much heavier than when he was simply the bishop of Florence. Urban was now concerned about the political fallout of such a book.

During this time, all books needed the permission of the church to be published. Somewhat tentatively, Pope Urban agreed to Galileo's pro-Copernicus book, with one stipulation: Galileo must be clear that Copernicanism and its belief that the

porter of astronomical research." Peter Harrison, *The Territories of Science and Religion* (Chicago: University of Chicago Press, 2015), 173.

20. John Hedley Brooke, *Science and Religion* (London: Cambridge University Press, 2014), 50. Brooke adds, "To wrench the earth from the sublunar region and to place it among the planets was to violate the entire cosmos. Certainly the Catholic Church had a vested interest in Aristotelian philosophy, but much of the conflict ostensibly between science and religion turns out to have been between new science and the sanctified science of the previous generation." *Science and Religion*, 50.

21. "But Galileo was certainly right to focus on the Jesuits, who were rapidly establishing themselves as the educators of the elite throughout Catholic Europe: there were 245 Jesuit colleges by the end of the sixteenth century. In Rome they ran what amounted to a research university, but one which trained educators who were sent out across the world. And he was right to think of the Jesuits as potential allies for the new science, for much of the early experimental science was done within the order. But there was a profound tension within the Jesuit enterprise. On the one hand, Jesuits were at the cutting edge of the new science; on the other, the order was committed to upholding the traditional learning of the Church as represented, above all, by St Thomas Aquinas." Wooton, *Galileo*, 115.

22. "Just when Galileo was feeling lonely and isolated, Maffeo Barberini, a Florentine, was elected pope on 6 August 1623, taking the name Urban VIII. He and Galileo had been on friendly terms since 1611, when Barberini had supported Galileo in a debate, conducted over the grand duke's dinner table: about why bodies float or sink." Wooton, *Galileo*, 176.

earth moved around the sun was *just a theory*. At no point did the church ever suppress Galileo's ideas. He was only asked to do the pope a favor by labeling them "speculative."

But for whatever reason—probably because of competition with those Jesuit philosophers—Galileo refused, and the book appeared with a splash, asserting as fact that the earth moved around the sun. Pope Urban was furious. And while Galileo was given a cold shoulder and much unwelcome treatment on trips to Rome, he was neither jailed nor tortured.

However, Galileo was tried, and after bending a knee to church authority, he was given his verdict. It was decided that he would face no punishment but house arrest, returning to a country villa outside Florence. He was even free to go to mass and visit his mistress. The plagues that ravaged Italy made him feel more caged in than he was. But there was no restriction on visitors, and his daughter, the nun, visited him often. Galileo even gave her convent financial support (not the actions of someone furious with the church). No doubt the church is guilty for suppressing Galileo's ideas for the good of their own political gain, but there is no truth in the rumors that Galileo was abused, or that Galileo, even in his exile, chose science over faith.

Never did Galileo see himself as anything other than a committed Catholic. It is a misunderstanding for Sasha and her friends to imagine that faith fears the size of the cosmos. The reason that the myth of Galileo's imprisonment seems to stick is because it is from his legacy that we are forced to confront how infinitely big this universe is. Facing the infinity of space is no doubt a struggle for all minds to comprehend, but Galileo's vision of its size never led him to be jailed or to personally give up his faith. Nevertheless, it leads many of our young people like Sasha to wonder, How can this big infinity of space allow us to still believe that the universe is bound in a personal order, minded by a personal God?

The scientific discovery of the big infinity of space no doubt raises this challenge for our young people. And within a few hundred years of Galileo, those following in his legacy would discover that the universe was not only infinitely big, but growing by the minute. It would be another man, a world away in

California, who would reveal that, indeed, the seemingly infinitely big universe was expanding. He too, using a telescope, revealed Einstein's greatest blunder. This man was Edwin Hubble.

13.

With a Bang

Galileo had moved us from the center; by giving us our first visions of just how expansive space was, he displaced humanity. The genie was now out of the bottle, Pandora was out of the box. And no matter how hard Jesuit/Aristotelian philosophers or priests wanted it back in, there was no return. The big infinity of the universe seemed to risk crushing us—at least Sasha wondered if it flattened the possibility of faith in a personal order, making the universe impersonal and arbitrary.

It appears to be a further irony of history (and one that additionally opposes the myth that faith and the scientific are enemies) that a Catholic priest educated in Jesuit schools would be one of the first to deduce the Big Bang. In 1927, Georges Lemaitre, a Belgian priest and budding professor of physics, published a paper that asserted (following Einstein's general theory of relativity) that the universe was expanding. He showed mathematically that there must have been a time when the universe was *not*. Through a huge explosion of expansion, it came to be, he asserted, and is continuing to stretch and expand even to this minute.

Four years before publishing his article, Lemaitre spent a year at Cambridge, studying under Arthur Eddington. It was Eddington, the uptight Englishman, more than anyone else, who made Einstein into a real Einstein, turning the eccentric German world-famous.

As we've already mentioned, 1905 was the year the young Einstein, who had experienced little more than failure in his adult life, published four papers while working as a patent clerk in Bern, Switzerland. These four papers started a revolution. Not only did they uniquely articulate the shape and expanse of the universe, pointing to the big infinity, but these same papers pointed to the small infinity as well. They proved that atoms (and even smaller realities) existed. In these 1905 papers, Einstein, like Galileo, recast our vision, now in the direction of both the big and small infinites. In 1915, Einstein further worked out his general theory of relativity, which changed the world. Yet, no one (other than pointy headed physicists) would know it until Eddington found a way to prove it.

In 1919, Europe was still coming to grips with just how bloody and utterly hellish the First World War had been. It was the first war to turn the technological pursuits of the scientific full bore toward mass killing. So the thought of an English scientist trying to prove the theory of an enemy German was too much for the world press to ignore.

Eddington had secretly been reading Einstein's papers for years (all German writing had been banned in England during the fighting). Eddington had a sense that Einstein was right. But all Einstein's breakthroughs had happened through thought experiments. Eddington began wondering if there was any actual experimental way to test Einstein's theories. Einstein's visions were so imaginative, Eddington wondered if it would take an "act of God" to prove his calculations. Lucky for Eddington, such an act came with an eclipse, which gave Eddington the chance he needed to see if Einstein's theory worked. If light was bent due to the eclipse it would prove Einstein's theory.

After a dramatic voyage to an African island called Principe, and a morning downpour, the skies cleared and Eddington proved Einstein correct. The next morning Einstein was featured on the cover of newspapers across the globe, as story after story presented him as a charming, playful, and brilliant scientist. From that day on, the name Einstein would be synonymous with brilliance, and Einstein himself would become one of the most famous persons in world history.

EINSTEIN'S HICCUP

But there was a hiccup in Einstein's theory of relativity. It wasn't so much in the theory itself, but in the presumption that went back to our story of Galileo. Einstein's theory seemed to show that the universe was indeed expanding, meaning at some point, it was small enough not to exist. Lemaitre had the math to show that it was indeed a big bang that ignited the universe from the smallest of infinites (from particles) to such a large one that even a great mind like Blaise Pascal would say, "The eternal silence of the infinite spaces frightens me."[1]

But this idea that the universe was expanding and therefore had a beginning stood against the Aristotelian presumption that the universe is eternal. Galileo had beaten up on Aristotle enough in moving the earth from the center and replacing it with the sun. Nevertheless, while Aristotle's science was wounded, it was still breathing. And though most agreed that the ancient philosopher was wrong about motion, mechanics, and the shape of the galaxy, he was still right, they assumed, about its eternal nature. Besides, in an environment where the social practice of "science" had found a secure enough place (in the nineteenth century), to assume that the universe had a beginning sounded *too* religious or theological (it's an irony that today creationists see the Big Bang as an enemy).[2]

1. Quoted in Stephen Barr, *Modern Physics and Ancient Faith* (South Bend, IN: University of Notre Dame Press, 2003), 158.

2. William Brown offers some background to the Big Bang being considered too religious: "As for the 'moment' when time and space had their genesis, the Big Bang model is frequently invoked as a scientific parallel to Genesis 1:1-3. When it was first proposed, however, the Big Bang model met stiff resistance from famous astronomer Fred Hoyle, who actually coined the phrase in a disparaging remark. Hoyle, instead, championed the 'steady-state' theory in part because the Big Bang, in his opinion, found too great a 'conformity with Judeo Christian theologians.' Regardless of any alleged 'conformity,' the Big Bang won. Nevertheless, caution is in order. First, some common misconceptions require correction. The theory of the Big Bang does not explain the origin of the cosmos but accounts for its evolution a fraction of a second after time zero (10–43 seconds), prior to which the laws of general relativity break down. Similarly, the first verse of the Bible begins not at the absolute beginning of

It would take the observations of another English-speaking scientist to prove to Einstein that indeed the universe was expanding, and that his cosmological constant was unnecessary. The engine of relativity was shown in the skies of California to be so sound that it was wrong to govern its limits.

THE TELESCOPE STRIKES AGAIN

Just a short drive from the sea of lights filling the Los Angeles basin, you can see the night sky, an ocean of starlight washing over you from billions of miles (and therefore years) away. The echoes of God's words to Job ("and who are you?") echo in the starlight that hits our eyes from such a distance that some of those very stars quietly twinkling in front of us no longer exist. Like Galileo 300 years ago, the vehicle that can take you from basin to the stars is a telescope.

On a mountaintop a few miles from Pasadena, the Carnegie Institute built an observatory that they hoped would be the greatest in the world. If Galileo could have seen it he would have been shocked and filled with wonder. In 1917 they installed a 100-inch telescope called Hooker. And in another spooky irony of history, the same year (1919) that Eddington was making Einstein world-famous, the observatory hired a young Midwestern cosmologist named Edwin Hubble. With this huge telescope, Hubble was witnessing how massively infinite the universe was, observing that it stretched beyond the Milky Way, and that galaxies themselves where farther away from each other than had been thought. "Some [of these galaxies] were millions of light-years away. (One light-year is the distance that light, which travels at 186,000 miles per second, traverses in a year. A light-year is about 6,000,000,000,000 miles.)"[3] The size was so massive that Galileo would have choked if he'd heard it.

As Hubble was mapping the big infinity, finding ways of calculating the space between stars, using the Doppler effect to discover that they were even farther away than had been assumed,

creation." *The Seven Pillars of Creation: The Bible, Science, and the Ecology of Wonder* (London: Oxford University Press, 2010), 56.

3. Barr, *Modern Physics and Ancient Faith*, 8.

he had an odd breakthrough. The distance between these stars seemed to be growing; the galaxies themselves were moving further and further apart. In 1929, two years after Lemaitre, Hubble published his findings. And like Eddington to Einstein, Hubble proved the Belgian priest correct—again, observation proved mathematics.

Building off of Einstein's theory of relativity, Hubble showed that spacetime was like a rubber sheet with galaxies drawn on top of it. As it was stretched in expansion, it moved galaxies further and further apart. The universe was indeed expanding. It was not only infinitely massive, but growing.

In the early 1930s Einstein was spending a few months in Pasadena at Caltech. One evening he jumped into a Pierce-Arrow touring car to drive up Mount Wilson, to see for himself what Hubble had spotted. When he did, Einstein asserted that his cosmological constant was indeed the biggest blunder of his scientific life. Why he ever added it, he didn't know. If he hadn't, if Einstein had stuck with his original assumption of 1915 that indeed the universe had to be either expanding or contracting, then it is possible that the Big Bang would be called the Einstein Bang—or maybe something more clever.

As it is, Hubble's Law stands. While Einstein had the equations that the universe was in motion, it was Hubble who showed that its movement was expansion. Galileo's few-inch telescope had knocked us off center, revealing that space was big and relativizing the earth next to other planets. Hubble's 100-inch telescope not only confirmed that our planet was not at the center of our galaxy, but also revealed that our Milky Way was not at the center of the universe. Spacetime is more infinite than we imagined, and it is growing!

YOUTH MINISTRY AND ASTROPHYSICS

Jared was surprised, and then surprised that he was surprised, that the week after the mathlete championship and pizza celebration, Lily—Sasha's teammate—came to youth group. That exuberant night after the victory, she'd made it clear that faith wasn't something she was interested in. But here she was. Jared couldn't help it—it felt weird, but in a good way.

But maybe the weirdness was Lily. She seemed different. Context has a way of bending perception, and Jared's first impression was shifting. In the pizzeria Lily had seemed so confident, but now, sitting next to Sasha on an old couch in the youth room she disappeared into its cushions. Jared now interpreted her large-rimmed glasses not so much as a bold statement, but as a disguise to hide behind.

As the night went on, Lily became more animated. She interacted with a few of the adult leaders, and the tension in her face at the beginning had faded away by the end. Jared even had the feeling that his talk on Romans 8 connected with her. At least she seemed to be paying attention, and she laughed at a few of his jokes, which was more than he could say about many of the regulars.

But odder than Lily's presence there, was that after youth group she hung around. Sasha usually was one of the first to leave, always rushing home to get back to her homework. But there they were, playing cornhole with a few other kids. Jared started to get the sense that they wanted to talk, and sure enough, as the rest of the young people departed, they asked to chat.

Lily began, "So, I came here tonight because Sasha said I should talk to you."

"Oh, cool," said Jared. "What's up?"

Lily looked at Sasha as if to ask, *Are you sure it's a good idea for me to talk to him?* Sasha gave a nod and Lily paused, and then nervously said, "So it's about my boyfriend . . ."

Lily paused again, blushing a deep pink hue. "Well," she continued, "so, he's in college . . ."

Where is this going? Jared wondered. He began mentally running through his protocol for teen pregnancy or abusive relationships. He wondered how messy this was going to get.

Lily steadied herself before speaking. "It's his mom."

Jared was now totally confused. "What?"

"Well, she's like this really conservative Christian, like, once she grounded my boyfriend for a week because he was reading Steven Hawking for fun."

Okay, Jared now understood Lily's righteous indignation around Galileo's mythical jailing. The church's hatred of "science" seemed true enough next to her boyfriend's experience.

"So our favorite show is *The Big Bang Theory*," she said, "so I got him a T-shirt for our two-and-a-half-month anniversary . . ."

Jared tried hard not to roll his eyes when she said anniversary.

Lily continued. "But when his mom saw it she got really pissed and said he wasn't allowed to wear it around her, saying that she thinks it's, like, an evil theory made up to distract people from following God."

Incredulous, Jared interrupted. "But it's a TV show!"

"I know, right?! Regardless, she went off about how God created the world and stuff, and about how that theory is evil."

"Now, that's crazy," Jared blurted, still not sure why she was telling him all this.

"So, Sasha told me her dad, who, like, *believes in God*, loves that show and is even a scientist. But I just needed to know how that was possible, so she told me to come to youth group and ask you."

"Ask me what?"

"I guess," Lily said, "how you can believe in God and the Big Bang?"

"Yeah," Sasha added, "how can you?"

Jared had no quick answer. Honestly, he hadn't thought much about it. So he asked his own question: "Why didn't you ask Sasha's dad?"

"Because we're asking *you*," said Sasha.

"Well, tell you what," Jared said, exhaling deeply. "What if I do a whole youth group night on the question? Why don't you two come back the next few weeks and we can plan a few things for a night on the Big Bang next month. Cool?"

"Yeah, totally!" Lily shot back.

"Okay. But just so you know, Sasha, I'm going to probably ask your dad to help me."

"Oh, you can talk to him," said Sasha. "Just don't invite him to come."

"Fine." Jared was now starting to think this whole mathlete MVP thing had gone to Sasha's head—but in a good way.

As the girls left, Jared wondered how he was going to pull this off.

14.

Finely Tuned

When they arranged it, Jared was sure that he would have no problem keeping up. Trent had about fifteen years and at least forty pounds on him. Jared was so confident, he wasn't worried that it had been months, probably closer to a year, since he'd gone out for a run. Actually he'd stopped right after getting the crushing news about Baby Brooklyn—running was a casualty of his depression.

So it took Jared a while to find his running shoes. But tying them on, he waited for Trent to arrive. Stretching in his front yard, Jared was surprised at how stiff he felt. It made him wonder if his body was communicating that he was older than he imagined—he decided not to dwell on it, ignoring that his T-shirt read "Senior Outing 2001."

As Jared waited, he assumed Trent would drive over. It was actually quite logical; Trent lived about four miles away. So Jared decided to keep his eyes open for Trent's car. This gave Jared an observation blindness. He was caught completely off guard when a large man in full running gear with a bottle belt around his waist and large GPS watch strapped to his wrist ran by and yelled "Let's go!" Jared was so startled he froze. "Come on, man," a fully geared-up and sweaty Trent yelled as he kept moving down the street.

Shaking himself from the cloud of confusion, Jared managed to catch up, but he had to run harder than he wished to.

"Where did you come from?" Jared asked.

Below his high-tech running glasses, Trent flashed a smile. "From home. I figured you wouldn't want to run my ten miles, so I thought I'd run over and pick you up." That's when Jared knew he was in trouble. As Trent's pace quickened, Jared's calves started to bark.

Trying his best not to show concern, Jared asked, "So, how long are we going?"

"Depends on how long you want to. Like I said, I'm going ten, but I figured you didn't want to go that long."

"Yeah," Jared said, trying to seem nonchalant as his breathing quickened. "I have something in a hour, so I don't think I can go that long."

"Okay," Trent said, "let's go about two and a half miles and we can talk about your questions. Then you can get back."

"Sounds good."

"So what did you want to talk about?"

Between gasps Jared mustered "The . . . Big . . . Bang . . . Tell me . . . about it."

Trent rehearsed some points from his freshman physics class and told Jared of a few interesting articles and chapters he should read. Jared thought about how to fulfill his promise to Sasha and Lily, and realized this was all very helpful. It was even more impressive that Trent could run at this pace and talk at the same time.

Jared was thankful for the Physics 101 overview, but he wanted to know a little more. So inhaling deeply, he said, "So do you believe it? I mean, I'd guess you do as a scientist, but what about as a Christian?"

"Man," Trent said, "that's why over a year ago I asked you to meet with me and Sasha. I'm not really sure how to make sense of that." Jared remembered clearly that conversation in the yellow restaurant.

"But surely you've thought about it," Jared said. "I mean, that's why you wanted to talk back then."

"Honestly, it was exploring the Big Bang that both led me to my career interest and into faith."

"Really . . . ?" Jared gasped

"Truly," said Trent. "It's all just a huge probability puzzle."

"What's that mean?"

"Like Sasha, I'm a major math nerd, and the more I studied the Big Bang, the more shocking it was to me that it happened. And it happened in such a massively huge way as to create such an infinite space!"

"Yeah," Jared interrupted, "but why? I mean . . . why is space . . . so huge . . . ? And doesn't . . . that lead you . . . to question . . . your faith?"

"Like Sasha, it does," Trent answered. "I doubt my faith all the time. But when I realized that this huge space is needed—it is completely necessary to get one thing. And when I thought about that, I was shocked, and moved."

"And what's that . . . one thing?" Jared's lungs burned like they were on fire.

"Life!" Trent exclaimed. "You can't get life without a universe *this* big and *this* old. When I began exploring the universe through the actuality that there is life in it, maybe only life on this small little teeny weeny planet, but nevertheless *life*, I couldn't believe how low the probability was."

"So math . . . led you to . . . God?" Jared asked.

"No, it's more complicated than that. Math can't prove God, and probabilities are probabilities. It is totally logical that life could be just an accident, a very low-probability accident, but nevertheless an accident. For me, it was just the mystery that there is life! It led me to pray, and when I prayed I felt something, particularly when I prayed with other people. So yeah, it led me to God, through the people I prayed with."

Trent then paused, and Jared was aware to respect the sanctity of the open space. After a minute or so, Trent picked up the thread again. "I don't know, I guess I'd say that contemplating the sheer size of the universe makes me doubt my faith, but contemplating its size through the fact that there is life makes me search for meaning and purpose, and this leads me to pray—and it was the praying with this group of other PhD students in Durham that changed me."

"Wow . . . that's . . . beautiful," Jared responded.

"Thanks." Trent said this as if he'd never really had the occasion to put those experiences together. "No, truly," and he said it again. "Thanks." He clapped Jared on the back with his large right hand, pushing the remaining air out of Jared's diaphram. Jared coughed, and Trent howled one of his laughs.

As they neared the two-mile point, Jared found a slight second wind, at least enough to ask Trent one more question. "But do you . . . really think . . . the Big Bang . . . is true? Or is it just . . . speculation? I mean . . . a lot of conservative Christians . . . like this lady Lily knows . . . claim it didn't happen . . . and there's no proof."

"What, besides the fact that we can hear it?" Trent asked with incredulity.

"Really?" Jared asked, dumfounded. "We can hear it?"

"Yeah, man, we can actually hear the reverberation of the big bang. It was the guys who discovered this that led me to want to be an experimental physicist!"

HEARING THE UNIVERSE EXPAND

In the early 1960s at Princeton University, the very place that Einstein, just a few years after looking through Hubble's telescope, decided to reside for the remainder of his life, a group of scholars had a theory. Particularly, Robert Dicke theorized that if Lemaitre was right and the universe started with a big bang, it would not only scatter the material particles for the creation of stars and planets, but would also release an enormous amount of radiation.

In 1964 two Bell technicians, Arono Penzias and Robert Wilson, were experimenting with radio waves, using a huge horn antennae in Crawford Hill, New Jersey (just thirty-seven miles from Princeton) to test how radio waves bounced off satellites. They were trying to figure out what the new satellite technology could mean for communications—like your phone. But they had a problem.

The antennae kept picking up interference. And what was peculiar is that no matter where they pointed the antennae, it was the same buzzing. If this feedback was everywhere, Penzias and Wilson assumed it must be an instrument failure. So they adjusted the antennae, troubleshooting for hardware malfunction. But still, the same feedback. After a little more searching, they were sure they'd found the problem—bird nests in the horn! Clearing the nests, they were ready to return to their communications tests, certain the interference would be gone. But to their frustration, it remained.

Soon frustration turned to an amazing realization. The interference was actually coming from the universe itself. Dicke had theorized that the Big Bang would leave cosmic microwave background radiation, and indeed that's what Penzias and Wilson were hearing. Penzias and Wilson called Princeton, having read Dicke's theory. Two of Dicke's younger colleagues (experimental physicists like Trent) were working on a way to decipher this background radiation. When Dicke hung up the phone, he said to his colleagues, "Boys, you've been scooped."

The Big Bang could now be mathematically demonstrated (by Lemaitre/Einstein), seen (by Hubble), and heard (by Penzias and Wilson). The discovery of the cosmic microwave background radiation showed that indeed a big bang, some 14 billion years ago, produced the universe. Aristotle's view that the universe was eternal, and therefore not made, was over. It was clear that the universe came into being, having a beginning and therefore, one day, an end.

When Lemaitre posited this, he was told it was far too religious. His math may be right, but his clerical collar was too tight, corrupting his physics by restricting the blood to his head. The comprehensive social practice of "science" accused the priest of positing a personal mind as the cause of existence. But soon enough the scientific findings could not be ignored, and indeed it was agreed that the universe had a beginning, a singular point of creation. So the same scientists who testified to the enormous infinity of space were asserting that this big infinity had a single inaugural instant that reverberates even now, expanding in continued creation this very second.

A LITTLE PROBABILITY GAME

To claim a personal order to the universe, we need to be able to see *cause*.[1] It would be easier to assume a cold impersonal universe if it had simply always been, frozen in a steady state, with no movement or direction. But to claim that the universe continues to expand, having a beginning and moving toward an end, calls for causality and makes us wonder about purpose. In other words, *why* did it begin? Who made it bang, and for what reason does it continue to expand? When Lemaitre, Hubble, and the others showed that indeed the universe begins and becomes, the ground was shifted, and a witness to the possibility of a personal, *hypostatic* universe was more plausible.[2] Rigid creationists, like Lily's boyfriend's mom, who curse the Big Bang, actually disparage a friend.

This doesn't mean that the Big Bang proves that a personal God exists. Rather, it sets up an interesting either/or, that without the Big Bang would not be so sharp. This either/or is framed like this: Either this massive, infinite universe is just the lucky outcome of probability, or something like a personal mind is directing it toward a purpose.

If it's a question as to the probability of there being *something*, like a universe of gravity, galaxies, meteoroids, and moon rocks, instead of *nothing*, then impersonal happenstance may be the best bet. We simply have a universe because of chance: like a random

1. Scruton offers a very insightful comment here and points in the direction of of cause and therefore the question Why: "There is a parallel here with the question that I raised in the first chapter: the question of God's presence in the world. If you look on the world with the eyes of science it is impossible to find the place, the time, or the particular sequence of events that can be interpreted as showing God's presence. God disappears from the world, as soon as we address it with the 'why?' of explanation, just as the human person disappears from the world, when we look for the neurological explanation of his acts. So maybe God is a person like us, whose identity and will are bound up with his nature as a subject. Maybe we shall find him in the world where we are only if we cease to invoke him with the 'why?' of cause, and address him with the 'why?' of reason instead. And the 'why?' of reason must be addressed from I to you. The God of the philosophers disappeared behind the world, because he was described in the third person, and not addressed in the second." Roger Scruton, *The Face of God* (London: Bloomsbury, 2012), 45.

2. Again this is similar to Torrance's position that the new physics started by Einstein breaks the hold of the static born from the enlightenment and Newton.

serendipitous occurrence, this big infinity of space just happens to be, born from the accidental meeting of gases and particles. It is improbable, but so was Sanjaya making it to the final rounds of *American Idol*.

But to make this bet, thinking of its odds, is to be a person with a mind that extends deeply into what you are not. It is to be alive. The probability of getting a universe of gravity, galaxies, meteoroids, and moon rocks is one thing. But for this Big Bang to deliver life, even single-celled bacteria, not to mention human persons that sing and celebrate, that love and hate, is a whole other thing. It is the very fact that there is *life* in the universe that opened up physicist Trent to mystery.

FEAR NOT

In a damp church basement, Scottish theologian T. F. Torrance was discussing the size of the universe, taking a group of laypeople into the big infinite. In the middle of the talk an older woman sitting in front blurted out "This scares me!"

Torrance stopped, looked her in the eyes, and said with an echo from the Gospels, "Fear not, for God created this huge universe so that you, so that life, could be."

Whatever direction we go with our either/or—either this world is here because of the impersonal outcome of probability, or, the world is here because of a personal cause—the universe has to be this big to deliver life. As the theory of relativity posits, space and time are so interconnected that they form a four-dimensional fabric called spacetime (the four dimensions are the three dimensions of space, plus time). Because time and space are essentially one fabric, you can't get one without the other. For space to be so massive you need enormous amounts of time (14 billion years). But also, to have the time for life to be, you need breathtaking amounts of space (stretching across 15 billion light-years). Therefore, we could say, with Torrance, that the universe is so large and so old because this is what it takes to produce life. Physicist Stephen Barr says something very similar: "If the universe were any smaller, then it would not have lasted long enough for life to have evolved. This is an absolutely crucial fact."[3] The Big Bang not only pushes the universe into existence, but also keeps it becoming, so that a womb for life might be.

And it's here where the small infinity—particles and quantum mechanics—enters our story, making some sense out of the big infinity that seems to scare us with its mass and age. We need this big infinity of spacetime so that the small infinity of particles that were released in the Big Bang can have the time and space to coalesce, interact, and create the conditions for life. For instance, it takes time for particles to coalesce into hydrogen, and millions of years for hydrogen to be pulled together to make a star. And it appears to take millions of stars, some too hot and some too cold, some too small and some too big, to get one just the right size. And this is where our story of big and small infinities starts getting spooky, and the edge of our either/or its sharpest.

It could be that the size and age of the universe are simply proof that life is a random happening. Put a heavy book on your computer keyboard, allowing it to randomly type letters. Leave it alone for tens of billions of years and at some point it will type out the lyrics of a Justin Bieber song. Time and size seem to make life just an accidental happening, just the probability of billions of light-years of spacetime. But take a closer look at what is actually happening with the small infinity and the picture is more complicated—a complication that led Trent into prayer.

A FINELY TUNED UNIVERSE

Einstein was the most brilliant and famous physicist in the history of civilization. But if you had to name a brilliant *living* scientist, the most famous would be Stephen Hawking. Hawking has been spoofed in numerous *Simpsons* episodes and even had an Academy Award–nominated movie about his life released in 2014, *A Theory of Everything*. What makes Hawking so captivating is that his brilliant mind is mediated to the world through

3. Stephen Barr, *Modern Physics and Ancient Faith* (South Bend, IN: University of Notre Dame Press, 2003), 160.

a computer and wheelchair. He's endured for decades with ALS. It was a Stephen Hawking book that got Lily's boyfriend into trouble and led her to Jared.

Hawking is far from an apologist for faith, but doing the math on the small infinites that make life possible in this universe has led him to point to the most finely tuned variables that make life possible. For instance, in his book *A Brief History of Time*, he states, "The laws of science, as we know them at present, contain many fundamental numbers, like the size of the electric charge of the electron and the ratio of the masses of the proton and the electron. . . . The remarkable fact is that the values of these numbers seem to have been very finely adjusted to make possible the development of life."[4] Alister McGrath explains further Hawking's position: "For [those] unfamiliar with the mathematical annotation, Hawking is suggesting that a difference of one part in ten billion in the rate of primal cosmic expansion would be sufficient to prohibit the emergence of life."[5]

4. Stephen Hawking, *A Brief History of Time* (New York: Bantam, 1998), 7, 125.

5. Alister McGrath, *A Fine-Tuned Universe: The Quest for God in Science* (Louisville: Westminster John Knox, 2009), 85. And this is only one picture of many of the precisely intricate realities that make it possible for life to be. Martin Rees, President of the Royal Society, has actually asserted, like in the TV show *Lost*, a mere six numbers have been so precariously tuned that if they were even slightly off, the universe and therefore life would *not* be. Along with McGrath, Rees explains the importance of these six numbers, as they are represented in six categories. Rees and McGrath explain:

1) The ratio of the electromagnetic force to the force of gravity.

If this were slightly smaller . . . "only a short-lived miniature universe could exist: no creatures could grow larger than insects, and there would be no time for biological evolution."

2) The strong nuclear force.

This force, which has a value of 0.007, "controls the power from the Sun and, more sensitively, how stars transmute hydrogen into all the atoms of the periodic table." If it "were 0.006 or 0.008, we could not exist."

3) The amount of matter in the universe.

The cosmic number Q (omega) is a measure of the amount of material in our universe—such as galaxies, diffuse gas, and so-called "dark matter" and "dark energy." Thus Q tells us the relative importance of gravity and expansion energy in the universe. "If this ratio were too high relative to a particular 'critical' value, the universe would have collapsed long ago; had it been too low, no galaxies or stars would have formed. The initial expansion speed seems to have been finely tuned."

4) Cosmic repulsion.

Cosmologists became aware of the importance of cosmic antigravity in controlling the expansion of the universe. . . . "Fortunately for us (and very surprisingly

Looking closely at these small infinites shows an intricate fine-tuning to allow for organic, carbon-based life. The universe must be as big and as old as it is for organic life—like you and me—to be.⁶ To get this world, from a mathematical perspective, seems highly improbable.⁷

to theorists), [antigravity] is very small. Otherwise its effect would have stopped galaxies and stars from forming. . . ."

5) The ratio of the gravitational binding force to rest—mass energy.

[This] is of fundamental importance in determining the "texture" of the universe. "If it were even smaller, the universe would be inert and structureless; if [it] were much larger, it would be a violent place, in which no stars or solar systems could survive, dominated by vast black holes."

6) The number of spatial dimensions . . . which is three.

"Life," Rees comments, "couldn't exist if [the dimensions] were two or four." McGrath, *Fine-Tuned Universe*, 120.

6. John Polkinghorne explains further: "Now what are we to make of all this? First, we must consider some scientific points. Maybe some of these apparently remarkable coincidences are actually just straightforward consequences of a deeper underlying theory, and so don't require 'fine tuning' at all. In fact, scientists have already recognized an example of this possibility. The necessary conditions in the very early universe—just the right rate of expansion and the right degree of smoothness—probably don't have to be written in, but are achieved automatically by a physical process called 'inflation,' which many think took place when the universe was a minute fraction of a second old. It's a kind of 'boiling' of space, and, although it's a guess that this happened, in my view, it's a pretty plausible guess. This doesn't mean that it would happen in just any old universe, though. Once again, it's only a very particular kind of universe that could boil up in this sort of way, and contrive to go off the boil in a controlled fashion. So I think that, although there may be other explanatory insights to come, it will still be the case that a world capable of evolving carbon-based life is a very special kind of universe." John Polkinghorne, *Quarks, Chaos & Christianity: Questions to Science and Religion* (London: Crossroad, 2005), 44.

7. Denis Lamoureux discusses further the elements of fine-tuning: "If the properties of water were not almost precisely what they are, carbon-based life would in all probability be impossible. Even the viscosity of ice is fit. If it were any greater, then all the water on earth might be trapped in vast immobile ice sheets in the poles. The fitness of carbon compounds for life is maximal in the same temperature range that water is a fluid. Both the strong covalent and the weak bond are of maximal utility in this same temperature range. Such coincidences are precisely what one might expect to see in a cosmos specially adapted for carbon-based life. Oxygen is a very reactive atom and it can only be utilized by biochemical systems because of a number of adaptions, including: the attenuation of its reactivity below about 500°C; its low solubility; the fact that the transitional atoms such as iron and copper have just the right chemical characteristics to manipulate the oxygen atom; that the end product of oxidation of carbon is carbon dioxide, an innocuous gas. Moreover, the reaction of carbon dioxide with water provides living things with a buffer—the bicarbonate buffer which has just the right characteristics to buffer organisms, especially air-breathing organisms, against increases in acidity. The chain of coincidences in the nature of things which permit higher forms of life to utilize oxygen provides further evidence

The same Robert Dicke who theorized about cosmic microwave background radiation and the possibility of hearing the Big Bang, asserted that gravity and electromagnetism had to be so finely tuned to get any life at all. Looking at the actuality of the large infinites through the small infinite has led another Princeton physicist, Freeman Dyson, to say, "it seems that the universe was waiting for us."[8]

It's as if you've been driving all day and are too tired to continue. You pull off the highway, seeing a sign for a Holiday Inn Express, La Quinta, and Hampton Inn. You randomly pick the Hampton Inn; it's the closest. After getting checked-in you go to your room, and notice some spooky occurrences. Playing on the TV is your favorite movie and the alarm is already set for your departure time. But then it gets weirder: oddly you notice a warm plate of your favorite walnut cookies—your grandma's recipe—resting on the bed, and looking at the nightstand you see a frame with a picture of your sister and your family dog. As you stare at the photo, the radio turns on, and it's the song of the first dance of your wedding. Freaked out, you race to the bathroom, noticing on the way a painting on the wall that your son made for you when he was four. As you enter the bathroom (for the first time) to splash water on your face, the medication you're taking is already there, the bottles open with a cold cup of water next to them. Spooked, you start to look for cameras or people; you'd likely assume someone (some personal mind) was watching you, preparing this room for you. But how could that be? You just randomly picked the Hampton Inn! And yet it is like it's been set up just for you. You're now sure you're not alone.

This would be a frightening and awe-inspiring experience. And one where you'd have to assume that some mind, or at least some personal force, had set the room for you. In a similar way,

of the unique fitness of nature for carbon-based life." *Evolutionary Creation: A Christian Approach to Evolution* (Eugene, OR: Wipf & Stock, 2008), 88.

8. To show further the place of this sharp either/or, "Steven Weinberg's oft-quoted conclusion in his book *The First Three Minutes*, 'The more the universe seems comprehensible, the more it also seems pointless.'" William Brown, *The Seven Pillars of Creation: The Bible, Science, and the Ecology of Wonder* (London: Oxford University Press, 2010), 194.

when we look at the small infinity, we see that this *unbelievably* big infinity is so finely ordered that it is hard not to wonder if it is personal. There is a possible overlap here between the epistemic goal of the scientific that asks, *What is the shape of the universe?* and faith, which asks, *What is the shape of existence?* This can lead someone like Trent to be drawn into mystery, wondering if this order that the scientific points to is a personal one.

After reading about this fine-tuning in the material Trent gave him, Jared called him up. Jared was so shocked by what he'd read, he forgot the decorum of introduction. When Trent answered, Jared just launched in, asking immediately, "Why have I never heard about this?"

"Well hello, Jared," Trent responded with a laugh. "It's customary to say 'hello' before bombarding the guy you called with a question."

"Sorry, Trent."

"So what now, Jared? What are you referring to?"

With the same intensity that started the call, Jared responded, "This whole fine-tuning thing . . . it scientifically proves God exists . . ."

Trent interrupted abruptly, "NO. No it doesn't. . . ."

15.

A Rebel's Birthday Party

"What?" Jared asked. "It seems to prove it to me."

"Well, very few scientists would agree," Trent said. "Now don't get me wrong, it is really unnerving and to me it is awe-inspiring. It leads me to wonder about a lot."

"But, wait. I thought you said you came to faith because of the Big Bang and fine-tuning!"

"No," Trent said. "I came to faith because of the people I prayed with. I came to faith because their prayers ministered to me, because I experienced the face of Jesus in their love and care for me."

"But, I thought . . ." Jared added.

"Right, I said the Big Bang theory played a part," Trent interjected. "And it did. The mystery of the fine-tuning led me into wonder. And after I experienced their prayers, I began thinking more and more about how a world where prayer and love happen could be. I began to wonder if this world was finely tuned for just these kind of experiences."

As Trent explained, Jared went right back to the day in Tanisha's office with Aly and her family, remembering Uncle Leon's words: "Faces and minds . . . science has a hard time with minds made for faces." Trent was being clear that the scientific indeed showed that the universe was finely tuned, but he wasn't allowing Jared to jump too quickly into what this meant.

"So how then do we explain fine-tuning?" Jared asked.

"Remember," Trent said, "that fine-tuning is about the existence of the universe, about how precisely mathematically tuned it is, so it can be at all. But the fact that we see it that way doesn't mean that it is a miracle. I mean, we're within it. We exist as the universe exists, so we might be predisposed to see something as amazing that really is quite normal. Kind of like people with a new baby; they think their own kid is so unique and does so many improbable things, like roll over at three and a half months. That seems amazing and improbable to them, but it is actually just normal. Maybe we look at the universe and see fine-tuning and mistakenly take the normal for amazing."

That really threw cold water on the fire of Jared's excitement.

"Or, similarly," Trent continued, "even if it is amazing, which I actually believe it is, it could just be chance."

"But, it can't be, right?" Jared jumped back in, recovering a little of his enthusiasm. "I mean, the odds are really against that, so it can't . . ."

"Oh, wait, no, if math says it is possible, it is possible; just because it is improbable doesn't mean it is impossible. Just think, it is a one- to three-hundred-million chance that someone will be president, and some years it is a one- to 18-million chance that you'll win the California lottery.[1] And yet someone wins. Just because the odds are against this universe being doesn't mean it couldn't happen, or that it needs a personal God to make it."

Trent paused. "And the fact that people, like a lot of them, buy lottery tickets when they have one- to 18-million odds, shows that my first point about our interpretation might be right."

"Well, Trent, thanks," Jared said with friendly sarcasm. "I

1. I've put the following argument of McGrath in the mouth of Trent: "Some argue that apparent cosmic fine-tuning is nothing more than an interesting happenstance. The fundamental constants in question had to have some value—so why not these ones? They need possess no further significance. To give an example: the population of the United States of America is (over) 300 million. There is only one president. The odds of any one American becoming president are thus 1 in 300 million. But so what? Someone has to be president. It may be highly improbable that any given individual should be president, but it is a certainty that someone will be. At one level, it is impossible to refute this argument. Yet it is clearly inadequate to account for the actualization of a highly improbable scenario: the emergence of a universe adapted for life." Alister McGrath, *A Fine-Tuned Universe: The Quest for God in Science* (Louisville: Westminster John Knox, 2009), 121.

thought I had something to discuss with the youth group, but now I'm back to zero."

"Not necessarily," Trent stated. "You keep mentioning my own story and how I came to faith. I have to say that when you do that, I felt really uncomfortable, Jared, especially because we were talking about scientific theories. I guess scientists try to keep subjectivity out of our thinking."[2]

"Sorry," Jared said.

"No, no," Trent continued. "What I've realized as we've talked is that my own personal experience of praying and having these friends help me through some tough times changed the way I looked at the universe. The experience of being cared for helped me see how the universe is a gift. I guess that could just be my subjective experience. But even though scientists like to project that we're objective, we come to our theories personally, through our personal subjectivity of encountering a pattern. So I guess what I'm saying is that through the experience of ministry, I began to see the universe patterned as a gift, as a unique place to receive the ministry of God. I started addressing the universe with a different *why* question, not the *why* of mechanical cause, like why does oil lubricate an engine, but with the why of reasons, like why do we exist in this massive universe, and why do I need people near me to love me, and why are we here at all? Looking at the Big Bang and fine-tuning through those questions drew me into faith."

"Wow, that's deep," Jared said.

"Of course, it doesn't change that it could be just a rare bit of luck that we're here, that the universe has produced the kind of beings that can ask why questions at all. My experience of being prayed for in Durham, I guess it just made the Anthropic

2. Trent is also echoing Ian Barbour's point about the Anthropic Principle (which I will discuss at length below): "I do not think that the Anthropic Principle provides a convincing design argument in the tradition of natural theology—partly because chance and necessity remain as options for the atheist, as we shall see. But I find the principle quite consistent with a theology of nature (an alternative form of the Integration model). The fine-tuning of the physical constants is just what one would expect if life and consciousness were among the goals of a rational and purposeful God. Such a theology of nature would have to draw from many fields in addition to astrophysics in articulating a coherent overall interpretation of cosmic history and human life." *Religion and Science: Historical and Contemporary Issues* (San Francisco: HarperSanFrancisco, 1997), 206.

Principle amazing to me. I mean, these people meant so much to me, like you did for Aly and her family, standing with them and caring for them. The Anthropic Principle was too amazing for me to not seek God."

"What's the Anthropic Principle?" Jared asked.

"Oh, man, you didn't read that part?"

"I don't think so."

"Check it out," Trent said. "I think this might help you with the youth group. They may like to debate the weak versus strong versions."

ANTHROPIC PRINCIPLE

Like a teenager who gets grounded for dating the wrong kind of guy, Galileo was put under house arrest for being too much a fan boy of Copernicus. Poor Nicolaus Copernicus was a devout Catholic, but after his death and the fallout of the Protestant Reformation, the implications of his theory made him a bad boy rebel. To move the earth from the center was to minimize the importance of humanity. And it was the human form that God had taken in Jesus to minister to the world.

Galileo was never kicked out of the family; he never saw himself as anything but Catholic. But he was grounded for his infatuation with that bad boy Nick, and it wasn't until 1992—350 years later—that the Catholic Church finally lifted Galileo's grounding. Copernicus never intended to be a rebel, but his heliocentric universe allowed for the creation of what some scientists[3] in the twentieth century called the Copernicus Principle:[4] that humanity had no important or privileged place in the universe. We are, they asserted, just meaningless carbon material tucked away in some small planet in an insignificant

3. Particularly Hermann Bondi.

4. David Wooton explains why this name is unfortunate and how Copernicus himself saw things: "Copernicus's universe was no longer Earth-centred, but it was still Earth-friendly, and there was no reason to think it was not the product of benevolent design. There was nothing in his argument which might imply that the Earth was just another planet, or that the universe had not been created for the benefit of human beings. The universe still had a centre, and the sun and the Earth were still unique objects." *The Invention of Science: A New History of the Scientific Revolution* (New York: Harper, 2015), 244.

solar system, in a typical, ordinary galaxy. The big infinity that Copernicus first pointed to crushed humanity into insignificance, making us and our world essentially meaningless carbon lost in massive space.

On Copernicus's 500th birthday a group of scientists and philosophers got together to celebrate the rebel, doing what scholars do for fun—presenting papers to each other![5] One of those papers (with a cumbersome academic title) was written by a theoretical astrophysicist named Brandon Carter.[6] Doing what you do at a rebel's birthday party, Carter decided to use the occasion to take a swing at the Copernicus Principle.[7] After knocking it down, he offered in its place what he called the Anthropic Principle.

Carter's point was that if the Big Bang actually was indeed how the universe came to be (and the microwave background radiation Dicke theorized about and the Bell technicians heard seemed to show it had), then the assumption, that our displacement from the center made us unimportant, was wrong. If the universe were in a steady state, and was not an expanding fabric of spacetime, then indeed it would be true that to displace us would be to relativize us to insignificance within a cosmological perspective.

Yet, Carter's main research area was on black holes. He was as aware as anyone that there were *many* parts of this massive universe, places in the big infinity where life of any kind was impossible.[8] So, he asserted that if the big infinity exists so that

5. In 1973.

6. Brandon Carter, "Large Number Coincidences and the Anthropic Principle in Cosmology," *IAU Symposium 63: Confrontation of Cosmological Theories with Observational Data* (Dordrecht: Reidel, 1974), 291–98.

7. Of course, it is worth saying again, that Copernicus himself probably would not have been a supporter of the principle that bore his name.

8. "Ward and Brownlee argue that most of the cosmos features 'dead zones' that are not hospitable for advanced living organisms. To cite a few characteristics supporting their contention, they note: 'The most distant known galaxies are too young to have enough metals for the formation of Earth-size inner planets. Hazards include energetic quasar-like activity and frequent supernova explosions. Although [globular clusters] contain up to a million stars they are too metal-poor to have inner planets as large as Earth. Solar-mass stars have evolved to giants that are too hot for life on inner planets. . . . [Elliptical galaxies and small galaxies] are too metal-poor. . . . Energetic processes [at the centres of galaxies] impede complex life. Many stars [at

the small infinity of particles and atoms have the ability to forge stars and planets, then the fact that we have (life has) found a place to *be* in the universe is a surprise. Carter wasn't necessarily saying that *we* (and other carbon life) were central to the universe. But, rather, that we had found some privileged space that was fine-tuned through the Big Bang for us to be. The theory of the Big Bang asserts that the universe changes over time. And what is amazing is that here, on this little patch, or even single thread of the fabric of spacetime, things had been fine-tuned to the most intricate level to allow life to be. The quantum material was just right to forge a space for living creatures.

So while the Copernicus Principle points to our insignificance, the Anthropic Principle recognizes that life itself is a rare occurrence. The Copernicus Principle looks at the big infinity and asserts that we are just carbon goo on the bottom of the universe's shoe. The Anthropic Principle examines both the big *and* the small infinity and recognizes how finely tuned the universe is through the Big Bang to allow life to be. What Carter showed is that if we are to take the Big Bang seriously, not returning to a steady-state theory that opposes Einstein and Lemaitre's equations, Hubble's Law, Dicke's theories, and Penzias and Wilson's observations, then the Copernicus Principle cannot be. The Big Bang and its mysterious fine-tuning gives us no other choice than to recognize an Anthropic Principle, and for some, to wonder how life got here at all.

Trent saw the Big Bang as a gift. He interpreted the Anthropic Principle as a wonder of the gift of life. But he interpreted it this way because he experienced a hypostatic encounter of ministry. *When others gave him the incredible gift of ministry, embracing his person, witnessing life out of death, he noticed how the Big Bang itself moved in a similar amazing pattern. The Big Bang seemed to deliver the sheer gift of life from death—from exploding stars, from covering nonbeing with being, from impossibility to something new.* Trent wasn't even willing to claim that the Big Bang proves God's existence; he would admit that it seemed to move in a similar way. The experience of receiving ministry led him

the edges of galaxies] are too metal-poor.'" Denis Lamoureux, *Evolutionary Creation: A Christian Approach to Evolution* (Eugene, OR: Wipf & Stock, 2008), 86.

to see the universe shaped uniquely for *hypostatic* encounter with God and neighbor. The Anthropic Principle opens up the possibility that indeed God desires a small part of the creation that God loves to be a place of ministry, a place finely tuned to allow life to testify to God's own *hypostatic* nature.

It had been a long time since Jared felt nervous before a youth group night. But this qualified. His anxious energy had its origin not only in the planned content. But he was also taking a risk with how he'd present it. Up against the subtle pit of anxiety in his stomach, he breathed deeply and reminded himself that he had promised Sasha and Lily. Jared got there early, and set up the youth room as a debate hall, with Jared wearing a black academic robe. As each kid arrived they received a piece of paper that said either "weak" or "strong."

As the night started, Jared stood before the youth group and said in a bad British accent, "Ladies and gentlemen, tonight we are in for a great debate, appraising the Big Bang!"

Jared explained that they *were not* going to examine if the Big Bang really happened. Rather, the scientific findings seemed clear that the vehicle that produced the universe was the Big Bang. The question still remained, however, if anyone or anything was driving this vehicle at all. Tonight they'd explore this.

Jared then took some time, and with the help of some videos (even one done by Trent) laid out fine-tuning and the Anthropic Principle. Jared showed that the Big Bang, rather than steady-state, seemed to make life important and improbable. "Ladies and gentlemen," he began, "it seems that most scientists agree that we live in an improbable universe, that, against all odds, created a place for life. But how do we understand this?"

Pausing, Jared continued, in his best orator voice with British accent for humor's sake. "Those who hold to this Anthropic Principle have given us a 'weak' and a 'strong' version. And tonight we will debate each. If you have a piece of paper with 'weak' on it, meet Linda and Todd in the education hall 2 room. If you have 'strong,' stay here and join Charles and Candi."

Linda and Todd, Charles and Candi were adult leaders who'd agreed to do a little work before the youth group night, reading a few short pieces Trent suggested, after meeting with them for forty minutes to discuss the topic.

WEAK VS. STRONG VERSIONS

We said above that the Big Bang sharpens an either/or. *Either* there is a personal mind in the universe driving the vehicle of the Big Bang *or* this is just all happenstance. Then to look at this either/or through fine-tuning and the Anthropic Principle is to look back at the universe through the actuality that we are observers, that there are those in the world who seek to know the universe, minding its shape. "[It] means at least this: human intelligence is uniquely designed to disclose the patterns of order hidden in the physical universe."[9] The Anthropic Principle keeps us from ignoring this fact.

Yet, this fact leads us further into an either/or. This either/or is what Carter and others have called a *weak* or *strong* version of the Anthropic Principle.[10] And when boiled down, it all comes down to the place of purpose/*telos*. It can't be denied that the universe is uniquely shaped for life (and this is proven by the Big Bang—something most Christians don't know). But the question remains, "Was this unique universe shaped for life by just random happenstance, like the Colorado River creating the Grand Canyon? Or did it have intention?"

To push the analogy, the Colorado River has no intention to create a great canyon; it is just doing its river-thing, and over GREAT amounts of time it creates amazing natural beauty. The Colorado River has no sense it has done anything; it has no mind for the canyon or beauty. Is the universe similar? Is it just doing

9. James Loder and Jim W. Neidhardt, *The Knight's Move* (Colorado Springs, CO: Helmers & Howard, 1992), 285.

10. Loder and Neidhardt offer a nice short definition of the weak and strong versions. "It should be noted that there are several forms of the anthropic principle. In its strong form, it states that it is so unlikely that the universe would produce conscious and intentional creatures like us that the universe must have been created for precisely that purpose—the production of life and consciousness. In a weaker form, the anthropic principle states that the universe is becoming conscious of itself through human understanding; or, weaker still, it simply points to the rootedness of human intelligence in our bodily existence and thus to our creaturely connection to the universe." *The Knight's Move*, 191.

its universe-thing, starting with the Big Bang, and then, over huge amounts of spacetime, presto! We get an amazing wonder called carbon life, that even has beings within it that can observe, document, and calculate this universe that has accidentally come to be! This is essentially what the Weak Anthropic Principle asserts.

Or did the universe, from the start, intend for life? This would assume that a kind of desire exists in the universe. But this wouldn't necessarily have to be God. Bees have intention to create intricate hives, propelled by some natural instinct to seek the goal of making honey. Maybe the universe is a natural phenomenon wired in such a way that it *must* produce carbon-life that will eventually deliver beings with minds to observe and know the universe itself. This is the Strong Anthropic Principle.

When scientists talk about the fine-tuning for life (or natural selection for that matter), they almost always talk as if the universe has a mind for agency. It may be just a rhetorical move, but they'll often say things like "then the universe decided . . ." or "the universe picked this over that" or "the universe was waiting for us." But a purely natural phenomenon doesn't make direct choices toward a specific *telos*.[11] Therefore, to claim that the universe was wired to create life leads us to ask who wired it, especially if it has made such intricate and numerous calculations to get life. The connected variables are so numerous, the odds of having them all connect is like having a squad of marksmen all at once miss you on your execution day—an analogy used by scientist John Leslie.[12]

11. "The difference between atheist and theist is, in the end, the argument from design, and the critical question is not whether the universe exhibits design and purpose but how to account for it." Richard Coleman, *State of Affairs: The Science-Theology Controversy* (Eugene, OR: Cascade, 2014), 106.

12. Polkinghorne discusses Leslie further: "John Leslie is a philosopher who shares my view, he does a lot of his philosophizing in the beguiling style of telling stories. In his book *Universes* (1989), he tells the following tale. You are about to be executed. You are tied to the stake and your eyes are bandaged. Ten highly trained marksmen have their rifles leveled at your chest. The officer gives the command to fire and the shots ring out. You find you have survived! What do you do, just shrug your shoulders and say, 'Well, here we are then, that was a close one'? Of course not, you will want to understand what happened, why you didn't die. Leslie suggests that there are only two rational explanations of your good fortune. One is that many, many executions are taking place today, and you just happen to be in the one in which

The fact that the universe is so finely tuned leads us to ask if there is not a personal mind directing the universe, intentionally creating persons who observe the mystery of the universe as a place to receive and give ministry.[13] This makes the Strong version compelling, and it allows for an overlap between epistemic goals of the scientific and faith. But as Trent made clear to Jared, we can only really make these claims if we've experienced ministry. If we've had others love and care for us, seeing and valuing us as persons, it becomes more difficult to look at the improbability of the universe and not see a personal order.

Recognizing the minuscule probability that we get carbon life that can observe and contemplate the universe by sheer luck, those advocating for a Weak Anthropic Principle have garnered a solution. They have called this the multiverse. The idea is simple yet grand. It agrees that from within our universe it is an amazing coincidence that all these variables by the smallest number are tuned just right to get us life. But this only seems amazing to us because we're locked into observing only our *own universe*. Rather, if there were millions, maybe even billions, of other universes, each like a bubble on the back of a lathered-up dog, then it would be a simple probability game that one of those billions of universes was fine-tuned for carbon life. In other words, give the Big Bang a billion shots at it and one will release just the right particles at just the right temperature at just the right speed to get persons who love, dream, and reach for understanding.

they all miss. The other explanation is that more was going on than you had realized; the firing party was on your side." John Polkinghorne, *Quarks, Chaos & Christianity: Questions to Science and Religion* (London: Crossroad, 2005), 46.

13. Polkinghorne adds to this: "In humanity the universe became aware of itself and, as a by-product of this reflexivity, science itself became an eventual possibility. Pascal said of human beings that, frail reeds though they appear to be on the cosmic scale, nevertheless they are greater than all the stars, for we know them and ourselves and they know nothing. Many of us cannot believe that this emergence of person-hood is simply a happy but meaningless accident, for it seems to be a most important clue to the nature of the reality within which we live. There is an authenticity in personal experience, both individual and communal, that demands to be treated with the utmost seriousness. Yet personal experience is always particular experience; it is always a view from somewhere and never a view from nowhere or from everywhere." John Polkinghorne, *Science and the Trinity: The Christian Encounter with Reality* (New Haven: Yale University Press, 2004), 174.

Then, again, we're back to a heavy book placed on a keyboard, randomly typing out a Justin Bieber song (or more exactly, his whole catalog). Essentially what the theory of the multiverse asserts is that there is not a sole keyboard randomly typing, but a whole airplane hanger filled with keyboards on top of keyboards, randomly typing. Give those billions of keyboards billions of years and eventually one will type out not only all of Justin Bieber's songs, but the whole Top 40 too.

There is *no* scientific finding that points to a multiverse; it is simply a metaphysical way to relativize and deal with the unique structures of the universe we inhabit.[14] In other words, to claim there is a multiverse is as much a statement of faith as any religion would propose. But it is a way to claim that the fine-tuned universe that seems to have a *telos* for carbon life has no mind and therefore is not personal. The multiverse is a creative way to uphold the commitment of the comprehensive social practice of "science" and keep at bay the spooky possibility that there just may a personal mind moving within the Big Bang, forging a contingent order that delivers living beings who care for and minister to creation.[15]

---

14. Polkinghorne says, "Scientifically, we have no reason to believe in the existence of any other universe than our own (people sometimes pretend that it is not the case for the many universes explanation, but, believe me, it is, if we are careful and scrupulous about what science can actually say)." *Quarks, Chaos & Christianity*, 47. Fisher, drawing from Polkinghorne, continues: "The postulate that there are other universes is unverifiable by science, and as such is inherently metaphysical. There is no empirical evidence for their existence; they are by definition unobservable. This is perhaps the most devastating critique of the multiverse theory—it is a metaphysical rather than a scientific explanation. The choice between infinitely many universes, one of which is bound to produce intelligent beings like us, or one universe, extremely fine-tuned by the will of God, may ultimately be a matter of faith. The multiverse theory at least has the same handicaps as the metaphysical assumption of God, and perhaps even a few more. Polkinghorne argues that since there are no observable ways to test related phenomena such as might be done in principle for the religious alternative, the multiverse option is inferior. God's existence can theoretically be verified using religious experience, answered prayer, the historical investigation of faith claims such as the resurrection or other metaphysical or philosophical considerations. Alternate universes are completely inaccessible except to the imagination." Christopher L. Fisher, *Human Significance in Theology and the Natural Sciences* (Eugene, OR: Pickwick, 2010), 257.

15. Robert Jenson has made the beautiful assertion that we are the animals that pray. I believe this is the struggle of the Anthropic Principle: How did this fine-tun-

THE DEBATE

When the young people returned, a representative from each group provided their three top arguments for either the weak or strong version of the Anthropic Principle. Between Jared's hamming things up as the debate master (he was now wearing a gray wig, with an unlit pipe in his mouth and calling himself over and again, in a terrible British accent, Professor Googleburn) and the adult leaders' pep-rally enthusiasm, the fun was palpable. After each point, the representing side would respond like contestants on *Family Feud*, shouting, "Good answer! Good answer!" Lily presented the arguments for the strong version. She started off nervous, but soon was laughing and playing up the bit.

After each group presented, the opposing group gave their counterargument, responding directly to the other group's points. Jared knew when moving into the counterarguments that things would become more serious. He hoped it would still be fun, but also more thoughtful as young people started thinking about the possibility of faith in a personal God next to these scientific findings. So as they transitioned, Jared dropped the British accent and allowed the room to turn more serious. Jared felt out on the edge and wished Trent was in the room, but he'd promised Sasha to not invite him. Overall, though, things seemed to be going well.

After the counterpoints, Jared slowly read parts of Psalm 139 and Psalm 19, while a slideshow with photos of space and human faces played behind him. The group then sat in silence for almost three minutes.

Jared then took off the robe and asked the group, "What was that like? I mean, we arbitrarily put you in a group and asked you to argue something you might not believe, or probably never thought about. What was that like?"

Jared was met at first with silence, but soon enough the comments started to come. Someone said, "I've never thought of the Big Bang that way."

"Yeah," Jared said. "Me neither."

ing come to create animals, but even more so, a group of animals that pray? See "Praying Animals," *Zygon: Journal of Science and Religion* 18, no. 3 (1983).

"It was cool," another young person said.

"I got shivers when you read the psalm," said a tenth-grader sitting next to Lily.

"What about the two positions? What do you think of those?" Jared asked.

"Actually," Sasha said, "I can see both sides. I mean, you can't deny the numbers in the fine-tuning, but we also can't see things outside our own universe, so maybe things would look different if we could—and not be so improbable."

"True," Jared responded.

Building off Sasha's statement, Hank, a senior interjected. "The thing I don't get is, like, if there is a God, why this super long process of creating? I mean, the fact that the Big Bang starts, I guess points to God, but, like, why all the billions of years and wasted space? Isn't that the way the Bible says it happened anyway, like six days? What do we do with that?"

Jared didn't know how to respond to Hank, but was sure that his journey would take him there. But as he looked at the alert, engaged faces before him, he noticed with some surprise that the question didn't scare him quite like it would have before.

Hank wasn't finished. "And it seems like having six twenty-four-hour days to get the world makes God more like, I guess, *God*. So I guess, even though it's amazing, I still don't get why it took so long. Why couldn't God just do it, like *boom, here it is!*, it wasn't and now it is? I don't get that part."

"That's what I don't get either!" Lily said.

"Yep, me neither," Sasha chimed in with her arms folded.

HYPOSTASIS IN THE BIG AND SMALL INFINITY

The fine-tuning of the Big Bang has upended the Copernicus Principle, replacing it with the Anthropic Principle. Jared recognized that he needed to always focus on the soteriological goal of faith as he engaged in conversations with the scientific. He realized that what young people like Sasha wanted to know was whether there was a place for the personal in the universe, or whether love, meaning, and hope were absurd accidents.

Most interesting to Jared was how the Anthropic Principle actually made a place for the personal, for the observer of the universe itself. It seemed to point to the possibility of a personal order, and opposed the commitment of the comprehensive social practice of "science." Brandon Carter upended the Copernicus Principle (an impersonal, faceless position) by showing us how the fine-tuning of the Big Bang had, against all probability, delivered carbon life that can actually see and proclaim the contingent order of the universe. We might not be at the center anymore, but clearly the universe seemed to know we were coming. It is no slam-dunk for God's existence, but it is an astounding mystery (and the odds so slim) that personal beings like us would *be*.

But maybe this shouldn't surprise us. It is a claim of faith, but one that is open to scientific theories and finding, to see the fine-tuning of the Big Bang, and the subsequent expansion of the universe, as a witness to the *hypostatic* nature of the universe itself. It was the *hypostatic* nature of particularities emerging from their relations that birthed the scientific from the logic of Nicene Christianity—both faith and the scientific claim that the universe operates as a person—a place where particularities are born through their relations (*hypostasis*). And these relations are so deep, contingent, and intricately in tune that human personhood (persons who can share in the life of one another as ministry) is forged. The universe is so fine-tuned through the Big Bang that out of its relation of particles and atoms come beings with observing minds who can receive and give ministry.[16] To show how this *hypostatic* reality spreads across the

16. Alexei Nesteruk, drawing from the Eastern tradition, shows the shape of human hypostasis. I'm pushing this concept further than Nesteruk, who draws a bold line between humanity and other realities in the universe. I'm following Zizioulas and pushing hypostasis further. Nesteruk says, "Hypostatic humanity is different from the rest of creation because of its similarity to God, as made in his image. Similarly to how God inheres all creation in his hypostasis, humanity is endowed with an ability to inhere the universe in its own subjectivity . . . which implies the ability to contemplate the universe, form its meaning and, ultimately, to act in the universe as its self-consciousness and self-realization. In other words, the existence of the non-human (i.e. non-hypostatic) can only be affirmed from within human hypostases. The very fact of existence of non-hypostatic matter is itself enhypostasized from within 'human matter'." *The Universe as Communion: Toward a Neo-Patristic Synthesis of Theology and Science* (New York: T&T Clark, 2008), 182. Nesteruk continues: "All

big and small infinity, we return to the story of Einstein, before picking up Hank's question to Jared at the end of youth group.

EINSTEIN TEASES BOHR

It became a thing, almost a sideshow, to watch Einstein aggravate Niels Bohr. Einstein had started quantum physics with one of those world-changing 1905 papers. It was clear that light came in waves, but the more closely it was observed the stranger it acted. Germany's greatest scientist, and the man who would be the first to see the genius of Einstein, was asked to help improve light bulbs. As he did, he noticed something strange. Light seemed not only to come in waves but also in a line. And when you looked closely at this line it was made up of dots, small pieces (or particles). Germany's greatest scientist, Max Planck, called these small dots, quanta. Einstein's paper would prove Planck's observation correct, taking us further into the small, quantum world than anyone ever had.

Einstein was a generation younger than Planck, and Niels Bohr was a generation younger than Einstein. Inspired by (and adoring) Einstein, the talkative, nervous Bohr dove deeply into studying the small infinity of the quantum world. Einstein had proven a deep relational interaction between space, time, mass, and energy. The big infinity of the universe is relative to (or better, interrelated by) the speed of light. Mass bends spacetime, because they are connected, having their particulates through their relations. Einstein, as we said above, saw a deeply contingent order, which I believe is fair to call hypostatic.[17] Though

other objects, such as physical particles, fields and their complex combinations are not hypostatic at all, so that their existence can only be manifested in the hypostasis of the other, namely in the hypostasis of human beings and, ultimately, in the hypostasis of the Logos." *The Universe as Communion*, 210.

17. Argyris Nicolaidis points to how this relationality of Einstein reflects hypostasis: "Einstein unified space and time into a continuum: spacetime. He achieved this by raising the speed of light (the speed of information transfer) to an absolute, a universal constant. The relational considerations that guided Einstein are evident; he insisted that different experiences in spacetime are linked together and reflect a unique, concrete, and unified nature. By accepting the Einsteinian point of view one must also accept the unity of nature or, phrased differently, that nature constitutes a hypostasis." "Relational Nature," in John Polkinghorne, *The Trinity and an Entangled*

Einstein saw God as impersonal[18] (he had a thing for Spinoza[19]), the universe he discovered was deeply relational.[20]

When Bohr looked into the quantum world he saw something odd. He discovered, with the help of his student Werner Heisenberg, that to examine a particle was to change it. It was impossible to describe and locate a particle (you could only do one or the other)—Heisenberg called this the Uncertainty Principle. The quantum world was deeply mysterious and appeared chaotic. Einstein hated the thought of this uncertainty (giving his famous line "God does not play dice," in rebuke of the theory).[21] Einstein's theory of relativity and the theory of quantum mechanics seemed to be opposing explanations of the physical universe, but both seemed true. This bothered Einstein greatly, and he sought, at first, to debunk Bohr's quantum mechanics.

World: Relationality in Physical Science and Theology (Grand Rapids, MI: Eerdmans, 2010), 96.

18. Below is an example of Einstein's unease with a personal God. As much as I personally love Einstein, this project opposes his conclusions here. Einstein says, "But I am persuaded that such behavior on the part of the representatives of religion would not only be unworthy but also fatal. For a doctrine which is able to maintain itself not in clear light but only in the dark, will of necessity lose its effect on mankind, with incalculable harm to human progress. In their struggle for the ethical good, teachers of religion must have the stature to give up the doctrine of a personal God, that is, give up that source of fear and hope which in the past placed such vast power in the hands of priests. In their labors they will have to avail themselves of those forces which are capable of cultivating the Good, the True, and the Beautiful in humanity itself. This is, to be sure, a more difficult but an incomparably more worthy task. After religious teachers accomplish the refining process indicated they will surely recognize with joy that true religion has been ennobled and made more profound by scientific knowledge." *Ideas and Opinions* (New York: Dell, 1976), 57.

19. "The final intellectual hero of the Olympia Academy was Baruch Spinoza (1632–1677), the Jewish philosopher from Amsterdam. His influence was primarily religious: Einstein embraced his concept of an amorphous God reflected in the awe-inspiring beauty, rationality, and unity of nature's laws. But like Spinoza, Einstein did not believe in a personal God who rewarded and punished and intervened in our daily lives." Walter Isaacson, *Einstein: His Life and Universe* (New York: Simon & Schuster, 2007), 84.

20. Again, thanks to the Nicene commitments of James Clerk Maxwell.

21. "For the rest of their lives, Bohr would sputter and fret at his repeated failures to convert Einstein to quantum mechanics. Einstein, Einstein, Einstein, he would mutter after each infuriating encounter. But it was a discussion that was conducted with deep affection and even great humor. On one of the many occasions when Einstein declared that God would not play dice, it was Bohr who countered with the famous rejoinder: Einstein, stop telling God what to do!" Isaacson, *Einstein: His Life and Universe*, 326.

Einstein, in his jovial way, spent most of his time at conferences (particularly, the Great Solvay Debates in 1927 and 1930) agitating poor Bohr by publicly giving him esoteric thought experiments and riddles, trying to undercut the quantum mechanics Bohr was birthing.[22] After Einstein's riddles (like, if the lid were opened on a box full of photons allowing just one to escape, it could be measured time-wise by simply measuring how long the box was open), Bohr would be spotted nervously walking the streets of the conference city working out Einstein's test in a jittery rhythm. To Bohr's credit, he always found an answer before the conference was over. At one level this irritated Einstein, but like a big brother, he took great pleasure in torturing Bohr. But the more Einstein's theory of relativity was examined, the more it was proven, and likewise, Bohr's quantum mechanics. The tension grew.

There seemed no clear way of reconciling these theories. Even the movie *Interstellar* draws from this fact: Matt Damon's character explains that plan A—to get all people off earth and onto a new planet—can't work because there is no way to reconcile relativity with quantum theory.[23] So Einstein's goal shifted. In

22. "'Einstein would bring along to breakfast a proposal of this kind,' Heisenberg recalled. He did not worry much about Einstein's machinations, nor did Pauli. 'It will be all right,' they kept saying, 'it will be all right.' But Bohr would often get worked up into a muttering frenzy. The group would usually make their way to the Congress hall together, working on ways to refute Einstein's problem. 'By dinner-time we could usually prove that his thought experiments did not contradict uncertainty relations,' Heisenberg recalled, and Einstein would concede defeat. 'But next morning he would bring along to breakfast a new thought experiment, generally more complicated than the previous one.' By dinnertime that would be disproved as well." Isaacson, *Einstein: His Life and Universe*, 346.

23. Loder and Neidhardt explain further the difference between Einstein and Bohr: "This same mindset that could never omit the significance of the observer in the examination of the whole also could not accept Einstein's confidence in a unified field theory because it essentially excluded Einstein—or the irreducible factor of the knower. But Einstein himself also recognized that even if a unified field theory were attained, it could not include or contain what was irreducibly human. The difference was that Einstein did not reason about the universe itself as if the knower per se had to be a part of the final explanation. We might say that Bohr and Einstein held two different views of universality: one ultimately and necessarily included human particularity, and the other recognized its importance but did not necessarily include it in the final analysis. Apparently, Bohr felt it was necessary to exchange ultimate objectivity for relationality as the price to be paid for a universality that could include human particularity." *The Knight's Move*, 188.

the end, he was consumed by a search for a Unified Theory that could explain both relativity and Bohr's quantum mechanics. Einstein would spend his final years walking Mercer Street in Princeton, his mind racing, probing for the Unified Theory that could explain it all.[24] He died still searching.

We are still waiting for a Unified Theory. Like relativity, quantum mechanics also seems to show a deep, even spooky, relational interaction in the universe—a demonstration of *hypostasis*.[25] Einstein himself discovered, in work done with two younger colleagues, that if particles at any point interact they'll forever correlate, even if separated by infinite space.[26] If one of the particles in union is transformed, immediately so too is the other (this is the quantum leap that moves faster than the speed of light that Sci-Fi shows have used imaginatively).[27] The particles remain distinct and particular, but their relation is so deep that what happens to one happens to the other. We could say

24. Here in Einstein's own words are his distain for quantum theory: "Some physicists, among them myself, cannot believe that we must abandon, actually and forever, the idea of direct representation of physical reality in space and time; or that we must accept the view that events in nature are analogous to a game of chance. It is open to every man to choose the direction of his striving; and also every man may draw comfort from Lessing's fine saying, that the search for truth is more precious than its possession." *Ideas and Opinions*, 326.

25. "Once two electrons (or any other pair of quantum particles) have interacted with each other, they possess a power to influence each other, however widely they subsequently separate. If one electron stays around here in the laboratory and the other goes 'beyond the Moon' (as we say), then anything I do to the electron here will have an immediate effect on its distant brother. In other words, there's a very surprising 'togetherness in separation' built into the fabric of the quantum world." Polkinghorne, *Quarks, Chaos & Christianity*, 70.

26. John Polkinghorne explains: "Albert Einstein, Nathan Rosen and Boris Podolsky discovered in 1935 that quantum theory implied a counterintuitive togetherness-in-separation (non-locality) for two quantum entities that had interacted with each other. If they separate from each other, even to a great distance apart, they nevertheless remain mutually entangled with each other, so that acting on the one 'here' (say, measuring one of its properties) has an immediate causal effect on the other, no matter how far away it may be." *Exploring Reality: The Intertwining of Science and Religion* (New Haven: Yale University Press, 2005), 30. Polkinghorne continues: "Einstein himself felt that the EPR phenomenon was so 'spooky' that its prediction showed there must be some shortcoming in quantum theory, but later experiments have confirmed that non-locality is indeed a property of nature. Even subatomic particles, it seems, cannot properly be treated atomistically!" *Exploring Reality*, 31.

27. What makes it Sci-Fi is that we've observed that particles can do this, but there is no way to imagine how something not at the quantum level could.

that once a particle shares in another (such as two people ministering one to other) there is relational entanglement that impacts
each particle's ontological state, while not imploding their
differentiation.[28]

This is very similar to how the Cappadocians understood
hypostatic encounter through the ministerial action of *perichoresis*.[29] The divine and human natures of Jesus are distinct, but in
their entanglement through the person of Jesus, they are forever
unified while not confused, bound but not swallowed, distinct
but forever linked. Though relativity and quantum mechanics
cannot be unified into one theory (as of yet), they both point
to the *hypostatic* structure of reality. Next to the Big Bang, fine-
tuning, and the Anthropic Principle, the universe, at both the
level of the big and small infinities, can be imagined as a place of
relationship, ministry.

This brings the scientific and faith together, but only while
affirming their difference. It allows faith to attend to its soteri-

28. "Polkinghorne points out that entanglement is not about communication
between the two particles. No communication can take place that is faster than the
speed of light. Rather he explains that 'quantum entanglement is a subtle form of
interrelationality.'" Heidi Ann Russell, *Quantum Shift: Theological and Pastoral Implications of Contemporary Developments in Science* (Collegeville, MN: Liturgical, 2015),
63.

29. Simmons provides a rich constructive theological discussion of how Trinitarian theology and quantum mechanics might reflect a hypostatic reality (though I
would not go as panentheistic as he does): "What I would like to argue at this point
is that perichoresis and entanglement can function as parallel metaphors, with quantum entanglement and superposition helping to explicate for today the meaning of
divine energy, activity, and relatedness within a panentheistic model of God. This
would allow us to talk about Trinitarian entanglement in such a way that the inner
life of the Trinity is entangled even as their functions become discrete in relation
to creation. This would also mean that the Spirit is always connected to the activity of the Father and Son in creation and that the Father and Spirit are connected to
the Son in incarnation, including crucifixion and resurrection. Divine entanglement
becomes a way of understanding the perichoretic expression of divine love and grace
in the creation. . . . Particles that are once interrelated can never be fully separated; so
too the mutually indwelling activity of the Trinity can never be dismembered. The
proposal is this: Perichoresis as entanglement can be understood as the energy of the
divine Trinity through which the creation is expressed. They exist in superposition
with the economic Trinity and evolve within the entangled life of God with the creation, thus supporting a panentheistic model of God. An entangled understanding of
the Trinity does indeed give rise to an understanding of God in which we 'live and
move and have our being.'" Ernest Simmons, *The Entangled Trinity: Quantum Physics
and Theology* (Minneapolis: Fortress Press, 2014), 144.

ological *telos*, while opening itself to the epistemic goals of the scientific. Faith looks at the scientific through the *hypostatic* reality of ministry. This is exactly how Trent understood his own experience. He came to faith (the soteriological) not through the findings of the scientific, but through the loving prayers of friends who shared in his life. But, once he encountered the life-transforming experience of ministry, he could see the logic of this encounter echoing within the scientific findings of the universe.

BUT THE NATURE OF GOD?

Although in these last few chapters, I have affirmed the Big Bang as a mystery of life and the deep echo of *hypostasis*, there remains the issue of *providence*. To repeat and rephrase one of Hank's comments at the end of youth group, "If God is really God, then why the need for this incredibly long and extraordinarily overgrown universe to get life?" The very age and size of the universe seem to point away from a personal, mindful God. If God is God, why not just make it so? Why the need for this massive fabric of spacetime to get life? If God only needs a small patch, or even thread, of this huge blanket to get life, then why the rest of spacetime?

The Anthropic Principle, in conversation with the soteriological goals of faith, leads us to see that God, indeed, has a particular desire for the creation of beings able to observe this universe, and to participate relationally as ministers. These beings are bound in the *hypostatic* by more than order; they participate volitionally in death for the sake of life (something we'll see more clearly in evolution in the next part). Particles, planets, and plants too participate in the *hypostatic* disposition of existence. They have their being through ordered relations. But it is only the human being who hears the direct call into ministry (the deepest form of *hypostasis*), to be our neighbor's keeper, and participate in the transforming power of love.

So why is the universe so old and large? For the sake of love![30]

30. "For in human life—and it can only be a human analogy—love is supremely manifest in self-limiting, costly action on behalf of the good and existence of

This simple answer needs some unpacking. First, the universe is so large because God seems to enjoy it, to love it. It may seem pointless or wasteful, but not to God. Even those corners of the universe billions of light-years away, where life could never be, God takes pleasure in, enjoying supernovas, black holes, and the birth of new stars. This seems to be at least part of the point of the book of Job. Astrophysicist Paul Wallace, in his book *Stars Beneath Us*, beautifully exegetes Job next to the mass of space.[31] God tells Job that God indeed loves the weird and supposedly insignificant—it is not a waste, but gives God pleasure.

But this doesn't get us any closer to understanding why God would use such a huge universe to bring about life as the Anthropic Principle suggests. Then, the second reason the universe *might be* so big, is because of the very nature of God's own being. The universe is so large and old because God is love, as 1 John asserts. And love that is the ministry of *hypostasis* (the relation of sharing in another) needs to take a particular shape.

By looking at the face of Jesus (as Nicene Christianity has taught us) we can see that the ministry of *hypostasis* is fused with *kenosis* (self-limiting or emptying, as in Philippians 2).[32] The God that the Bible says creates the world is a minister, coming to

another. The designation of God as 'Love' is, of course, a specifically Christian insight and I am not suggesting that without the revelation of God in Jesus the Christ we could have known this explicitly simply by reflecting on the world. But such reflections leading to the notion of God's self-limitation of his omnipotence and omniscience at least render it meaningful to speak of the vulnerability of God, indeed of the self-emptying (kenosis) and self-giving of God in creation." Arthur Peacocke, *Theology for a Scientific Age: Being and Becoming—Natural, Divine, and Human* (Minneapolis: Fortress Press, 1993), 123.

31. *Stars Beneath Us: Finding God in the Evolving Cosmos* (Minneapolis: Fortress Press, 2016).

32. Moltmann nicely shows how the self-emptying of kenosis does not mean self-defeat, but is bound in a Trinitarian reality. As this section continues this will become clearer. Moltmann says, "So kenosis is not a self-limitation and not a self-renunciation on God's part; it is the self-realization of the self-surrender of the Son to the Father in the Trinitarian life of God. By virtue of limitless love, the inner life of the Trinity takes its impress from the reciprocal kenosis of the divine persons in relation to one another. The Son by virtue of his self-surrender exists wholly in the Father, the Father wholly in the Son, the Spirit wholly in the Father and the Son. Kenotic self-surrender is God's Trinitarian nature, and is therefore the mark of all his works outwards (the creation, reconciliation, and redemption of all things)." "God's Kenosis in the Creation and Consummation of the World," in John Polkinghorne, *The Work of Love: Creation as Kenosis* (Grand Rapids, MI: Eerdmans, 2001), 141.

Israel to bring freedom from bondage, setting them apart not for themselves but to minister to the world.[33] The incarnation shows us that God's own action comes not with the force of imposed power, but with the love of ministry, mediated through personal (*hypostatic*) encounter, like a mother to a child.

To read the Anthropic Principle through the soteriological goals of faith is to see God's *kenotic* (self-emptying) act of loving and slowly molding the universe so it might produce ministers made in God's image who might love God and care for the universe as God does.[34] It takes so much time and space because God chooses to love the universe. God *kenotically* ministers to the universe itself, shifting and tuning it so that it might produce not raw stuff, but living things that need the ministry of others. These living things come to be through being with each other, and thus witness over and again to the *hypostatic* nature of God's own Trinitarian self.

But this only makes sense if God is a minister and not a super-hero. The universe is so large and so old because God chooses to form it through the *kenotic* act of ministry, and not through magic (Acts 8 shows that divine action cannot be confused for magic). God could impose force on nonbeing, cutting and hammering it into immediate shape. Or out of the ministerial love of the Trinity, God could speak being out of nonbeing, ministering to beings in love, giving it space and time to unfold as God lovingly ministers to and enjoys it, parenting the universe, so that it might become an environment where there are persons who reverberate and reflect the loving being of the God who is three *hypostases* (fundamentally relational beings) bound in love.[35] God is hidden in the mass of time and space because

33. It is no wonder then that Israel first experiences the ministry of God in exodus or in exile and then writes its creation stories. Like Trent's experience, the experience of ministry frames one's conceptions of the universe.

34. Polkinghorne highlights a similar point I'm seeking to make: "I believe that the answer lies in the recognition, already acknowledged, that God's creative action necessarily has a two-step character. First, in a kenotic act of allowing the creaturely other to possess its divinely granted independence, God brought into being a world that exists at some metaphysical remove from its Creator. The gift given by Love is that creatures should be allowed to be themselves and to make themselves in the veiled presence of God." *Science and the Trinity*, 165.

35. I personally resonate with Polkinghorne's discussion below—both his move-

God is active within the universe as a minister, slowly fine-tuning the smallest parts of the universe to produce being with the mind for ministry.[36]

Just as Jesus is Lord and true God of true God by emptying himself for the sake of ministering to humanity, so the Father creates through the *kenotic* act that allows a Big Bang to shatter nonbeing with something. God, slowly but lovingly, allows being the space to be, ministering to it slowly so that it might produce a space for a *hypostatic* encounter called ministry. God works through small, seemingly insignificant means (like a poor man from Nazareth born in a Bethlehem stable), where the life-giving love of ministry might shine like a million suns in the universe.

ENDING WITH ALIENS

There they were again, awkwardly waiting around. Jared knew exactly what it meant this time—they wanted to talk. So he walked right up to Sasha and Lily and said, "Hey, what's up?"

"Oh," Sasha said, trying to hide that they were obviously hoping to talk with Jared now that youth group was over.

"That was really good," said Lily, her thick-rimmed glasses sliding down her nose.

ment away from panentheism and his connection to the East. He says, "I certainly believe that the distant God of classical theism, existing in isolated transcendence, is a concept in need of correction by a recovered recognition of the immanent presence of the Creator to creation. However, I do not believe that this requires us to embrace the too-inclusive language of panentheism. All that is necessary is to reaffirm that creatures live in the divine presence and in the context of the activity of the living God. A concept that seems to be of value here is the distinction made in the thinking of the Eastern Church, and particularly in the writings of Maximus the Confessor and Gregory Palamas, between the divine essence (God's being, ineffable to creatures) and the divine energies (God's activity in creation). An appropriate understanding of the latter can provide a strong account of effective divine presence without endangering the distinction between creatures and their Creator. I wish to consider the energies as immanently active divine operations *ad extra*." *Science and the Trinity*, 98.

36. "On the one hand, anthropic coincidences feature a non-verbal divine noticeability that reveals evolution to be a loaded process intended for humans to appear. On the other hand, fine-tuning in nature also displays an aspect of divine hiddenness." Denis Lamoureux, *Evolutionary Creation: A Christian Approach to Evolution* (Eugene, OR: Wipf & Stock, 2008), 96.

"Yeah, It was super good," Sasha added in her usual serious tone.

"Well, I promised you two I'd do it, and I think it worked well," Jared responded.

"It did," Lily said.

"It helped me understand what my dad was talking about," Sasha added.

"What do you mean?" Jared asked, honored that somehow the youth group night had touched on something Sasha and Trent had been discussing.

"There really are a lot of biological, or just, *issues* of life, to consider when thinking about aliens."

"What do you mean?" Jared asked, trying not to smile that the aliens thing had come up again.

Sasha paused for a few seconds, clearly putting her thoughts together. Finally she said, "I guess, I mean that life is so fine-tuned that the odds seem really slim that there is life beyond us. And because the universe is still expanding, it means there is a whole timing issue with life. I guess to me what the Anthropic Principle shows is that it is totally possible that there is life on other planets, but if there was, it would be an amazing miracle—like the miracle that there is life here. And I guess for the first time tonight, thinking about life on other planets made me more open to God. I had been thinking it would exclude God, but looking at the science of life in space helped me see it differently. I mean, if God is lovingly creating life, then to find life on other planets would, I guess, point further to God's work in the universe. I think that's what my dad was trying to say . . . you just said it *way, way* better."

Jared laughed hard, sure she was wrong, reminding her that Trent had actually helped him plan the night. But what really amazed Jared was how Sasha was putting things together he hadn't really thought about. He was amazed to see how the *permission* to think these thoughts next to faith had been so important to Sasha.

"Well, that's great; I'm glad you two challenged me to do it," he said, wrapping up the conversation.

"Oh, but that's not what we wanted to talk about," Sasha said.

"No?"

"No," said Sasha, "actually Lily wanted to know if there are still any spots left for the mission trip? She wants to go."

"You do?" Jared asked, trying to hide his surprise. He flashed back to their first meeting and Lily's skepticism about Christian faith, accusing Jared's people of jailing poor Galileo.

"Yeah," Lily responded. "I like hanging out with you guys, it's fun . . . and interesting. I didn't think churches liked science."

PART III

(Part Martin)

16.

Martin and the Coming Mass Extinction

"I thought you should know that Sarah was just fired."

The group responded with shock that quickly turned to indignation. But Jared couldn't join, because to his shame he couldn't remember who Sarah was. Knowing it would be inappropriate to ask, he remained silent and just slowly shook his head, joining the group's frustration.

This was the first meeting of the denomination youth ministry leadership team in months. If Jared was honest, his excitement for the group had waned. He still believed in its importance and thought their leadership was as meaningful as any in the denomination. But he personally wasn't feeling it. He'd worked himself into this group at a time when his ambition was running hot. He wanted to be important and listened to, and he saw this group as the road to just that. He wrapped his ambition in language of leadership and giftedness, but now Jared was pretty sure he'd wanted in on the group because he was bored with his work in ministry.

When ministry gets flattened into program building, the only next step is to take your ideas public and teach others the secrets of your success. But Jared's failure to be selected for the church plant had pushed him onto a new path, and walking with Aly through the loss of Gena shifted something significant within him. Ministry was now a deep sharing in personhood, mediated in the most direct way by the act and being of God. The boredom had been almost completely exorcised; he now felt like ministry wasn't about building something, but about receiving, over and again, a gift.

A year ago Jared would have been sitting in the leadership team meeting thinking to himself, "How can I interject myself? How can I get more influence?" But now it surprised him that he had none of those thoughts. Instead Jared found himself just wanting to get back to his young people, remembering the privilege it was to wrestle with Sasha and Lily's questions.

Pulled back to the conversation at hand, Jared heard someone say, "Yeah, she totally got fired because some parents, and other church members, didn't like what she was teaching."

"Wow, she'd just gone full-time!" someone else added.

Still not able to place Sarah, Jared asked, "What was she teaching?"

"I guess, evolution," someone answered.

Jared's brain lit up, suddenly remembering who Sarah was, taken back to his workshop at the January training conference. It had been Sarah who asked him about helping small groups address difficult questions. Jared remembered her saying that faith and evolution were like two totally different operating systems, one Android and the other iOS, both good but unrelatable.

"What happened?" Jared now intensely asked.

"Well, the story is that there had been some conflict between some people, Sarah solidly among them, and others who were really into Ken Hamm. A rift started between those who were comfortable without the six days of creation being a literal twenty-four hours and those who weren't."

"Yeah, that's what I heard too," someone else added, picking up the thread of the story. "But I guess they thought they had it solved when they hired a new pastor. He'd been really involved in origins stuff for years. When he talked to Sarah he was clear that he wasn't a creationist like Ken Hamm. I think that got Sarah confused."

"What do you mean?" Jared quickly added.

"Again, I'm not completely sure, but what I heard is that she thought this meant that the new pastor was okay with evolution. So in a small group she told some young people that they could totally be Christians and be into evolution. I guess the pastor freaked out and fired up the termination machine. Ten days later she was gone. And now I hear she says she's out of church ministry and never going back."

"But wait," Jared said, now on the edge of his seat. "I thought her pastor said he wasn't a creationist or whatever?"

"He did and he isn't; but I guess, he's like in an Intelligent Design group or something, and they totally hate Darwin, and pretty much think evolution is bogus."

"Man, that's confusing," Jared shook his head.

"It is, and I guess that's what screwed Sarah. She thought because the pastor said he wasn't a creationist it meant that he saw some validity to evolution. But that sure wasn't the case. And to make matters more confusing, Sarah thought when he said he was into Intelligent Design that this fit with her assumption that somehow God used evolution to get us the world we now have. But clearly, to assume some intelligent mind in the process of evolution isn't the same as being a member of the Intelligent Design group."

"Wow, she must be so hurt," someone observed.

"I heard that what sealed her fate was when she told a young person that it was okay, and even noble, for Darwin to be his hero. The personnel committee and the pastor flipped out. They told her that Darwin's whole point was to lead people away from faith, and that Darwin was one of the greatest enemies the church has ever had."

"That's right!" someone else added. "I actually heard that one of the elders said to her that Darwin's ideas were so dangerous they'd be more comfortable if she had sanctioned drag racing in the church parking lot than encouraged them to admire Darwin."

"Yep, I heard that too. I guess after the pastor told her she'd be terminated he repeated three times, like a spell in a movie, 'The dangerous ideas of Darwin cannot be tolerated, the dangerous ideas of Darwin cannot be tolerated, the dangerous ideas of Darwin cannot be tolerated.'"

17.

When the Rocks Speak

Darwin's dangerous idea seems, at least in part, to follow
Galileo's space travels. If Galileo used the telescope to travel to
the moon and beyond, showing us that space was so expansive we could no longer assume ourselves (and our little planet)
at its center, then the tissue that holds Darwin's "dangerous"
idea together is similar. It is the exponential expanse of time.
(Of course, thanks to Einstein, we know something that neither
Galileo nor Darwin ever did—that space and time are not separate, frozen entities, but so relationally bound that they form a
single fabric called spacetime.)

The two sharpest edges of Darwin's dangerous idea are 1)
that all living things are connected, from plants to animals to
humans (to even microscopic bacteria which Darwin didn't have
the technology to see—he had a microscope, like Galileo had a
telescope, but not a high-powered one that could see these tiny
forms of life), and 2) natural selection, the idea that it is the fittest
that survive, mutating and changing to thrive in their environment. What *seems* to make these edges so sharp is the massive
amounts of time needed for selective adaptation to move from
trees to turtles to Taylor Swift. Just as we choke on the universe
expanding for more than 14 billion light-years, our minds can
barely comprehend that this little planet we call home is 4 billion
years old.

All this would be hard to believe if not for scientific findings. Thanks to the telescope and the eyes of Galileo, Hubble, and so many others behind it, we know that the universe is massive. And thanks to *rocks*, we know our planet is old, really old.

Like the assertion of Jesus that the rocks will cry out in praise (Luke 19:40), in the nineteenth century people began to hear the rocks telling a story. First, it was discovered that limestone had clear layers, and soon it was calculated how long each layer would take to compress into stone. Calculations of mass and compression showed us how long it took to get each layer. Yet, things would get even more precise as we became more astute at looking at the small infinities of molecules and atoms. Soon we discovered that stones had their own internal clocks. For instance, we discovered that a particular form of uranium turned into lead in a stable, consistent way.[1] So, observing the decay, we could count the approximate age of the earth. These molecular clocks were ticking at billions and hundreds of millions of years old.[2]

---

1. "One cannot, of course, assume that there was no lead in the rock to begin with. Thus there needs to be a way of estimating how much lead was there in the beginning when the rock was first formed. There is a simple way of doing this. The lead formed from uranium is known as lead-207. But there is another form of lead known as lead-204, and extensive data show that, chemically speaking, lead-204 and lead-207 behave identically. Thus when a mineral is first made (that is, when a rock is forming), the chemical process of mineral formation cannot distinguish between the two lead isotopes. When the rock is forming, each of the two lead isotopes would be chosen in a non-distinguishing manner; they would be in the same relative amounts as they are in the earth's crust in general. Now we come to the important point. If uranium-235 were incorporated into the rock when it was first formed, it would slowly decay to produce extra lead-207 but not lead-204. If the rocks are only a few thousand years old, there would be almost no measureable extra lead. However, if it was hundreds of millions of years old, there would be much more of it. The amount of extra lead is precisely equal to the amount of uranium-235 that has decayed." Darrell Falk, *Coming to Peace with Science: Bridging the Worlds Between Faith and Biology* (Downers Grove, IL: IVP, 2004), 65.

2. Falk explains further: "As we examine the age of a particular very old rock, let's assume that there was no lead in the rock when it was first formed. If this were true, then if we found that a particular mineral in a rock contained equal amounts of uranium and lead, the rock would be 713 million years old. All the lead would have come from decayed uranium. If the elements were now equal in amount, that would mean half the uranium had decayed, giving a half-and-half mixture. If, on the other hand, the sample contained about three times as much lead as it did uranium, we would say that only one-quarter of the original uranium is still present and that the rock is now 1.426 billion years old." *Coming to Peace with Science*, 64.

CREATIONISTS AND THEIR ID COUSINS

The more skilled we became at reading these molecular clocks, the more difficult it was to argue against the rocks. Fundamentalist Christians, to their credit, had seen at the beginning of the twentieth century how the comprehensive social practice of "science" was gaining strength and using these rocks to further their goal of impersonalizing the universe. Yet, to their shame, they decided, particularly in the 1960s, that the only way to answer the challenge of the social practice of "science" was by asserting all the louder that earth was truly young, created literally and directly as Genesis 1 and 2 said—in days, interpreted by them as twenty-four-hour units of time—making the rocks wrong, and the earth only 6,000 years old (6,000 versus 4 billion is a *big* difference).

But no matter how direct and confrontational their rhetoric was, the rocks still told another story. So to silence the rocks, they drowned them! Noah's global flood became the rebuttal to the testimony of the rocks. Fossils and limestone layers only *seemed* to be old because of how the Genesis flood impacted them.[3]

He continues: "The molecular clock, like the daily use of a tissue, is ticking. One click, one day—time moves on. The difference, however, is that the molecular clock ticks, not for three hundred days, but for millions of days, indeed for millions of years. All down through the eons of time, the clock in the rocks has been ticking. In a sense, then, the uranium-containing mineral has also been 'held hostage.' In this case it has been 'captured' in a rock, and its decay product, lead-207 atoms, like the used tissues, has remained locked up inside of that rock since the moment it was first formed—hundreds of millions, perhaps billions, of years ago." *Coming to Peace with Science*, 65.

3. "In 1957 the Russians launched Sputnik, the first space satellite, and US alarm at falling behind in the space race led to reforms in science teaching, including increased emphasis on the teaching of evolution. This in turn helped to boost interest in Henry Morris and John Whitcomb's new book *The Genesis Flood*, published in 1961, a reformulation of the ideas in Price's New Geology. Within a quarter of a century *The Genesis Flood* went through 29 printings and sold over 200,000 copies (Numbers 2006). The interest stimulated by this book led to the formation of the Creation Research Society (CRS) in 1963 and other creationist organizations since that time. Whereas the earlier creationist movement of the 1920s still maintained that the earth was very old, the late twentieth-century movement initiated by Morris and Whitcomb promoted the idea that the earth is only about 10,000 years old, a belief not otherwise widely held since the eighteenth century. The term 'creationism' began to be associated specifically with this brand of 'young-earth creationism.'

The scientific findings never really added up to support this flood thesis, making the group all the more rigid. Now calling themselves Young Earth Creationists, they battled more fiercely for cultural/political space. When Sarah started at her church she was confused, because she too believed the universe was created. So she felt like she was a kind of creationist, but not in the way of drowning rocks and fighting for an earth only 6,000 years old. Soon enough, though, the Ken Hammites in her church made it clear that she was out of bounds and not a "creationist" at all.[4]

What ultimately fueled the formation of the creationists in the 1960s was fear for young people.[5] The fire that burns within

Various forms of anti-Darwinian creationism are held by around 40-45% of the US population, whereas in European countries the level of creationist beliefs is generally much lower (Spencer and Alexander 2009)." Denis Alexander, "Creation and Evolution," in J. B. Stump and Alan Padgett, *The Blackwell Companion to Science and Christianity* (London: Wiley-Blackwell, 2012), 236.

4. "We have to use the word 'creationist' or creationism very carefully. Historically, Christians and Jews and Muslims are all creationists because they believe that God brought the world into existence. A creationist was not a person historically who had any particular views on the origin of biological species, but was one who held certain theological views about the universe and about the soul. The definition of 'creationist' became narrowed in the seventeenth century and in the eighteenth century. At this time, people were discovering a great deal more about the natural world and were classifying individual species and grouping these species in larger and larger groups. And it became a matter of belief during the seventeenth and eighteenth centuries that each of these species, each of these biological species of plants and animals—tens of hundreds, thousands of species—had been individually created by God in their first pair in the Garden of Eden." Krista Tippett, *Einstein's God: Conversations About Science and the Human Spirit* (New York: Penguin, 2010), 101.

5. Ronald Numbers explains how origins of Christian disdain for evolution revolved around young people. It was William Jennings Bryan, three-time presidential candidate, who was the key prosecutor in the Scopes trail. Numbers explains that what moved Bryan in his passionate direction against evolution, was the experience of young people. Numbers explains: "About the time that Bryan discovered the alleged Darwinian origins of the war, he also became aware, to his great distress, of unsettling effects the theory of evolution was having on America's own young people. From frequent visits to college campuses and from talks with parents, pastors, and Sunday-school teachers, he heard about an epidemic of unbelief that was sweeping the country. Upon investigating the cause, his wife reported, 'he became convinced that the teaching of Evolution as a fact instead of a theory caused the students to lose faith in the Bible, first, in the story of creation, and later in other doctrines, which underlie the Christian religion.' Again Bryan found confirming evidence in a recently published book, *Belief in God and Immortality* (1916) by the Bryn Mawr psychologist James H. Leuba (1868–1946), who demonstrated statistically that college attendance endangered traditional religious beliefs. After the much-publicized 1924 trial of Nathan Leopold and Richard Loeb for the kidnapping and murder of Robert

the debate on the earth's origins is often stoked by concern for the young—making it odd that Protestant youth ministry has mostly avoided scientific discussions. The creationists of the 60s assumed that the scientific teachings of an old earth buttress the comprehensive social practice of "science," and therefore risk destroying the possibility of the young having biblical faith (Ken Hamm is the champion of this position today). Confrontation became the only way to beat back the social practice of "science" and to use such fierce rhetorical force that scientific findings and theories would become collateral damage. To save the kids, creationists fought for the Genesis creation story to be taught with an equal, or even privileged, place next to evolution. Creationist intensity was so high that they could never see how they were shooting at established scientific findings as much as (if not more than) the pursuit of the social practice of "science" for an impersonal universe.

In the 1990s a group recognized that the creationists would never meet their political goals because in their warring they had become unscientific, so the courts would never allow young people to be exposed to anything but evolution in (most) public schools. This group shared the overall political/cultural goals of the creationists, but decided to enter the cultural debate with a new strategy. They tried to stick with *just* the science.[6] Instead of pushing for the Bible story to be taught in public schools from the start, they made it their pursuit instead to expose evolution as bad science. Returning in new ways to arguments from design

Franks, Bryan and other antievolutionists commonly added this heinous crime to their list of charges against the teaching of Darwinism, prompting one frustrated critic to point out that Jesse James was a fundamentalist and that 'Memphis, Tennessee, where Evolution is outlawed . . . has more murders in proportion to population than any other city in the United States.'" Ronald Numbers, *The Creationists: From Scientific Creationism to Intelligent Design* (Cambridge, MA: Harvard University Press, 2006), 56.

6. Deborah and Loren Haarsma provide more texture in explaining ID: "Supporters of Intelligent Design theory use the ideas of probability and pattern to argue against the theory of evolution. Their claims can be phrased this way: First, it is highly improbable that complex biological features such as the bacteria flagellum could have evolved via the mechanisms of evolution. Second, it is reasonable to believe that some intelligent being would want to intervene during the history of life to create these complex biological patterns." *Origins: Christian Perspectives on Creation, Evolution, and Intelligent Design* (Grand Rapids, MI: Faith Alive, 2011), 217.

that existed before Darwin, they tried to show that evolution just didn't add up. To meet this new goal, Darwin himself became Enemy Number One. They'd even put Darwin on trial as a bad scientist.[7]

This new group called themselves Intelligent Design (or ID). "ID places its major focus not on how the first self-replicating organisms came to be, but rather on perceived failings of the evolutionary theory to account for life's subsequent stunning complexity."[8] Their goal was to show that a theory of an *intelligent* design was just as scientific (in their minds, more so) than evolution.[9] *And that Darwin and his ideas were dangerous.*[10]

It was mainly her indirect acceptance of Darwin's "dangerous idea" that got Sarah fired. She had no idea that ID was uneasy with Darwin, and no sense that "design" was code for anti-evolution. She was particularly confused because it seemed that her pastor was so scientific. But not seeing the fault lines, she stepped over them and caused a violent tremor. Sarah believed that God, as an intelligent, personal force, formed the universe, that indeed

7. "ID's founder is Phillip Johnson, a Christian lawyer at the University of California at Berkeley, whose book *Darwin on Trial* first laid out the ID position. Those arguments have been further expanded by others, especially Michael Behe, a biology professor whose book *Darwin's Black Box* elaborated the concept of irreducible complexity. More recently, William Dembski, a mathematician trained in information theory, has taken up a leading role as expositor of the ID movement." Francis Collins, *The Language of God: A Scientist Presents Evidence of Belief* (New York: Free Press, 2006), 183.

8. Collins, *The Language of God*, 183.

9. Francis Collins summarizes ID in three propositions. All three see evolution and Christian faith as an either/or. He says, "The Intelligent Design movement basically rests upon three propositions.

  Proposition 1: Evolution promotes an atheistic worldview and therefore must be resisted by believers in God.

  Proposition 2: Evolution is fundamentally flawed, since it cannot account for the intricate complexity of nature.

  Proposition 3: If evolution cannot explain irreducible complexity, then there must have been an intelligent designer involved somehow, who stepped in to provide the necessary components during the course of evolution." *The Language of God*, 183–86.

10. The "dangerous idea" actually comes from Daniel Dennett's book *Darwin's Dangerous Idea*. Dennett actually means for his reader to see this positively. Dennett, along with others, represents a kind of fundamentalist neo-Darwinism, and makes the wrongheaded ID seem a better option than the dogmatic atheism of Dennett and others.

there is purpose and meaning in the mass of spacetime. Sarah just thought the process God used to create was evolution. Little did she know that this assumption would shake her church like an earthquake, making her job the core casualty.

In part 1, we saw Sarah as a representative of NOMA (non-overlapping magisteria), a position that essentially believes that the scientific and faith can be good neighbors if (and only if) they make (and stay behind) good fences, keeping each in their separate zones. This is what Sarah meant back in January when she said that evolution and faith were like Android and iOS.

Yet, Sarah's experience months later shows that NOMA can really only work at relating the scientific and theological at the academic level. She had tried to keep them separate, telling young people that Darwin had nothing really to do with faith, and because he didn't, he could be your hero as much as LeBron James could. But this is what got her fired. In the context of ministry, next to the lived/concrete experience of young people, it is important to spot overlaps between the scientific and faith. Sarah's experience *may have* been different if she'd been able to speak of how evolution and faith overlap (at the epistemic level).

Or maybe not! Her senior pastor was more than clear that Darwin was a damaging enemy of faith, more dangerous to young people than drag racing. Like Voldemort, once Sarah uttered his name in the walls of the church, she was doomed. After all, her pastor emitted his own incantation three times: "The dangerous idea of Darwin cannot be tolerated."

But this might not be true. Faith may not only be able to tolerate the dangerous ideas of Darwin, but may actually claim an epistemic overlap between them. To see if this is possible we have to explore how a true English gentleman, a man not that different than Lord Grantham on *Downton Abbey*, became a monster, more threatening than Darth Vader and Hannibal Lecter combined.

18.

A Clergyman's Dangerous Ideas:
The Story of Darwin

Like Galileo before him and Einstein after him, the first stage of Charles Darwin's life was filled with more confusion and false starts than success. Few of the great figures of the history of science were like Mozart, child protégées who were clear masters at young ages. Yet, even in childhood, both Galileo and Einstein showed unique mathematical abilities. Poor Charles lacked even these basic early signs. He was no dummy, but forgettable and average in every way. His family, however, was anything but.

The Darwins were solidly part of the British ruling class, true ladies and gentlemen, rubbing shoulders with men and women of title, accompanied by butlers, housemaids, and footmen. Like all British nobility, this privilege came as a birthright, but the Darwins also earned it. They had been major players in the Midlands Enlightenment and were some of the most devoted Unitarian Christians in England. Erasmus Darwin, Charles's grandfather, was a famous physician. After him, medicine became the core family business. The steps on the path of this foreordained destiny were clear and worn. At the right age, each Darwin man would leave England for Scotland and the University of Edinburgh. Edinburgh was *the* place in the nineteenth century to receive medical training. Before Charles would place his foot on this path, his father (who was known as "the Doctor") and his older brother Erasmus (who bore the name of his famous grandfather) had already successfully taken the journey to Edinburgh and the calling of medicine.

But like Galileo before him, Charles would flop as a medical student. He couldn't stomach it, both literally and figuratively. Acute pains in his stomach caused him problems that would last the rest of his life, often chaining him to his bed. The work of medicine, too, made him uneasy. Watching operations and procedures was sometimes unbearable for him. Once, famously, he ran from an operating room because a suffering child's agony was too much for him to witness. Charles was a sensitive soul, and the inducing of pain for the hope of healing, which medicine called for in the nineteenth century, was more than he could take. For Charles, the path to healing had to go too directly through the inducing of suffering.

To get away from the haunting of what he saw as medical torture, and to find the fresh air his own illness called for, Charles picked up a new hobby: beetling.[1] Like today's hipster hobbies of knitting or brewing your own beer, in nineteenth-century England, beetling was all the rage. Walking through forests and springs, looking under rocks and logging new specimens was the fad of the time. Beetling was the first step into many people's new curiosity with nature. This was the time where coal-burning machines were pumping black smoke and soot all over London—and a return to trees and springs, logging and classifying rocks, plants, and insects became a big draw. And Charles was particularly good at it. Edinburgh not only gave him many natural sites for beetling, but also connected him with a handful of other naturalists who encouraged his new interest.

Yet, the Doctor wasn't going to pay the high price to keep fledgling Charles in Edinburgh for the sake of beetles and nature walks. The Darwins had a name and lineage to consider. It soon

---

1. Adrian Desmond points to the significance of beetling and its place at Cambridge, which Charles will be headed to next: "Beetling in Cambridge had become just as competitive as cricket or rowing—but with one difference. It was no team sport. A painstaking observer could win the student accolades. Charles, such a disappointment to his father, became obsessed with the idea." *Darwin: The Life of a Tormented Evolutionist* (New York: Norton, 1991), 58.

became clear that aimless Charles and his bug interest would be best directed into the pastorate.

To be a clergyman was a high noble office in England at this time; and Charles seemed particularly wired for a country parish. After all, many clergymen were particularly into beetling and naturalist activities (again, we see how those in the church were supporting the new science). So the Doctor made the arrangements for Charles to matriculate at Cambridge, seeking a divinity degree at Christ's College. It is more than a little ironic that the monster with the dangerous ideas was an aimless, sickly young man who loved beetles and studied for the ministry.[2]

Failure at the family legacy of medicine and the call of the ministry put Charles, who would become the greatest scientist of the nineteenth century, at the same university as the greatest eighteenth-century scientist, Isaac Newton. Yet when Charles arrived in Cambridge, no one would have guessed his future. Things started choppy, and the academic work was a struggle. But soon Charles was faring much better as a divinity student than as a medical student. He eventually did so well that, in another great irony of history, he was given the dorm room named after the theologian William Paley.[3]

Like Darwin, Paley was a Unitarian, writing his most important book, *Natural Theology*, at the very end of his life. In this book, Paley offered one of the most famous arguments for creation as design, using the analogy of a watchmaker. Paley explained that if you found a watch, looking at it you'd be sure

2. Haught adds a little texture: "By his own admission, Darwin's formal studies at Cambridge could scarcely compete with his enthusiasm for riding and shooting small animals. And collecting beetles. Still, during the latter part of his Cambridge period, he won the patronage of two instructors, John Stevens Henslow and Adam Sedgwick, both of them clerics as well as scientists. Their own love of nature along with their kindness and encouragement, aroused in the young Charles 'a burning zeal to add even the most humble contribution to the noble structure of Natural Science.'" John Haught, *Making Sense of Evolution: Darwin, God, and the Drama of Life* (Louisville: Westminster John Knox, 2010), 6.

3. "In the elegant stone-cased front court of the college, on the south side, up G staircase to the first floor, were the rooms traditionally inhabited by the theologian best known to students for his pellucid, passionless prose, the author of their set texts, *The Evidences of Christianity* and *The Principles of Moral and Political Philosophy*, the Revd William Paley. On All Saints' Day 1828, with the arrival of a new tenant in Paley's rooms, the nameplate on the door read 'C. Darwin.'" Desmond, *Darwin*, 64.

that there was someone who had designed it. The design itself, with all its working parts, witnessed to a designer. In the same way, he argued, when you look at nature you can't help but see an intricate design that promises a designer—case in point, the eye. Paley explained that there was no other way to understand the order and direction of nature than to recognize a maker behind it.

Like all Cambridge students of his day, Darwin read Paley, and while he couldn't put his finger on why, it didn't sit well. Perhaps because by this time Darwin was even more into his hobby, learning more sophisticated ways of classifying insects and animal species, even gaining skills at taxidermy and geology. The more the young Charles dug his hands into the soil of the natural world, the more Paley's apologetics seemed banal. Not to mention, there were signs of a coming revolution. Unease with the elitism of the highborn was starting to spread throughout England, and frustration with the privilege and high salaries of the clergy was the first salvo.

Yet, this didn't keep Charles from studying hard for his exams, successfully completing his divinity degree. His next step was to take the ordination exams and receive his country parish, where he could spend the rest of his days preaching and collecting bugs.

THE *BEAGLE*

The Doctor was pleased that Charles now had the prospects of an honorable profession before him, with a satisfactory salary. A clergyman was a suitable profession for an English gentleman, and so the Doctor could exhale. But it wasn't long before the Doctor's ease dissipated, when Charles informed him that a vessel named the *Beagle* was in search of a naturalist for its voyage around the world.

The Doctor refused to permit Charles to go. Not only was any sea voyage dangerous in the mid-1800s, but even more worrisome, years spent with unsavory sailors would corrupt Charles for the church. The Doctor believed Charles was both too sickly and too highborn for such a venture. It was the high-born piece that ultimately got Charles the position.[4]

The *Beagle*'s captain was a man named Robert Fitzroy, who had both adventure and seawater coursing through his veins. But he was anxious. Reports of an earlier voyage were haunting the hardened captain. The skipper of another vessel, all the equal of Fitzroy, had killed himself, driven mad by the pressure of his command. Fitzroy had the idea that he could save himself from a similar fate by ensuring that his naturalist was an English gentleman, able to share his dinner table with the gifts and decorum of conversation. Fitzroy reasoned that he'd beat back the demons of insanity with the tonic of English manners.

And so Charles departed for South America, not to see jolly England again for a long five years. These years were filled with enough adventure to make Forrest Gump or Walter Mitty blush. Wild storms, naked tribal warriors, raucous mutinies, murderous raids, excessive riches, and undiscovered rivers and new landscapes met Charles nearly every day. When he was not being the salve that kept Fitzroy sane, Charles was immersing himself in the hobby that was now his responsibility: collecting every animal, insect, and plant that he could find, documenting them and loading them into the ship's hull. For the first time in his life Charles was finding his own voice; on the edge of the world he stumbled into a confidence that gave him new insight after insight. And these breakthroughs would be ignited thanks again to the rocks.

Charles had learned much from his naturalist mentors about geology during his days in Cambridge. And when he and Fitzroy stood looking at the cliffs of South America's coastline, both knew there was just no way that anything but HUGE amounts of time were needed to form them. The arising of these

4. Desmond explains the Doctor's concern: "By the next morning, 30 August 1831, his sisters had briefed the Doctor. His refusal was a cruel blow, and neither Henslow's nor Peacock's endorsement would budge him. It was further evidence of his son's aimless preoccupation with enjoying himself. The voyage would be a useless, dangerous distraction. The unsettling years in the company of sailors would taint Charles and spoil him for the Church. It would ruin his professional chances again. Besides, why was a naturalist being sought with only weeks to spare? Something must be wrong with the vessel, the voyage, or FitzRoy. No, the whole plan looked reckless, and Susan, Caroline, and Catherine agreed." *Darwin*, 102.

cliffs needed eons to shift and shape. The more Charles examined the animals that made their homes in these unique environments, the more the old story of the rocks seemed suitable to the animals' own unique fit for the environments. Time and environmental adaptation became central to Charles's imagination. His experience in the Galápagos would only bring these thoughts into sharper vision.

These thoughts and connections found their way deep into Charles. But they were only thoughts, the beginning of a theory. For now, he had the Andes to summit, Tahiti to taste, New Zealand to explore, and Sydney to fall in love with.

When the *Beagle* was headed for the horn of Africa, a few of Charles's letters to a fellow naturalist friend were published in England without Charles's knowledge. Somewhat like posting a tweet and then shutting off your phone for a long flight, Charles landed and discovered he was a phenomenon. In the dark of the sea voyage Charles had no idea that these letters, now articles, had made him a name all across the British Empire. Even the Doctor, who was sure that this voyage was a bad idea, was now converted, buying up copies and proudly telling all within earshot that his son, once sickly, underachieving Charles, was a famous naturalist. Charles, five years earlier, had left England a shy boy, only to return branded a naturalist hero, a title he'd hold for the rest of his life.

THE DAYS AFTER THE *BEAGLE*

When Charles placed his feet back on English soil, there was no returning to the life of a country parish pastor, but not for the reasons the Doctor had feared. It wasn't the external perceptions, or the corruption of sailors, that moved Charles away from the church, but Charles himself. In one sense there was no reason any longer for a pastor's life. Charles had wanted to be a clergyman so he could have the position and salary to follow his naturalist interests. Thanks to his articles and soon-to-be-published books about the *Beagle*'s voyage, Charles had no lack for funds or reputation (he was quickly elected into the esteemed Royal Society).

Yet, in another sense, the clergy life was undercut by Charles's own inner doubts. Despite today's misinformed view of Darwin as a monster, he saw an important place for the church, even writing about the importance of missionary work across the world (though this may have had more to do with colonialism than ecclesial appreciation).[5] Charles never wished to upend the church or the moral directions it set for society. Yet, Charles couldn't shake Paley. William Paley had argued that the more you look intently at nature the more you saw the reflections of the design of a Designer. Charles had a completely different experience. His voyage on the *Beagle* led him to look more deeply than most into the eyes of the natural world. In so doing, Charles had to admit that he saw design, but not necessarily the reflection of a designer. Rather, from looking at the rocks, environments, and adaptive changes of the animals, Charles saw how the design or order of the world might rest within its own natural mechanisms. At this point in his life, Charles didn't doubt the Christian faith as much as its simple conception of design. The natural theology of Paley couldn't work with scientific observation—Darwin believed.[6] But these were personal thoughts that Charles wished not to share. He had too much respect for the church and its place in English society to go raiding.

5. Desmond's lines are revealing: "These 'worthy men' had done their best, and the weeks in Tahiti and New Zealand convinced FitzRoy and Darwin that the missions were a success. For both, Christianity came as a civilizing package, and most of all they applauded the noble-mindedness of the missionaries. In these outposts of empire, a genteel class of white man was making shores safe for Britannia's sailors, preaching good manners and promoting good government. Their 'political agency' was needed wherever ships put in and lands were being settled." *Darwin*, 175.

6. Brooke speaks powerfully of what the upending of Paley would mean: "It should not be difficult to see why intelligent people have often taken the view that Darwin's theory, properly understood, and Christian conceptions of an active providence are not merely incompatible but belong to two mutually exclusive worlds of thought. This does not mean that it was impossible to build bridges between them. Theologians could adapt as they had to the scientific innovations of the past. But from the standpoint of twentieth century humanism, Darwin's theory was the focus, if not the cause, of a transition into a modern world in which humanity could no longer delude itself that there was a caring providence, that pain and suffering had an ultimate rationale, or that there was any destiny other than engineering the future course of evolution." John Hedley Brooke, *Science and Religion* (London: Cambridge University Press, 2014), 416.

LOVE AND LOSS

There were many sufferings during the five years at sea, but a particularly acute one was the loss of Charles's true love. After months of writing her love letters, Charles was informed that she had chosen another suitor. In the world of Jane Austen, love and position were intertwined, and Charles had lost out. Returning, it seemed most suitable to marry his cousin Emma Wedgwood. Emma's only concern in marrying Charles was his position on the Bible. Emma had experienced loss, and reading the Gospels had been a particular comfort. Charles assured her that while he had his doubts about the creation story, he supported the church (both in spirit and financially) and hoped in eternal life.

After their wedding they moved to the country, always Charles's wish. They procured the Downe House, and filled it with servants, and their own children. As Charles internally debated marriage, he knew choosing Emma and life in the country would mean never traveling again. But given his own stomach pains and the assurance that his stint on the *Beagle* had provided enough adventure for a lifetime, he chose a wife, the country life, and children.

Charles and Emma brought ten of them into the world. The first was a son, named William Erasmus, the second, the pearl of Charles's eye, Anne. Like the Doctor with Charles's sister, so Charles had a soft spot for Anne. They had a particular connection. Unfortunately, it stretched as deep as shared stomach pains. These pains became particularly bad at the end of Anne's ninth year. Charles was devastated, in no small part blaming himself for her illness. The country doctor could only help so much, so as things worsened, Charles took Anne to a special spa that he too had used when his own stomach pains became severe.

Now with five children at home and Emma in the last weeks of another pregnancy, she couldn't travel, leaving it to Charles, who as a young man in Edinburgh couldn't take the sight of a child suffering, to nurse his little daughter. Charles watched at her bedside as Anne cried in pain, moving in and out of fever. Emma could only receive updates by letter, bearing the agonizing wait for news as baby Horace prepared to enter the world.

Three weeks before his birth, as her beloved father watched, Anne died, leaving a gash in Charles's spirit that would never heal.

After her death Charles never again went to church. When asked about his Christian faith, he'd honestly say that he had left it—never because of the implications of evolution or his theory of natural selection, but rather because poor, sweet Anne had been ripped so painfully from his side.[7]

Charles Darwin is not Darth Vader with a British accent, no raging monster seeking to stomp out faith. More rightly, he was a wounded father whose tears had run too dry to mount the steps of the church. After Anne's death, Charles, like Galileo even after he bent his knee in Rome, continued to financially support the church in Downe, even entering into many conversations with its vicar. But never again did he attend a service. Each Sunday he would walk with his family to church and leave them at the door. Then he'd turn and head instead into the forests and springs that had sung the healing chorus to his sensitive soul since his days in Edinburgh.

THE THEORY COMES TO LIGHT

There were others before Darwin who were moving in the same direction.[8] Some of their thoughts Darwin had built on

7. "Annie's cruel death destroyed Charles's tatters of belief in a moral, just universe. Later he would say that this period chimed the final death-knell for his Christianity, even if it had been a long, drawn-out process of decay. He was also freer to hold his beliefs in the home. Through nine pregnancies, always difficult and dangerous, Emma had needed the security of thinking that they belonged to each other for ever. With no more babies, the threat of separation lifted. They would certainly be together for many years to come. Charles now took his stand as an unbeliever." Desmond, *Darwin*, 387.

8. Haught here shows that Darwin wasn't quite the villain or hero that he is often made to be. "I cannot count the number of times I have heard or read prominent evolutionists and Darwinian scholars insist that it is natural selection rather than divine creativity that explains design. For example, Janet Browne, one of Darwin's best biographers, writes that after returning from his *Beagle* voyage in 1836, he came to believe 'that living beings were not created by divine fiat.' This kind of claim is typical of countless contemporary Darwinians. I doubt that Darwin himself ever intended to leave things at that. True, he placed natural selection in opposition to special divine creation, but in general his language did not formally exclude a deeper

in his books on the *Beagle* (and other scientific articles).[9] Charles wasn't creating his theory of evolution totally out of the blue, but his observations from the *Beagle* were leading him to deeper connections. Charles was now seeing a clear way to move past the unease he had with Paley's theory from back in his student days.

This clear way was the theory of natural selection. It would both add something unique to evolution, and in turn, make Paley's watchmaker analogy as obsolete as a sundial. Adding natural selection to evolutionary adaptation made a clear path for design without the action of a designer. Natural selection, Charles could show, could get you a watch, or a long-beaked finch, without necessarily having a watchmaker or a finchmaker. Darwin wasn't *against* a designer. While a lapsed church member, he was not an atheist.[10] If there was any iconoclastic spirit in Charles (which is debatable) it was not toward God, but simply toward the theory of William Paley.

Charles knew the ramifications of this idea of natural selection, fearing that it could too quickly lead the opponents of the clergy (who were already brooding) to strike, fronting the assumption that Darwin was giving us a world without a God and in turn an England without need for elitist clergy. Fearing this interpretation, Charles sat for years on the theory; his respect for the church's impact on society too high.

Yet, the writing that Charles did publish drew around him a handful of fellow budding scientists who were building on and pushing forward his ideas. One of them informed Darwin that another naturalist named Alfred Russell Wallace was working on a theory similar to evolution by natural selection. Recognizing that he might get scooped, Charles reluctantly decided to publish *On the Origin of Species.*

Wallace was happy he did. Wallace's mother was English and

role for a 'divine fiat,' for God's creative 'Let there be.'" *Making Sense of Evolution*, 18.

9. One thinks here in particular of Jean-Baptiste Lamarck.

10. "Darwin was no atheist. He accepted that all this resulted from God's natural laws, and if it looked like leading to a godless conclusion, a 'Man . . . would more earnestly pray "deliver us from temptation."'" On the other hand, accepting this evolutionary determinism could transform human conduct, for a father would 'strive to improve his organization for his children's sake.'" Desmond, *Darwin*, 261.

his father (like Maxwell and Torrance) was Scottish. Wallace's Scottish family tree stretched directly back to William Wallace, the leader who won Scottish independence in the thirteenth century (and was played by Mel Gibson in the movie *Braveheart*). Alfred Wallace was no raiding warrior, but a slim man who wielded not a sword, but a butterfly net. He had been building off Darwin's work and admired him deeply (Wallace too, because of Darwin, became a naturalist on a long sea voyage). Wallace found the full fleshing out of Darwin's theory wonderful, though he wasn't sure it meant that the created realm was only a natural (impersonal) place. Wallace wondered if, instead, natural selection was a way for God to steer the created realm. Wallace didn't see evolution by natural selection as eliminating a personal God.[11] But Wallace never had the ghost of Paley haunting him, was never annoyed by the incessant winding of a watchmaker.[12]

Like Paley, Darwin was a Unitarian, meaning that both men denied the doctrine of the Trinity. I've argued throughout this book that Nicene Christianity was not only an early harbinger of scientific rationality, but possesses a logic for doing the science itself. Nicene Christianity provides ways to hold together particularities through their relations, allowing for seeming opposites, like light as wave and particle (like divine and human

11. Ian Barbour adds about Wallace, "In his later writing, Wallace went further and claimed that natural selection cannot account for the higher human faculties. He pointed out that the brain size in primitive tribes, which is comparable to that in highly civilized groups, actually provides a mental capacity far beyond the simple needs of their aboriginal patterns of life, for which a much smaller brain would have sufficed. 'Natural selection could only have endowed savage man with a brain a little superior to that of an ape, whereas he actually possesses one very little inferior to that of a philosopher.' And how can one explain musical, artistic, or ethical capacities that contribute nothing to survival? Wallace felt that such 'latent powers' possessed in advance of the need to employ them indicate that 'some higher intelligence may have directed the process by which the human race was developed.' More recent opinion has not supported Wallace's idea of 'latent powers,' but it has tended to agree with him in holding that human evolution involved distinctive processes that had been neglected by Darwin." Barbour, *Religion and Science: Historical and Contemporary Issues* (San Francisco: HarperSanFrancisco, 1997), 60.

12. Once you understand Darwin and his annoyance with Paley's watchmaker analogy, the iconoclastic and bombastic writing of Richard Dawkins (whose personality is very, very different than Charles Darwin's) makes sense. One of his most famous books is titled *The Blind Watchmaker*.

natures), to nevertheless be one. It is possible, but only a guess, that Darwin's anti-Trinitarian background impacted his ambivalence, keeping him from seeing divine action as something very different than a watchmaker.[13] This may have kept Darwin from the vision that Wallace, and, as we'll see, Asa Gray possessed, seeing how natural selection could remain a completely natural reality and yet nevertheless could be steered by a personal God who transcends the world by entering it in a *kenotic* movement of ministry. "A theology of divine humility makes room for true novelty to spring spontaneously into being—a feature logically suppressed by deterministic materialist interpretations, as well as by the notion that the universe is simply the unfolding of an eternally fixed divine design or plan."[14]

We'll have to explore this possibility in the next chapters. But for now, it is enough to wonder if Nicene Christianity might allow us to see evolution by natural selection as bearing the marks of divine action as the movements of *hypostasis* as ministry.

BULLDOG BITES

Immediately upon publication of *On the Origin of Species*, debate raged. Was natural selection a planned, steered process by a personal God? Wallace and Gray thought so. Darwin was ambivalent. The death of Anne assured him that nature was a tragic place, red in tooth and claw. A few of those younger admirers of Darwin, particularly Thomas Henry Huxley, screamed "Hell, no!" to any sense that evolution could be steered.

On the Origin of Species would encompass the first of Darwin's supposed dangerous ideas. Now with the encouragement of young radicals like Huxley, Charles found the confidence to

13. My point here, which I'll develop below, is that the work of God can only be explored through the face of Jesus Christ, and therefore God cannot be seen as a watchmaker, but as a minister. Evolution by natural selection, in my mind, must be explored through our experience of God as minister. Of course, this was something Charles couldn't see, or didn't experience, in the loss of Anne, and it therefore haunted him as much as the banality of Paley's analogy.

14. John Haught, *God After Darwin: A Theology of Evolution* (Boulder, CO: Westview, 2000), 54.

release his second big (supposedly) dangerous idea. Eleven years after *On the Origin of Species*, Charles would release *The Descent of Man*. This book would argue that all living things evolved from each other, dropping the bombshell that would shake proper British society.

The ramification of Darwin's theory is that dukes and ladies had descended from apes. British society was feeling the strain of the underclass, pushing against the privileged protégé and the centuries-long (even millennia-long) commitment to the right of bloodlines. But now Darwin (one of their own) seemed to be saying, no matter whether you share blood with a duke or duchess, *all* of us can trace our line back to monkeys! This was not appreciated by British society, and particularly not their chaplains—the gentlemen of the clergy class that Charles had ditched after the fame of the *Beagle*.

But Thomas Henry Huxley couldn't help himself; it was delicious. Huxley was a brilliant but underemployed biologist. He watched, and resented, the clergy class that received high salaries to go to balls and do half-baked science (all of which couldn't hold a candle to the rigor of his own work).[15] He had no patience for these hacks, and was bent to bring down the privileged clergy. While Huxley found Darwin's science to be right, even more so he saw it as a weapon with which to attack the clergy and those other Oxbridge elites.

15. Desmond gives a little texture to Huxley: "Copies of Spencer's article went out to 'leading men,' who acknowledged them politely. One went to an astute, dark-eyed young naturalist, making his name with a series of technical studies on seasquirts. This was Thomas Huxley. Twenty-seven years old and fiercely ambitious, he had returned from a four-year stint on the surveying ship *HMS Rattlesnake* just in time for the Great Exhibition. Angry, down on his luck, out of money, he had been eking out an existence, searching in vain for a job." *Darwin*, 403. He continues: "Huxley was livid: in science England wanted all the credit without paying the cost. One had to be an independent gentleman to make a vocation of it. Here he was, a newly elected Fellow of the Royal Society, living in tawdry St John's Wood. He could not even afford decent lodgings, let alone bring his fiancée from Australia where they had parted three years before. Talk about Malthusian 'moral restraint'—this was ridiculous; it drove him 'wild.' Months of lecture-grubbing and other profitless pursuits left him in despair. How he had envied Hooker at the British Association a year ago, destined to succeed his father as the Director at Kew, and engaged to Professor Henslow's daughter, who was sitting by his side. Huxley's mother had just died, leaving his own father a dependent wreck. When Spencer's article arrived in September, Huxley was close to a break-down." *Darwin*, 404.

Huxley became known as Darwin's bulldog, and he loved to bite. But Darwin himself never felt completely comfortable with the conflicts, and he chose to quietly remain a gentleman and church supporter while Huxley and his hounds howled.

Without a doubt, those peacocking for the comprehensive social practice of "science" have used Darwin's theories as the core mechanism to get a universe that is so self-contained that its personal order is evicted. These thinkers, moving from Huxley to Dawkins and Dennett, are often called "neo-Darwinians," the high priests of the social practice of "science." But what's clear from actually looking at Charles Darwin's life is that he is no neo-Darwinian, no raider for the social practice of "science."[16] He no doubt stumbled into scientific findings that challenge the commitments of faith. But because these findings are bound in the epistemic goal of the scientific, faith must not discard (or caricature) these findings, but must enter into dialogue with them. The epistemic goal of faith calls us to actually and honestly wrestle with the findings of Darwin next to the soteriological *telos* of faith. Darwin and his theories could only be discarded without rigorous engagement if we assume them to be propaganda—cheap shots used for nothing more than disruption and chaos. But Darwin's own story makes such an assumption impossible.

Or we could say it this way: too often when our young people think of evolution, they picture not a sickly man with amazing adventures on the sea, dragging behind him a broken heart, appreciating a church he was once trained to serve. Rather, they imagine that Darwin is Huxley, barking and bragging, seeking to use science to win a cultural battle—ironically or not, creationists and ID supporters now use anti-Darwinian ideas in

16. Merlin Donald explains this dynamic more, explaining Darwin's gentleman side. "Of course, this is exactly what Darwin feared might happen to his ideas. Victorian gentleman that he was, he delayed the publication of his first book on evolution for two decades, and his ideas on human origins were held back for another fifteen years, because he feared where they might lead. But most modern neo-Darwinians do not worry about any of this. They have seized what they perceive as the moral high ground. It is irrelevant, they claim, whether Darwin would have approved their agenda. He was a man of the nineteenth century, and here we are in the twenty-first." *A Mind So Rare: The Evolution of Human Consciousness* (New York: W.W. Norton, 2001), 2.

their cultural battles. This is exactly what those who fired Sarah assumed, thinking that Darwin's whole goal was to take down the church. But this is undermined by his story. Charles wanted none of that. He was too sensitive and shy, too respectful and responsible, for such pursuits. And always far too sick.

Soon enough the stomach aliments that had plagued him for nearly his whole life and had taken Anne would have their way with Charles. When he died, the family's plan was to place him in plot at the cemetery in Downe. But before the funeral arrangements were complete, the invitation came to lay Charles in Westminster Abbey. Some wondered if this could be done. Darwin had confessed great ambivalence to faith, and his ideas were taken by some to further impersonalize the universe and relativize the importance of humanity. Was burial in the holy Abbey of Westminster appropriate? Despite the many bites suffered from Darwin's bulldogs, it was clear that Darwin, a man weighed by the doubts of a broken heart, was nevertheless a great credit to England, and all of British society. There was no better place than the Abbey for this shy, unassuming boy who loved beetles, now to be laid before a God he knew was no watchmaker, but *maybe* still his Lord.

19.

Darwin's First Dangerous Idea

It was an odd blend of envy and gratitude. These two seemingly contradictory emotions were coming in waves, cresting and falling, one after the next. Sitting on tenth-grader Aaron's patio, watching the pool glisten and shimmer, Jared wondered why he didn't have a pool of his own. And yet he was hit with gratitude that Aaron's parents, Christine and Chet, so happily hosted the Bible study. Speaking of the Bible study, Jared was thrilled to be doing it, grateful to be reading the Bible with young people again—it had been months since he had done a formal Bible study. But he also felt a few ticks past annoyed that this Bible study was mandated by the senior pastor. It was an initiative Tanisha dropped on the staff at their last meeting. She wanted to connect all generations of the congregation with her sermon series on Genesis.

Jared wasn't sure why Tanisha had decided to do a sermon series on Genesis. Issues of origins weren't her thing. Jared got all sorts of questions about evolution from young people, and parents sometimes asked him for advice. But outside these impromptu questions and concerns, it wasn't a topic of discussion. There were no Hammites or ID raiders, like in Sarah's church. Tanisha did explain that the point was to discuss the *imago Dei* (the image of God) and explore how sin entered a perfect creation.

Before Jared could get past his internal conflict, one more wave came. Jared was disappointed that after planning this Bible study, only three kids had showed. *What would it be like to be at another church, where it wasn't so damn hard to get kids to show?* Yet, it also felt right and sacred that nevertheless here sat Aaron, Tegan, and Martin, eating pretzels and volleying sarcastic comments at each other. It wasn't surprising that Martin had come. He came to everything, and Jared was sure that his sarcasm was a front for deep loneliness. Martin acted like he only cared about basketball and hip-hop, but Jared knew, particularly from discussions on the mission trip, that there was more going on under Martin's front than he allowed most people to see.

To calm his inner turmoil, Jared decided to start with a direct but basic question: "So why did each of you come?"

Aaron responded quickly, "It's at my house, so . . ."

". . . you had to be here!" Jared finished his sentence with a chuckle.

"Pretty much. But no," he continued, "I like this stuff too. I mean whatever *this* is."

Tegan just shrugged her shoulders.

"And how about you, Martin, why are you here?" Jared asked

"Dinosaurs." Martin responded with a cocksure attitude.

Both Tegan and Aaron cracked up.

"Really?" Jared responded with a tone of fatigue, "You're here because of dinosaurs?"

"H-e-l-l, yeah," Martin said. "Dinosaurs are the bomb. Of course, that's why they're all dead because a bomb called a huge meteorite hit the earth."

The laugher erupted again from Tegan and Aaron. It was like rain on the parched earth of Martin's confidence.

Tegan was now completely taken with Martin's attitude, and Jared worried he was seeing a love connection before his eyes. A mutiny worse than any Fitzroy could imagine was about to take over Jared's boat if he wasn't careful. So he decided his only strategy was to enter into the lunacy. As he did, though, he discovered that it wasn't lunacy at all, but echoed back to the deepest conversation Jared had had with Martin on the mission trip.

Martin, with that same cocksure attitude, said more directly, "I'm here because I want to know why Genesis doesn't say anything about dinosaurs. Why? And why are they dead? If God created everything, then why is so much of the created stuff dead?"

DINOSAUR DEATH

Evolution seems to fit so well with the comprehensive social practice of "science," taking on the sharp edges of neo-Darwinism because the limits of evolution's findings can be re-dressed for ideological pursuits. As a natural scientific theory, evolution can say nothing about God and God's action in suffering. From within the boundaries of biology, evolution says that suffering and death have no meaning, no "purpose," other than ruling one adaptation more fit than another. Again from within the theory itself, evolution is indifferent to death. Dinosaurs are destroyed, becoming fossils, because they simply do—randomly (and apparently abruptly) their environment changed. And when environments change, things not equipped to survive perish. It is right here that the social practice of "science" sweeps in and takes these limited assertions as the conclusive truths of reality, emphasizing that those who are mature can face the fact that death and suffering have no meaning. And those that keep looking for meaning are immature babies.

But this search for meaning is exactly Martin's search. It leads him to wonder if moving beyond the boundaries of evolution allows us see an epistemic overlap between evolution and the claims of faith. After all, Christian faith boldly asserts that suffering and death are not meaningless (proving an impersonal universe), but are profoundly filled with purpose and significance—so much so that God promises, in the perishing face of Jesus, to be forever present, ministering to us in and through death itself.[1]

1. "History, recorded and interpreted, as some basis for our countering the flow of time toward entropy and death must be reversed and reinterpreted in light of the incarnational, crucifixion, and resurrection, in which we have the decisive demonstration in history of the end of history—according to God's time. This proleptic significance of the Christ event is where we can begin to re-envision the arrow of time,

Nevertheless, mass extinctions have been proven—again, by the rocks. These rocks have told us that not only is this planet billions of years old, but that eras of ice and oceans, lizards and fish have come and gone, leaving fossils of species that have thrived for a time, only to disappear. Much like Sasha, who considers the mass of space and wonders how the soteriological goal of faith could stand if aliens contacted us. Similarly Martin searches for how the soteriological *telos* of faith could be if evolution is right and nature is so red in tooth and claw that whole species—particularly these strange conscious ones called *homo sapiens*—could be drowned in their own blood. Like Sasha with aliens, Martin isn't necessarily looking for a direct answer about mass extinction, but needs to know how evolution and the claims of Christian faith might intersect.

MOVING INTO THE DANGEROUS IDEAS

As we saw in the last chapter, Darwin's two *supposedly* dangerous ideas are encompassed in his two books *On the Origins of Species* and *The Descent of Man.* It was actually Daniel Dennett who most famously coined the phrase "Darwin's dangerous idea(s)," rebranding the beetle-hunting sickling into the leader of a motorcycle gang. Dennett boldly asserts that any belief in a personal order and a divine being is a stupid, childish thought. Darwin is awesomely dangerous, in Dennett's mind, because he provides a way to finally bury the thought that there is anything outside nature itself, showing that it is only and finally natural mechanism (natural selection) that gets us this world, even these beings that think about thinking and will choose death for the sake of love.

Those on the opposite end, who put Darwin on trial, actually fall into Dennett's trap and indeed make Darwin a supposed menace to society (something he historically was *not*). They too see Darwin's ideas as dangerous, and, oddly, for almost completely the *same* reasons. The only difference between Dennett's

historical time, and our personal lifetime from the standpoint of God's time." James Loder and Jim W. Neidhardt, *The Knight's Move* (Colorado Springs, CO: Helmers & Howard, 1992), 141.

New Atheists and the ID raiders is that one group welcomes the dangerous ideas and the other fears them.[2]

Neither position can help Martin. His own experience, at least for now, won't allow him to give in and admit that life and death have no meaning and purpose. He can't help but ask, why did the dinosaurs die? What is the point of living things if they all go extinct? And if we, human beings, will eventually go extinct, because *all* we are is natural and material, then what are these nonmaterial realities we experience and claim as central to our being, like love, compassion, and friendship?

Martin also can't deny evolution, however. It is a story that makes too much sense out of the rocks, variations, and diversity of the biosphere. Not to mention that genetic research done long after Darwin has proven the interconnected descent of living things. So Martin gets himself to the Bible study not wanting arguments for one position or the other, but a way to understand how the theory of evolution might connect (or co-exist) with the soteriological *telos* of faith. Martin essentially wants to know if faith has anything to say to Darwin's dangerous ideas—and if in the end they are really dangerous at all.

THE DANGEROUS IDEA ONE:
NATURAL SELECTION

Like Einstein who had the first antecedent to his 1905 breakthrough back when he was sixteen, dreaming about what it

2. Haught insightfully shows that these neo-Darwinians too are stuck in heavy design and providence talk. "Darwinians such as Dawkins and Dennett, for example, seem unaware that by using the expressions 'alternative to,' 'instead of,' and 'rather than' they reveal their underlying assumption that evolutionary biology and theology are both trying to do the same thing: to provide an ultimate explanation of design. The difference is that to evolutionary naturalists, the idea of natural selection does a better job of it. They believe that in the quest to find a foundational understanding of design, science and religious faith are locked in a contest to the death. Theology and biology are rivals for explanatory primacy, and one of them has to lose. If it were not for the fact that they see biology as a substitute for theology, it would make no sense for Dawkins and Dennett to insist that a naturalistic account rather than a theological one has now come out first in the contest. By putting it this way, however, they simply show that they are still bewitched by theology. They are not yet doing pure science." John Haught, *Making Sense of Evolution: Darwin, God, and the Drama of Life* (Louisville: Westminster John Knox, 2010), 19.

would be like to ride a light beam like a bull, so Darwin had the first inklings of natural selection back in 1838. Just two years after the *Beagle* docked back in England, Charles read Thomas Malthus's *An Essay on the Principle of Population*. In the essay, Malthus predicted (thankfully wrongly) that population would double every twenty-five years, quickly outstripping food production. Darwin saw a connection with his observations on the *Beagle*. A species would always overpopulate beyond available resources; therefore only those in the population with certain adaptations, predisposing them to *win* in the fight for resources, would survive. Surviving, they'd pass along these winning mutations to their offspring, giving them a fitness to survive. This would do it![3] It would execute Paley's watchmaker, giving us a fully natural mechanism for the design of nature. The environments Darwin saw from the bow of the *Beagle* seemed anything but harmonious. "Violent" was a better word for them. Nature was a war, not a ticking timepiece.[4] And now Malthus's essay seemed to affirm Darwin's observations.

Just about three months after reading Malthus and putting together the first bricks of the theory of natural selection, Charles had lunch with a friend named Joseph Dalton Hooker. Hooker brought with him an American colleague named Asa

3. "By now he had it down pat: overpopulation and competition led to a 'Natural Selection,' as the victors emerged triumphant from the 'war of nature.' This was the mechanism of descent. Everything at the present day was related. But animals were not steadily advancing up a Lamarckian ladder, one behind the other, with each grading into the next. Life had a tree-like pedigree; we could relate mammals—say the 'horse, mouse, tapir, elephant'—by searching back through the genealogy for the 'common parent.'" Adrian Desmond, *Darwin: The Life of a Tormented Evolutionist* (New York: Norton, 1991), 293.

4. Haught adds to this, showing us the challenges of natural selection. "It should not be difficult to see why the theory of natural selection is so theologically troubling. For one thing, the variations that constitute the raw material for selection are said to be completely random, that is, undirected by any intelligent agency: This accidental or 'contingent' aspect of evolution suggests that the universe is not governed by a divine providential intelligence after all. Next, the competitive 'struggle' in which the weak (the reproductively unfit) are so ruthlessly eliminated reveals a universe apparently untended by divine compassion. And finally, the disinterested way in which natural selection works—Dennett refers to it as 'algorithmic'— evokes the suspicion that we live in a remorselessly impersonal universe, hardly one residing in the bosom of a personal deity." John Haught, *God After Darwin: A Theology of Evolution* (Boulder, CO: Westview, 2000), 24.

Gray, a visiting botanist from Harvard. Charles and Asa hit it off, enjoying each other's company. But circumstances would keep them from interacting much for the next decade and half, as well as keeping Charles from furthering his theory of natural selection. Charles was busy; he needed to publish books about the *Beagle*, to get married, to become deathly ill, and to have children. As we saw above, one of those lovely children, Anne, would be killed by the same stomach pains that Charles survived.

Anne's loss never left Charles, but eventually he was able to get back to work. Needing some information on American flower species, Charles wrote Asa the first of what would become three hundred letters. In these letters Charles most directly worked out the theory of natural selection, even providing Asa with an early outline of *On the Origin of Species* in an 1857 correspondence. Asa was sure that when the book was released in 1858, it would be groundbreaking, so much so that it was Asa Gray who got the book onto American soil, becoming Darwin's main interpreter and supporter in North America.

Convinced by Darwin, Asa too saw evolution by natural selection as the shape of nature. But what Asa could not see was why this eliminated divine action. He couldn't quite see how Charles's scientific findings removed a personal order. In a letter, Asa wrote, "God himself is the very last, irreducible causal factor, and, hence, the source of all evolutionary change."[5] Asa saw evolution as the process of God's action, and natural selection the human interpretation of divine cause. Asa, like James Clerk Maxwell (and T. F. Torrance), came from Scottish Presbyterians.[6] Nicene Christianity ran through his veins, and he was not shy about claiming it.[7] Asa saw no reason that a God

5. Randy Moore, *Evolution in the Courtroom: A Reference Guide* (Santa Barbara, CA: ABC-CLIO, 2002), 125, 307.

6. "Moses Wiley Gray was of the first generation of his family born in America. His father, Robert Gray, had been among an early group of Scottish Presbyterians who emigrated from the north of Ireland." Hunter Dupree, *Asa Gray: American Botanist, Friend of Darwin* (Baltimore: Johns Hopkins University Press, 1959), 2.

7. Quoting Gray, Dupree shows his commitment to Nicene Christianity. "As he entered the final great period of activity after his retirement in 1873, Gray was able to put down with some precision his own idea of his religious position and his relation to Darwin. He was still 'a humble member of the Christian church, & as for orthodoxy, I receive & profess, ex animo, the Nicene creed for myself, though with no call to deny the Christian name to those who receive less.'" *Asa Gray*, 358.

revealed in the *kenotic* act of Jesus Christ, entering death so new life might be, could not use evolution as Darwin imagined. Darwin, I believe, was hung up on Paley's rigged natural theology, believing that clear observable design was the only lens in which to see divine action.

With Anne's death, Malthus's theory, and Paley's theology all mixing within Charles, his purview of death and struggle were narrowed. Paley's theology of a watchmaker asserted that creation was made of intricately tooled gears, ticking in perfect harmony. But Anne had been caught in these gears, and the rocks had crushed more species into nonexistence than could be counted. Darwin couldn't see how a personal God was acting in the world (though he wished he could). And he couldn't because, even in his opposition to Paley, he ironically conceded his view of God to him. Darwin was right; if you started with a God who was a firm technical watchmaker (as opposed to a kenotic minister—which the Bible points to), then natural selection and divine action were in opposition.[8]

When Gray told Darwin that he saw the possibility of divine action in the theory of evolution by natural selection, Charles wrote him, telling Gray directly that he agreed that his theory was "not at all necessarily atheistical," but Paley's ghost and Anne's screams were too haunting for Darwin. Charles responded, "I feel most deeply that the whole subject is too profound for the human intellect. A dog might as well speculate on the mind of Newton."[9]

8. Dupree explains Gray's take on scripture and his centrist position. "A literal belief in the Bible was no part of his version of evangelical religion. He did not even resort to symbolic interpretations to reconcile science and the Scripture. No need for reconciliation existed. Science was one of the things which, as he remarked to his brother George, the Bible did not teach. The Bible was simply not a textbook in science." *Asa Gray*, 136. Dupree continues: "The tendency of materialists to take over Darwin's idea and to go to war on religion Gray of course resisted. The tendency of the clergy and other defenders of the faith to attack Darwin and all science as atheistical not only filled him with dismay but struck him as very faulty tactics." *Asa Gray*, 281.

9. Charles Darwin (January 22, 1860). "Letter 2814, Darwin Correspondence Project" (Letter to Asa Gray). Retrieved January 1, 2015. Dupree continues: "Gray could . . . conclude, 'I dare say I am much more orthodox than Mr. Darwin; also that he is about as far from being an atheist as I am.' Did Darwin 'deny the existence of a Creator'? Gray's answer was, 'certainly not.'" *Asa Gray*, 359.

While Asa agreed that such a subject was certainly infinitely deep, he was willing to claim that his mind, in some small way, had touched its possibility. It is speculation, but worth imagining, that Gray was willing to see the mind of God in the supposed chaos of evolution by natural selection because of his experience as a deacon. Gray was a devout deacon at First Church in Cambridge, Massachusetts. In Presbyterian and Congregational churches, deacons are ministers. They may be laypeople, but they are nevertheless called (even ordained) to the direct ministry of the congregation, blessing the sick, praying for the young, and reaching out to the shut-in.[10]

Gray may have seen something different in evolution by natural selection than Darwin, because Gray had participated in ministry, and he also saw reality through the logic of Nicaea. Charles was seeking to upend ideas in the theology of Paley, but Asa was experiencing the very action of God in ministry itself. Gray may have experienced how from death springs *new* life, how in death itself a personal force seemed to promise new possibility in and through perishing.[11] While Charles saw nature as red in tooth and claw, Asa saw a ministerial paradigm that from death comes life.

While this might be plausible but self-servingly speculative in relation to Asa Gray, it is exactly the experience of Francis Collins, which we'll explore more fully below. It was from the experience of ministry that Collins (the leader of the Human Genome Project) not only found faith, but also saw how evolution and faith might overlap.[12] Collins and those that follow him stand in the legacy of Asa Gray, seeing evolution as possessing cause within itself.[13] But this cause is inextricable from

10. "Gray spent busy Sabbaths teaching a class of black boys at Sunday school and listening to the latest preaching attraction among the Presbyterian ministers, the Reverend Thomas H. Skinner, fresh from Andover Theological Seminary." *Asa Gray*, 50.

11. Again, possibility through perishing is to echo Eberhard Jüngel.

12. Francis Collins says, for instance, "Truly it can be said that not only biology but medicine would be impossible to understand without the theory of evolution." *The Language of God: A Scientist Presents Evidence of Belief* (New York: Free Press, 2006), 133.

13. For disclosure as these next few chapters unfold, I find myself close, though hopefully in new ways, to Collins's take on Theistic Evolution. He describes the

the kenotic nature of God, who forms a distinct place, forged through ministry, to echo ministry across the universe.[14]

Through the lens of ministry we *can* see evolution by natural selection as the process God uses to shape those with minds for ministry, giving us, in turn, a world that yearns, even in its smallest particle, for ministry through its evolutionary interconnection. God uses evolution to create the *hypostatic* beings God wishes to share God's image as ministers.[15] Evolution becomes

position as follows: "There are many subtle variants of theistic evolution, but a typical version rests upon the following premises:

1) The universe came into being out of nothingness, approximately 14 billion years ago.

2) Despite massive improbabilities, the properties of the universe appear to have been precisely tuned for life.

3) While the precise mechanism of the origin of life on earth remains unknown, once life arose, the process of evolution and natural selection permitted the development of biological diversity and complexity over very long periods of time.

4) Once evolution got under way, no special supernatural intervention was required.

5) Humans are part of this process, sharing a common ancestor with the great apes.

6) But humans are also unique in ways that defy evolutionary explanation and point to our spiritual nature. This includes the existence of the Moral Law (the knowledge of right and wrong) and the search for God that characterizes all human cultures throughout history." *The Language of God*, 200.

14. "I am suggesting that those who envisage the universe as enfolded by such infinite love and promise will be able to appreciate aspects of 'Darwinian' evolution that those committed to a more tragic spin on things might take as a reason tor cosmic despair. St. Paul (Philippians 2:5–11) portrays Christ as one who 'though in the form of God' did not 'cling' to his divine status, but instead 'emptied himself' and took the 'form of a slave.' It is to this image that Christian theology must always repair whenever it thinks about God's relationship to the world and its evolution." Haught, *God After Darwin*, 111.

15. I think Haught here is pointing to the ministerial nature of God and God's creation: "Consequently, any respectable theology after Darwin will not insist that the Creator is so petty as to function like an engineer tinkering mechanically with life. Theologians in the biblical tradition normatively understand divine creativity, providence, compassion, and wisdom as inseparable from the more basic motifs of liberation and promise, notions that do not correspond easily with that of engineering. Israel's idea of God is shaped above all else by its experience of the exodus from Egypt, and Christianity's God is inconceivable except in terms of the experience of being delivered from the most profound forms of enslavement, sin, and death. The God of Abraham and Jesus is a promising God, a God who seeks the transformation of all things, who dreams of renewal beyond the deep freeze of design, and who opens up the future even where it seems to mortals that there are dead ends everywhere." Haught, *Making Sense of Evolution*, 64.

a kind of species-bound school, a shared environment, which forges beings with minds for ministry.[16] It does this by hard-wiring us with a sensitivity and openness to nothingness. For it is out of the death of nothingness that divine action brings forth new possibility, and it is when we walk into nothingness, embracing others as they grieve the loss of their job or spouse, or into the nothingness of nature, sitting with a bird as it dies on the sidewalk, that we encounter the mystery of God's own being.[17]

Evolution implants a death-to-life paradigm within us that is haunting outside the ministerial action of God. But within it, this paradigm delivers beauty and promise through the frequency of ministry. Through ministry we experience that out of nothingness and death comes the new—not through the force of a watchmaker, but through the love of a self-giving minister.[18] It is through perishing that God brings new possibility, and evolution wires this not only into our own being, but into the being

16. Haught points in part to this school that I'm referencing. He adds, "A theology of evolution extends the Christian vision of divine fidelity into the depths of nature and evolution. Only an everlasting fidelity distinct from, but deeply related to, the universe itself could truly redress the fact of perpetual perishing. Furthermore, since in human beings the universe has been lifted to an unprecedented intensity of awareness (at least on earth), and evolution has now become conscious of itself, it is inconceivable that any truly cosmic redemption would tolerate the final snuffing out of the very consciousness to which the natural world has been straining so long to give birth. Our hope for conscious, subjective survival of death makes very good sense if the universe and evolution have an everlasting importance to God." *Making Sense of Evolution*, 105.

17. Fisher provides a theological take on why death is bound in the universe. This is an idea I'll further develop below. But here it communicates the paradigm of from death to life. Fisher says, "Because the creation is from absolute nothing, there is no component of nature that is everlasting; otherwise, it would have qualities that only belong to God, making nature and God the same in a substantial way (Pannenberg has a similar idea in his belief that 'God alone has unrestricted duration'). If nature is not everlasting, then death for nature is inevitable—not only the death of all individual created entities, but the death of the entire cosmos itself. The cosmos is mortal by nature." Christopher L. Fisher, *Human Significance in Theology and the Natural Sciences* (Eugene, OR: Pickwick, 2010), 156.

18. "In the symbol of the cross, Christian belief discovers a God who participates fully in the world's struggle and pain. The cruciform visage of nature reflected in Darwinian science invites us to depart, perhaps more decisively than ever before, from all notions of a deity untouched by the world's suffering." Haught, *God After Darwin*, 46.

of all living things, pushing us to enter the nothingness of one another and the created realm, as the way into divine encounter.

> After Darwin and Einstein, a good way to think about God is as the ultimate source of ordered novelty, as a disturbing lure that seeks to intensify the world's beauty. . . . Such a God is not interested in perpetuating the status quo, but in making the universe become more than what it is now. It becomes more, however, especially by intensifying its beauty and the aesthetic capacity of beings to enjoy this beauty.[19]

As we said above, the universe itself operates as a person. And it does this because every part of it is covered in this death-to-life paradigm. All parts of existence *are* through contingency and connection, finding particularity and distinct novelty, through relational connection that forges what was nothing into something.[20]

Darwin couldn't see this because of Paley's brainworm. William Paley, no Nicene Trinitarian, saw everything hinging on design.[21] The face of the second person of the Trinity, Jesus,

---

19. Haught, *Making Sense of Evolution*, 83.

20. William Brown speaks of the inherent death in nature: "But the perpetual recycling of cosmic gas and dust cannot last forever. Likewise for life. So many processes that generate and sustain life do so by taking life, with new generations built on the death and decay of previous ones. It is unlikely that we would be here without the mass extinction of the dinosaurs some 65 million years ago. The alternations between life and death are written into the very heart of evolution. A time for extinction and a time for recovery. Regardless of whether much of life on Earth as we know it will survive the crushing weight of our carbon imprint, possibly leading to a sixth great extinction, in the far grander scheme of things, the recycling of life will ultimately be interrupted by cosmic forces that lie beyond anyone's control. There are many ways that the 'cosmos wants to kill us,' notes astrophysicist Neil deGrasse Tyson, from killer asteroids to the sun's explosive death to galactic collisions. And one could also include a nearby supernova, black hole formation, or the collapse of a massive star. It's only a matter of time, the ancient sage would remind us." *The Seven Pillars of Creation: The Bible, Science, and the Ecology of Wonder* (London: Oxford University Press, 2010), 188.

21. "Christian belief, at any rate, does not depend for its credibility on the existence of a world without design flaws. Among notable Christian thinkers, Cardinal John Henry Newman (1801–90) expressed an exceptionally strong distaste for any theology that supports itself by leaning on the vapid criterion of design. Even before Darwin published the *Origin of Species*, Newman had written in 1852 that William Paley's design-oriented natural theology could 'not tell us one word about Christianity proper,' and that it 'cannot be Christian, in any true sense, at all.' Paley's brand of theology, Newman goes on, 'tends, if it occupies the mind, to dispose it against

was vague in his theological imagination. Paley became infatu-ated with order and couldn't see the death-to-life paradigm that Jesus' very body represents. This made apologetics for design more important than novelty—the reality that nature unfolds into newness, bringing from death new possibilities.

Paley and Darwin faced off over how design occurred in nature. Paley claimed that there could only be design if there was a designer. Darwin showed otherwise. But what Asa Gray saw was how evolution begot newness. Evolution from natural selection, no doubt, provided a way to have design without a designer. But Gray also saw that it could witness to the contin-ued creating action of God who takes what is dead and brings new (novel) life out of it. As Haught says, "The point . . . is that the place to look for God is not in the design but in the drama of life."[22]

Darwin could only see evolution as a war because the infatu-ation with design drew his attention backward. Darwin tells a captivating story, but it is a drama that it is only retrospective, ignoring that there are actually persons telling this story. From the place of strict backward-looking design, the death of dinosaurs and other mass extinctions seem to show no personal mind moving in the world. But if we change perspective and peer into the advent of newness, we can see that from death comes new life, bringing new possibilities. The dinosaurs play their part in bringing forth novelty, in and through their death. Without their existence, life would not have spread. And with-out their death, and the end of the lizard era, mammals would have lacked an environment to grow and prosper. And what ultimately can't be ignored is that this evolving newness eventu-ally delivers conscious beings that possess the *hypostatic* capacity to minister. Like the Anthropic Principle we discussed in the last part, all our thinking about design must be done with a recog-nition that evolution led to *us*, uniquely novel beings who pray.

Whether evolution is examined through the lens of design

Christianity.' For Newman, in other words, it is not the task of theology to dis-cover a divine designer lurking immediately beneath or behind the data of biology or physics." Haught, *Making Sense of Evolution*, 64.

22. John Haught, *Making Sense of Evolution: Darwin, God, and the Drama of Life* (Louisville: Westminster John Knox, 2010), 58.

or novelty often determines our metaphysics—whether we believe the world is bound in an impersonal or personal order.[23] Similar to cosmology and physics, when we see evolution as the story of how conscious (ministering) life came to be, we are freed from needing a watchmaker, and instead are given a minister, who, through every novel turn, is bringing new life out of death—even the death of dinosaurs.[24]

23. Haught explains further using Teilhard. Taking us full circle in this chapter, he discusses Dennett's own metaphysic. "Toward the end of his life the famous Jesuit paleontologist Teilhard de Chardin (1881-1955) observed that traditional theological reflection has conceived of God's influence on nature too much in terms of Aristotle's notion of a prime mover pushing things from the past (a retro). Evolution, Teilhard said, requires that we think of God not as driving or determining events from behind or from the past, but as drawing the world from up ahead . . . toward the future." John Haught, *God After Darwin: A Theology of Evolution* (Boulder, CO: Westview, 2000), 81. "In the case of Gould and Dennett, both of whose 'scientific' thinking is determined in great measure by an a priori commitment to materialist metaphysics, it is not Teilhard's science that really arouses their disdain, but his demand for an alternative metaphysics. They are disturbed by Teilhard's own 'dangerous idea,' namely, that metaphysical materialism is incompetent to make full sense of the actual discoveries of evolutionary science. . . . What really repels them is Teilhard's suggestion that a metaphysically adequate explanation of any universe in which evolution occurs requires—at some point beyond the limits that science has set for itself—a transcendent force of attraction to explain the overarching tendency of matter to evolve toward life, mind, and spirit." *God After Darwin*, 83.

24. For the interested reader, Alister McGrath provides a discussion of dinosaur mass extinction. "So what caused this mass extinction? How are we to explain this unusual event? It must be immediately conceded that a multiplicity of explanations can be devised, many lying beyond the scope of the scientific method, as strictly interpreted. Most recent work on the K-T extinction has focused on the theory that a meteorite, or even a small asteroid, collided with Earth at this time. The Chicxulub Crater, named after the nearby village of Puerto Chicxulub, is widely regarded as resulting from such a massive bolide collision with Earth. The impact of an item approximately 12.5 miles wide left an egg-shaped crater of between 90 and 125 miles across the undersea Yucatan platform of Mexico. This impact, reckoned to be equivalent to an explosion of 100 million megatons of conventional explosive, would have caused a massive tsunami, with massive expulsion of dust and debris into Earth's atmosphere, possibly preventing photosynthesis from taking place. This vaporized and molten debris, including glass spherules and iridium, would have risen high above the atmosphere to be deposited across the entire globe as it slowly drifted downward. Acid rain might have resulted from the sulfur-rich rock of the impact site. Yet although the evidence for a massive impact on Earth at this time is strong, it is impossible to determine whether it was the cause of the extinction event, or whether it arrived, coincidentally, during an established extinction process. The patterns of extinction cannot all be explained by the impact of a meteorite." Alister McGrath, *A Fine-Tuned Universe: The Quest for God in Science* (Louisville: Westminster John Knox, 2009), 91.

20.

Darwin's Second Dangerous Idea and All Those Other Hominids

It is rare for an academic debate to turn into a Comedy Central roast, with zingers and barbs flying and audiences erupting in laughter. Academic debates tend to be events with intensity and anxiety. It's understandable that sometimes those involved might innocently put words in people's mouths that were never spoken, or recount rebuttals they wish they'd said as if they had. It is more than likely that the details around the most famous English debate of Darwinism wears these marks of exaggeration —but even so, it reveals the unease with Darwin's second supposed dangerous idea.

On the Origin of Species had appeared only seven months earlier. But a section of the British Association for the Advancement of Science was meeting in Oxford to discuss and debate it. Charles, himself, wasn't present. But some other pretty big names were, like Bishop Samuel Wilberforce, Joseph Dalton Hooker (who years earlier had introduced Charles to Asa Gray), and none other than Robert Fitzroy, the skipper of the *Beagle* who had given Charles the opportunity to become the great naturalist he now was. And, of course, the Bulldog, Huxley, was also present. Huxley had actually considered skipping the session but when he heard that Bishop Samuel Wilberforce would be opposing Darwin in the debate, he couldn't resist coming.

Wilberforce was just the kind of man that the Bulldog couldn't stand, a clergyman with an unearned scientific platform, a member of the elite, with proper speech, who, in Huxley's mind, had no real sense of science. The Bulldog's hackles were up around such men.

What actually happened in the debate is debatable.[1] But unequivocally, Wilberforce agitated Huxley and he bit. Whether it was a nip or full-force bite is an open question. But the more dramatic version asserts that in a moment of open discussion, Wilberforce cornered Huxley. Bishop Wilberforce had been doing his best to debunk Darwin, painting the Bulldog into a corner. He asked him with a sneer if it was from his grandfather or grandmother's side that Huxley claimed his descent from monkeys? Supposedly, the Bulldog went for the throat, shooting back like the roastmaster Jeffery Ross, at the man with title and position:[2] "If I had to choose, I would prefer to be a descendant of a humble monkey rather than a man like you!"[3]

1. See David N. Livingstone's "That Huxley Defeated Wilberforce in Their Debate over Evolution and Religion," in Ronald Numbers, *Galileo Goes to Jail: And Other Myths About Science and Religion* (Cambridge, MA: Harvard University Press, 2009). Here Livingstone nicely lays out the myth and how many have used it against religion. I'm using it here only to show the uneasiness with the second dangerous idea.

2. Brooke explains further: "Women were in the audience when T. H. Huxley and Bishop Wilberforce had their encounter at Oxford in 1860. One fainted, according to some reports, and had to be carried out—so tremendous had been the spectacle of a man of God slain by a man of science. The bishop had asked whether Huxley would prefer to think of himself descended from an ape on his grandfather's or his grandmother's side, thereby touching the sensitive nerve of female ancestry. Huxley's retort that he would rather have an ape for an ancestor than a bishop—or words to that effect—has come to symbolize not merely the conflict between Darwinism and the Bible but the victory of science over religion." *Science and Religion*, 55.

3. Actually, even in the dramatic version that more than likely didn't happen. Huxley is reported as saying, "If I had to choose, I would prefer to be a descendant of a humble monkey rather than a man who employs his knowledge and eloquence in misrepresenting those who are wearing out their lives in the search of truth." *Science and Religion*, 55. Other more reliable reports have Huxley's rebuttal as "whether, in the vast shaky state of the law of development, as laid down by Darwin, any one can be so enamoured of this so-called law, or hypothesis, as to go into jubilation for his great great grandfather having been an ape or a gorilla?" or "it was of little consequence to himself whether or not his grandfather might be called a monkey or not."

The crowd erupted, bouncing on their knees, hands over their month, some shouting "Ohhhh" while others yelled "Snap!" Of course, that isn't true. We're not sure how the audience reacted, but we do know that the media found it captivating, and the English public, disconcerting. Was it really possible that we came from apes? Was the bishop's Christian commitment to the *imago Dei* over? It's assumed, now thanks to evolution that there is nothing really unique about human beings. That we are nothing more than apes with alphabets, made more in the image of monkey than of God.

THE DESCENT TO THE APES

Over a decade after the debate, when *The Descent of Man* was released, the implications of *On the Origin of Species* were made explicit. The first of Darwin's dangerous ideas was loose and making its impact. Natural selection provided a clear way (with a certain metaphysic) to have a diverse, adaptive world without the need for a watchmaker. Indeed, the world was no designed timepiece but a bloody battlefield for survival. Asa Gray saw something different in natural selection.[4] And I think it possible that this "something different" was engendered from the experience of ministry, seeing that the kenotic God so personally enters the world that nature itself wears the mark of beautiful newness—life coming out of the impossibility of death. Death, then, is suffered, but so that death is imbued with new possibility. To me this is a way to see an important connection between evolution and the soteriological *telos* of faith.

Yet, we're still left with Darwin's second dangerous idea and the implication of *The Descent of Man* itself. While overall the first dangerous idea is in more direct tension with faith (giving us design without the need for a designer), nevertheless the second is often more disorientating than the first. It is this second

---

4. "Darwin himself, though not a Christian believer, had affirmed that he thought it was perfectly possible for someone to be both a theist and an evolutionist. It was only in the first quarter of the twentieth century that rejection of Darwinian ideas began to grow in fundamentalist Christian circles." John Polkinghorne, *Science and Religion in Quest of Truth* (New Haven: Yale University Press, 2011), 30.

idea that Huxley used as the fangs when Darwin's bulldog bit Wilberforce. The second idea asserts that when following the branches of natural selection we discover that you and I are just well-groomed apes.

This is a dangerous idea because it not only upends our sensibilities, but also implants a "nothing-but" form into our reasoning. Charles himself worried about this, fearing that the implications of *The Descent of Man* could undercut the moral fabric that the church supported and England needed. The neo-Darwinians of today, following more in the footsteps of Huxley than Darwin, find this point delicious, seeing a kind of exhilarating freedom within it. The "science" shows that we can stop all this searching for a personal order, because we are just apes, bound only to a natural impersonal world.[5]

It would be much easier to deny this perspective and call it ideological if the scientific findings didn't so clearly support it. Both the archeological record and genetic testing show that Darwin is right. We are, because of the adaptive jumps, descended from ape-like creatures. Our ancestors, like those of gorillas, are now extinct primates. Huxley was right; we are creatures, and no high culture or technological advance can hide this fact of our embodied, material animal-ness.

But do these scientific finding eliminate the claims of faith, that we are creatures, sure, but unique ones made in the image of God?

We saw that Darwin's first dangerous idea was anything but, when we free ourselves from a metaphysic that peers backward, missing the beauty of novelty and the act of a ministering God who brings life again and again out of death.[6] To see if there is

5. Stenmark explains further: "Evolutionary biologists cannot find any propensities in the organic material they investigate which make the development of human beings likely. Therefore, human life lacks a meaning in the sense that we were planned by God or anything like God to appear in natural history. . . . The argument then seems to be that all biological events taking place in evolutionary history, including the emergence of our species, are random with respect to what evolutionary theory can predict or retrospectively explain. Therefore, there is no ultimate meaning to human life. Humans are not planned by God or anything like God to be here." Mikael Stenmark, *How to Relate Science and Religion* (Grand Rapids, MI: Eerdmans, 2004), 159.

6. "And yet, I am convinced that numerous puzzles that arise in our reflections on evolution will simply fall away as pseudo problems if we situate the Darwinian pic-

overlap between faith and Darwin's second supposed dangerous idea, we must do the same.

MARTIN AND THE DINOSAURS AGAIN

The Bible study *wasn't* supposed to focus on origins. That's not what Tanisha, the senior pastor, had in mind when she set up groups across the generations of the church to connect with her sermon series. But no other group had Martin in it. The more the group dwelt on Martin's questions about dinosaurs and their extinction, the more Jared saw a surprising connection.

Martin kept flipping back and forth, saying things like, "We're just animals, like other animals, so we'll go extinct too—someday—it's just a matter of time. We're nothing special." But then Martin would add later, "But we're really weird animals! We have schools and zoos! Like, even think about a stupid little kids' shows like *Dinosaur Train* on PBS; it's a show where, like, dinosaurs act like humans, living in families, teaching lessons, and telling stories. No other animal does that! We're so weird we make up stories about other animals that act like humans. That's crazy."

It was crazy, and oddly seemed to connect with Lily and Sasha's questions around the Big Bang. When looking into the mass of the universe, as we've said, we're stuck with an either/or. The mass of the universe means that our planet, and the life on it, is meaningless. We're so small and insignificant; how can we matter? This is the unfortunately named Copernicus Principle. But when peering into the mathematics of the fine-tuning of this mass space, we can see something different. We can spot that the Big Bang happened against all odds with just the right temperature, speed, and particle release to create life. This

ture of things within the framework of a theological metaphysics of the future. Why is nature ordered and yet open to disorder? Why doesn't contingency or chance, so prominent in evolution, prevent order from emerging? Why is natural selection so rigorously lawful and yet open to indeterminate new creation? Why does the world have the temporal character that allows evolution to occur at all? These are all questions that remain without answer when we view them through a metaphysics of the eternal present or of the deterministic past. But if we place them within the horizon of the coming of the future, then evolution not only begins to make scientific sense but also—at last—to have 'its own God.'" Haught, *God After Darwin*, 96.

is called the Anthropic Principle. So looking at the mass of space, it depends on where you put your focus—on sheer mass or the life that exists within the mass.[7]

THE SECOND BIG BANG

What Martin seemed to be echoing in his statements is something similar,[8] but this time as it relates to evolution. Darwin's second dangerous idea can be seen in a way similar to the Copernicus or Anthropic principles. Either we are nothing but furless apes or we are uniquely strange animals that sing, pray, love, and hope. Just like with Darwin's first dangerous idea, so with the second, it depends on where you focus.

While at first, reading that last sentence seems deeply apologetic (even pious), as though I'm saying that if you look at the origins of humanity with religious glasses you'll see God. But that's not what I mean. Rather, this debate around where you start is embedded within scientific work itself. For instance, paleontology is a scientific field that seeks to explore ancient plant and animal fossils, getting as far back to the origin of species as possible, giving particular attention to climates. This

7. I'm following Haught with the direction of this chapter. This quote is an important one: "Like it or not, in our big bang universe at least, the evidence shows that since life's beginning almost four billion years ago, evolution has been feeling its way toward more intensely conscious kinds of being. Is this purely by accident or purely by necessity? Or is it the product of the blend of contingency, law, and time that makes nature an adventurous narrative and not a mere succession of states? The biologist will be satisfied—and rightly so, scientifically speaking—to explain the emergence of mind simply as the product of natural selection. But a layered approach to explanation can add that, at another reading level, the dramatic arrival of mind and freedom in life's evolution is due to the non-coercive lure of an infinitely good and wise divine presence completely hidden to Darwinian grammarians." *Making Sense of Evolution*, 77.

8. Mithen explains more what I mean by this "Big Bang," helpfully dating it: "'The big bang of human culture'. We will see that when the first modern humans, Homo sapiens sapiens, appeared 100,000 years ago they seem to have behaved in essentially the same manner as Early Humans, such as Neanderthals. And then, between 60,000 and 30,000 years ago—with no apparent change in brain size, shape or anatomy in general—the cultural explosion occurred. This resulted in such a fundamental change in lifestyles that there can be little doubt that it derived from a major change in the nature of the mind." Steven Mithen, *The Prehistory of the Mind: The Cognitive Origins of Art, Religion and Science* (London: Thames & Hudson, 1996), 15.

attention backward (even hundreds of millions of years before mammals), often leads paleontology to minimize human uniqueness, mainly because the focus is elsewhere.[9]

But another scientific field, paleoanthropology, starts somewhere very different. Its focus is on hominids, seeking to explore the fossil and archeological record for clues on how *homo sapiens* came to be, and why all the other hominids died out. This focus has led some paleoanthropologists to speak of a second Big Bang.[10] Their point is that just like the first Big Bang, which brings what is not into being against great odds, so too the jump from primates and lower hominids to *homo sapiens* is such a cataclysmic leap that it can only be seen as an explosion into uniqueness.[11] It depends on where you look. If you follow paleontology your attention is drawn before this second Big Bang. A paleoanthropologist, however, like a particle physicist, peers directly into the explosion—this time, the eruption of human uniqueness.[12]

9. Ian Tattersall explains: "Most paleontologists seek to uncover and explain the evolutionary histories of diverse groups of organisms; they are looking for the origins of arrays of species. In stark contrast, paleoanthropologists have seen their job essentially as one of tracing the origins of the single species Homo sapiens as far back into the remote past as possible." *Becoming Human: Evolution and Human Uniqueness* (New York: Harcourt Brace, 1998), 88.

10. I'm thinking particularly of Ian Tattersall.

11. Van Huyssteen explains Ian Tattersall's perspective of a Big Bang of uniqueness, giving us some background: "Tattersall also examines chimpanzees and other primates that offer the best comparative models for understanding the cognitive capacities of early hominids. Where Darwin and most neo-Darwinians have held that the anatomical and cognitive traits of modern humans gradually arose in tandem, and faint beginnings would be ascribed to our remote ancestors and greater capacities to our more proximate relatives, Tattersall distances himself from this gradualist position and argues that the emergence of human uniqueness was achieved in one quantum leap. He finds theoretical support for this belief in Stephen Jay Gould and Niles Eldredge's punctuated equilibrium model of hominid evolution. This theory suggests that hominid evolution was punctuated by rapid speciation events, usually caused by dramatic changes in climate or geography, during which groups split from one another, creating new species that might then remain morphologically and behaviorally stable for hundreds and thousands of years." Van Huyssteen, *Alone in the World? Human Uniqueness in Science and Theology* (Grand Rapids, MI: Eerdmans, 2006), 188. Mithen believes something very similar: "There was a cultural explosion in the fourth and final act of our past. This happened in the time period 60,000-30,000 years ago." *The Prehistory of the Mind*, 150.

12. Again, I'm not saying that all paleoanthropologists see it this way. But I am following the likes of Tattersall and Mithen, who do.

Darwin's second dangerous idea, then, is threatening only if we pave over (and somehow ignore) this second Big Bang.[13] What seems to make Darwin's second idea so dangerous is that it relativizes the human being, making us nothing special. On one hand this could be a helpful gift, keeping humanity from the triumphal stance of superiority that I believe is unbiblical, and has had terrible ecological consequences. Darwin's second idea reminds us that we are indeed creatures like all others, bound to the universe. But on the other hand, it quickly leads us to see our uniqueness. As Martin says, no other creature has schools and zoos. Or as the theologian Karl Barth stated, no other animal "tells jokes and smokes"—Barth was a mid-twentieth-century man who loved to think and discuss big ideas over puffs of a pipe.[14] So to see if there might be an overlap between Darwin's second idea and the soteriological *telos* of faith we must peer directly into this second Big Bang.

OUT OF AFRICA

It was the way she walked! It caught everyone's attention, making her uber popular. She got her name from a Beatles song. And she was about the same age as Martin or Tegan when she unfortunately met her demise. But her story didn't end. Actually, it only began 3.2 million years later when paleoanthropologist Donald Johanson dug her up from African soil and named her "Lucy," after the song that had been playing on loop at his excavation site. Lucy became world-famous, proof of one of our earliest ancestors. If Wilberforce had asked Huxley in the 1860s about monkey grandparents after Johanson's finding in the 1970s, Huxley would have a name to give, claiming Lucy's people as his ancient kin.

13. "It is quite easy to think of the Middle/Upper Palaeolithic transition as a cultural explosion, or a big bang—the origins of the universe of human culture. Indeed a 'big bang' is the shorthand description I will use." *The Prehistory of the Mind*, 152.

14. "Barth did appreciate the fact that Titius ended his arguments for human distinctiveness by paralleling Barth's own approach of basing anthropology on Christology, but he quips: 'What a pity that none of these apologists considers it worthy of mention that man is apparently the only being accustomed to laugh and smoke!' (cf. 82f.)." Van Huyssteen, *Alone in the World?*, 136.

But if Huxley had, it would have been as correct as it was confused. It's true that Lucy is proof that we've evolved over millions of years, and in that sense she is our ancestor. But there are light-years between her and us, a chasm as wide as a Big Bang. If you saw Lucy, and not just her bones, you'd be sure you were looking at a primate, a kind of monkey and a particularly slow one.[15] Lucy would have had no name and no story to tell, for what makes Lucy scientifically interesting is that her brain was that of a monkey, small and primitive, but her legs showed that she walked upright, having a gait close to our own.

Lucy is interesting because she walks like us, but she is far from talking like us. We're about three million years and another Big Bang away from jokes and smokes. But Lucy is scientific proof that at some point, in Africa, creatures left the trees for the tall grasses of the savanna, straightening their backs to better see and walk long distances.[16] As years unfold, these creatures continued to adapt to their environments. And they became more sophisticated in the process, using tools, like sticks, eventually with flint spearheads, to hunt. From Africa, groups of early hominids spread across the globe. But if we'd encountered these hominids we'd be sure they were more like Lucy than Martin. Even millions of years after Lucy, the world was still lacking in jokes and smokes.[17]

15. Mithen adds to this point. "Yet such studies have ultimately proved unsatisfactory, because while the chimpanzee is indeed our closest living relative, it is not very close at all. We shared a common ancestor about 6 million years ago. After that date the evolutionary lineages leading to modern apes and humans diverged. A full 6 million years of evolution therefore separates the minds of modern humans and chimpanzees." *The Prehistory of the Mind*, 10.

16. "Historically, then, South Africa will always retain its singular importance as the area from which truly early hominids were first reported; but currently its foremost significance is in providing us with some of the best evidence for hominid species diversity in the period between 3 and 1.5 myr ago." Tattersall, *Becoming Human*, 125.

17. I mean this in two ways. We were far from cultural realities that would allow for agriculture, commerce, and the overall culture to kick back and smoke. Also, it is unlikely that any of these early hominids had mastered fire. It is a debate whether Neanderthals did, or whether fire is a distinctly human activity.

ENTER THE SELF-CONSCIOUS BEINGS

It was only recently, in the last sixty thousand years (if not shorter), that the second Big Bang happened in places like southern Africa and southern Europe. Small little evolutionary pops were occurring, maybe every five hundred thousand to a million years, with groups of hominids. But these were relatedly small, measurable, and next to the passing of time, minuscule. Yet, the measure of evolution is survival. And these small adaptations proved successful. But then out of nowhere—like a massive explosion, metaphorically on a scale with the Big Bang—a whole new strategy was forged, which brought with it joking and smoking animals.

Remember that before the math of Lemaitre and the observations of Hubble, the accepted scientific position was that the universe was eternal, bound in a steady-state. Einstein, unfortunately, fudged his equations to keep spacetime steady.

There is a similar misconception in evolutionary theory. We imagine that adaptation of one species into another happens in a steady-state, slowly but surely mutating through the generations. This concept has led creationists to claim that evolution simply can't be true because the fossil record doesn't show transitions (though it does, but never mind that).[18] Yet, just as the universe is not in a steady-state but continues to explode into newness, not statically being, but always becoming, so evolution happens as explosions, as events (dare we say, revelations) into newness. What this means is that evolution always happens in stops and starts; it is a jerky process, and not a steady unfolding. And more importantly, *only* populations, not individuals, evolve.[19] Evolution is a communal reality, not an individual one.

---

18. "For years paleontologists had been dimly aware that fossil species often appeared to be 'real' in a way that the Synthesis didn't allow. Instead of gradually transforming one into another over the aeons, new species tended to appear suddenly in the geological record and to linger for varying periods of time. When their time was up, they would vanish as abruptly as they had arrived, to be replaced by other species that might or might not be their close relatives. As far back as Darwin, the fossil record's failure to agree with the expectation of gradual change had been explained by its famous incompleteness." Tattersall, *Becoming Human*, 91.

19. "In short, then, individuals don't evolve; populations do. But which populations? In one sense, of course, it is the reproductively cohesive species that constitutes

Like overthrowing the idea of the steady-state of the universe, this view of evolution as explosion into newness opposed what's called the synthesis theory, or the steady, gradual evolving of species.[20]

We now have proof that in the southern tip of Africa, but

the definitive population. But in another—and equally important—sense, species are essentially abstractions. For, as just noted, they usually consist of multiple local populations that occupy a variety of environments—or at least of microenvironments. The critical consequence of this is that evolutionary tendencies within species will not tend to be unidirectional. Rather, such tendencies will be toward divergence, as each local population within the species plows its own adaptive furrow in its own local habitat. And we know for a fact that local populations do routinely develop their own heritable peculiarities, even though it's possible to argue—though I don't recommend it—that in most cases, natural selection is something that we have to assume, rather than something we can know. Only extremely recently, for example, has any direct experimental evidence at all become available to confirm that natural selection does indeed function within populations." Tattersall, *Becoming Human*, 100.

20. In this long footnote, Tattersall explains the Synthesis theory and why it was upended. This provides good background to our discussion. "Long periods of species stability interrupted by brief events of speciation, extinction, and replacement: a very different vision of life history from that of the Synthesis. True, the framers of the Synthesis had scrupulously acknowledged that rates of evolutionary change could vary enormously. But they had ascribed such variation simply to fluctuations in the strength of natural selection. For them, evolutionary change was an essentially continuous process that would promote better adaptation to static environments when it was not producing accommodation to shifting ones. Eldredge, in contrast, was proposing that in the case of his trilobites, speciation had been the basis of evolutionary change, rather than its passive result. The dominant signal he discerned in the fossil record he had so closely examined was one of stability, not of gradual change. And with thousands of specimens to work with, he wasn't prepared to explain away what he saw as the product of an inadequate record. Eldredge may not have fully realized it at the time, but he had set the stage for paleontologists of all stripes to go back to their fossil data and to rethink their views of the evolutionary process." Tattersall, *Becoming Human*, 93. Tattersall continues: "Eldredge and Gould were, in fact, proposing that evolution is not a gradual process, but rather one that proceeds by fits and starts ('evolution by jerks,' as an unkind early critic put it). Species, far from being nothing more than arbitrarily defined segments of lineages, are real entities. Like individuals, they have births (at speciation), life spans (of greater varying lengths, but unmarked by significant change), and deaths (at extinction). What's more, on the wider evolutionary stage, species play a role similar to the one envisaged for individuals in traditional Darwinian theory. Species can become extinct for many reasons, including being outcompeted by other species, among them their own descendants: in other words, just as individuals vary in their ability to compete with each other, so do species. Trends in the fossil record—such as human brain-size increase with time—are often cited as evidence for gradual, directional change; but it is in fact much more probable that trends result from the winnowing of species by competition among them, than from directional selection within lineages." *Becoming Human*, 94.

more conclusively in southern Europe, a population, a community of hominids exploded onto the scene with an all-new strategy and capacity. With abilities never seen before, these new beings could actually *think about thinking*. Like an event that came out of nowhere, they appear to jump the track of other hominids and become distinct, unique animals with adaptable minds.[21]

These beings are light-years different than Lucy. Huxley would be right to claim Lucy as a relative, but this would be like claiming gases pre–Big Bang as a relative to the universe. Of course, it is true that pre-Bang gases are the universe's antecedent, but to equate one with the other is to miss the incredible unique singularity of spacetime itself. Hydrogen is essential to getting us spacetime, but it is not spacetime, just as Lucy is essential to getting us conscious human beings, but her mind was far from *homo sapiens*.

THE SMOKING GUN PICTURES
OF UNIQUENESS

The scientific smoking gun of this uniqueness, the visual evidence of this second Big Bang, are the cave drawings in Southern France and Spain. Deep inside these caverns are 35,000-year-old drawings of stags, buffalo, and birds.

So what? We might ask at first glance. Any four-year-old can draw a picture. Never mind that these paintings display sophisticated artistic ability; the very fact that a four-year-old can draw animals is amazing. That makes a human four-year-old a creature like no other. To draw a picture takes the unique ability to hold something in your mind, flip, twist, and then represent it in a medium disconnected from the context of your original witness of it. Wentzel van Huyssteen writes, "More than simple, decorative pictures, these paintings were gateways to the

21. "In fact, if there is one single thing that distinguishes humans from all other life-forms, living or extinct, it is the capacity for symbolic thought, the ability to generate complex mental symbols and to manipulate them into new combinations. Tattersall correctly argues that this is the very foundation of imagination and creativity, of the unique ability of humans to create a world in the mind and then re-create it in the real world outside themselves." Van Huyssteen, *Alone in the World?*, 190.

spirit world, panoramas that, in their trance experience, shamans could enter and with which their own projected mental imagery could mingle in three animated dimensions."[22] This is a mental capacity, a form of consciousness that no other animal (living or extinct) has even been close to possessing. No other animal can extend their consciousness across spacetime.

This is exactly what inspired the Anthropic Principle, the fact that there are beings in the world with extended consciousness, who are able to discover the size of the universe, as well as theorems and equations to describe it. The universe existed for billions of years, the earth 4 billion, and complex life on earth hundreds of million years until, just a very short 35,000 years ago, a Big Bang of consciousness exploded into existence. "For the first time," as Polkinghorne says, "the universe became conscious of itself." Suddenly there were minds able to think about thinking, to extend and share the mind of what they were not.[23] Or as paleoanthropologists say, for millions of years we get the smallest of advances in hominid innovation. For instance, "after the initial appearance of the hand axe at 1.4 million years ago, we have a single major technical innovation at around 250,000 years ago with the appearance of a new production technique called the Levallois method."[24] That's it! But then, BANG, a small community explodes and within tens of thousands of years (an incredibly short time) we get language, art, religion, agriculture, cathedrals, governments, Paris fashion season, cars, and HBO (streaming!). Darwin and Huxley are right: we are the descendants of Lucy. But we can only name her Lucy and give her a story, writing a book like *The Descent of Man* or angrily pointing our finger at a bishop in debate, because we are

---

22. Van Huyssteen, *Alone in the World?*, 209.

23. Tattersall makes a bold statement here for a scientist, a statement I'm trying to highlight for theological purposes: "For if the last chapter established anything at all, it showed that with the arrival of behaviorally modern Homo sapiens, a totally unprecedented entity had appeared on Earth. For the first time since the adoption of upright walking—or perhaps stone tool-making—a new kind of hominid was around of which it could not be said that it merely did what its predecessors had done, only a little better, or even just a little differently. Homo sapiens is not simply an improved version of its ancestors—it's a new concept, qualitatively distinct from them in highly significant if limited respects." *Becoming Human*, 188.

24. Mithen, *The Prehistory of the Mind*, 116.

the unique animals that have minds for joking and smoking. In other words, because we have minds for the divine.

WHAT ABOUT GOD?

Nearly every paleoanthropologist agrees that whatever else the earliest *homo sapiens* had their minds on, clearly it was God, spirits, or the transcendent.[25] The paintings in the caves were used in worship, and burial sites show sophisticated views of the afterlife. Paleoanthropologist Steven Mithen has constructed an interesting theory on the evolution of the *homo sapiens* mind. Mithen compares the mind of *Neanderthals* with those of early *homo sapiens.* This is interesting because *Neanderthals* are agreed to be closest in hominid genus to us. But when paleoanthropologists explore *Neanderthals* and their ancient environments, it is clear that there is a world, a Big Bang, of difference between them and us.[26] Mithen shows, from the archeological records, that though the *Neanderthals* had an environmental intelligence, they lacked a fluidity in their thought.[27] Unlike *homo sapiens,*

25. "Among all those organisms that we can study in the world today, it appears that only modern human beings show 'spiritual self-awareness' in William James's sense; and even his 'social self-awareness' appears to differ dramatically in quality between humans and nonhuman primates." Ian Tattersall, "Origin of the Human Sense of Self," in Wentzel van Huyssteen and Eric Wiebe, *In Search of Self: Interdisciplinary Perspectives on Personhood* (Grand Rapids, MI: Eerdmans, 2011), 39.

26. "During the Upper Paleolithic transition, which in Western Europe lies between 45,000 and 35,000 years ago, the Neanderthals gave way to Homo sapiens, with the two forms living side by side, at least in some areas, for some thousands of years. This transition clearly was an immensely important period in the human story: it is during this time that human consciousness and intelligence emerged, and with it creative, artistic, and religious imagination. For this reason this important period is also called the Upper Paleolithic Revolution or the 'Creative Explosion.' What clearly emerged in the Upper Paleolithic was a distinct morphological gulf between the Neanderthals and the Upper Paleolithic people. The most recent version of the Out of Africa hypothesis will pick up on this important issue and not require that Neanderthals evolved into Upper Paleolithic or Cro-Magnon people." Van Huyssteen, *Alone in the World?*, 64.

27. But none of this is to belittle the Neanderthals. As Tattersall nicely says, "It is, of course, profoundly misleading to see the Neanderthals simply as an inferior version of Homo sapiens, for there are many ways to play the evolutionary game, and the Neanderthals played to a different set of rules. With changing circumstances, their rules eventually let them down—as ultimately could ours." *Becoming Human,* 166.

they lived in much smaller pods. And while they buried their dead, they did so with no ritual,[28] had no art, and, it appears, no sense of any transcendent quality to existence.[29]

Yet in sheer volume, *Neanderthal* brains were bigger than ours. "Although the *Neanderthals* (200,000–30,000 years ago) had brains as large as ours today, their culture remained extremely limited—no art, no complex technology and most probably no religious behavior."[30] Mithen explains that minds are structured with modes, or zones, of expertise. These modes come to us through the stops and starts of evolution. For instance, *Neanderthals* and tigers have mental modals for recognizing weather patterns and tracking prey. But these expertises are instinctual (nonreflective), given by evolution. What Mithen explains is that what is experienced in one mode is locked forever in that mode.

What makes *homo sapiens* unique is that the modes of our mind are fluid. Using the analogy of cathedrals, Mithen explains that other animals' minds, even other hominids, are structured like an ancient cathedral. The walls between rooms are thick and what happens in one room stays in that room. But the *homo sapiens* mind, while smaller in gray matter, is structured not like a fifth- but a sixteenth-century cathedral.[31] There are windows between modes, allowing experiences in one mode to inform experiences in another.[32] For instance, *Neanderthals* might see

28. "What's more, it's far from clear that Neanderthal burial ever involved the sort of ritual that is invariably associated with this practice among modern human populations—and which, as we saw in the first chapter, is so dramatically evident in many burials of the Upper Paleolithic." *Becoming Human*, 161.

29. "Most Neanderthal sites are small (or if large, consist of numerous small successive living spaces, implying quite severely limited group size at any one time); Cro-Magnon sites embrace a much larger range of sizes, suggesting that, at least seasonally, much larger groups assembled." *Becoming Human*, 178.

30. Mithen, *The Prehistory of the Mind*, 11.

31. Mithen explains further: "With regard to our cathedral of the mind analogy, consciousness was firmly trapped within the thick and heavy chapel walls of social intelligence—it could not be 'heard' in the rest of the cathedral except in a heavily muffled form. As a consequence, we must conclude that Neanderthals had no conscious awareness of the cognitive processes they used in the domains of technical and natural history intelligence." *The Prehistory of the Mind*, 147.

32. "My explanation of the big bang of human culture is that this is when the final major re-design of the mind took place. It is when the doors and windows were

fire in the forest after a lightning strike, know it is hot and its smoke harsh, and have the mind to avoid it.[33] The *homo sapiens* has the same evolutionarily imposed instincts, but her fluid mind leads her to wonder, *what if?* Extending her mind to feel again what it is like to be cold at night, her mind runs fluid and she sees what the *Neanderthal* has no mind to see, that this fire is more than a threat; it might also be an opportunity.

Her fluid mind makes her a great problem solver, but it also does something else. It pushes her to seek meaning, to both contemplate and experience transcendence. She is the first animal that jokes because her mind is fluid enough to share in other minds. Teasing these other minds, she plays with language, allowing her mind to fluidly enter another's, recognizing what is funny. It takes a fluid mind beyond pure instinct to have a sense (a mind) for humor.

Yet, her mind is open to something more than humor. Now that she can think across modes she sees connections and causes, her eyes are open to encounter mystery. She can contemplate the meaning of existence. She can now hear a word whispering through the universe. A personal force seems behind all things, beckoning to her to receive and give ministry to her neighbor and to the earth she inhabits. She now has a mind for personhood, for the *hypostatic*, to laugh and love with others as they together contemplate, in prayer and worship, the mystery of the universe.

No other animal does this!

---

inserted in the chapel walls, or perhaps when a new 'superchapel' was constructed." *The Prehistory of the Mind*, 153.

33. It is a debate within paleoanthropology if Neanderthals had mastered fire. Some believe that ancient sites prove they did. Others think that these sites were actually early *homo sapiens* locations that Neanderthals raided and inhabited. "Clearly, the mastery of fire was a major event in human prehistory, carrying with it symbolic overtones as well as practical consequences in terms of protection against predators, cooking of food, and so forth. Certainly, it cannot fail to evoke echoes of humanity. The trouble is that these isolated cases fall a million years or thereabouts before we have any concrete evidence of the control of fire in hearths, so it is difficult to know exactly what to make of them. Milestone tools, once invented, rapidly became a regular part of the hominid repertoire, fire use seems to have been rather intermittent until quite a late stage." Tattersall, *Becoming Human*, 140.

THE *IMAGO DEI*

The theological tradition has thought of the *imago Dei* (the image of God) as an essential piece of faith's soteriological *telos*. So while we can see that Darwin's second dangerous idea is anything but dangerous, if examined through the Big Bang of human uniqueness, we must still ask, How does this connect to the image of God?

There have been three common ways to think about the *imago Dei*. It has been described as substantive, functional, or relational. The substantive position asserts that the image of God is bound in capacities, like reason, rationality, and intellect. We are made in the image of God because we have these abilities and other animals do not. Others have argued that the image of God is bound to functions. With these unique capacities we are to be God's representatives in the universe. Like in Game of Thrones, we human beings are the "Hand of the King," able to have dominion (power and rule) over the world because we bear the image. Finding this second position domineering, others have seen the imago as relational. This third position asserts that the image of God has nothing to do, necessarily, with capacities or functions, but is about relationship. We are made in the image of God because God simply elects us to be the creatures who are persons—able to be in person-to-person relationships—most directly with God. We are the unique creatures that recognize the personal order, and in turn, respond to it in prayer and worship.

None of these perspectives are undercut by the scientific findings of evolution or Darwin's second idea, that we descend from primates. As a matter of fact, following the scientific theories, there is a way of holding all three of these positions together, seeing them not as opposed but interconnected.

For example, scientist Michael Tomasello, in his book *A Natural History of Human Thinking*, seeks to explore the evolutionary origins of language. He shows through studies with great apes that they simply lack the minds for gesture-reading.[34] They have

34. "And so, the first step in our natural history of uniquely human thinking is the cognitive mechanisms of joint intentionality that evolved to coordinate humans' ear-

the intelligence, and can be taught that when you see a pointed finger,[35] don't look at the finger but the thing the finger is pointing to, but they have no innate hardwiring for doing so.[36] Human beings, on the other hand, are different. We read complicated gestures, like facial expressions, within months of our birth.[37] We innately seek the fluid act of entering the mind of others.[38] Even as babies, our survival mechanism is profound.[39]

liest species-unique forms of small-scale collaboration and, later, cooperative communication." Michael Tomasello, *A Natural History of Human Thinking* (Cambridge, MA: Harvard University Press, 2014), 38.

35. Justin Barrett says something similar: "Some of these foundations are rare or even entirely absent in other species. Consider declarative pointing—gesturing to direct another's attention. It might be that no other animal naturally produces such behaviors or is naturally sensitive to them. Even chimpanzees, very clever social animals, do not appear to use declarative pointing and require enormous socialization by humans to even begin to follow the pointing gesture to a target instead of merely looking at the pointer's fingertip. Similarly, humans make distinctively heavy use of eye-gaze to anticipate the actions of another or even to infer mental states: if someone looks at that object in a sustained manner, she might want it. Other social animals naturally shy away from looking each other in the eyes." Justin Barrett, *Cognitive Science, Religion and Theology: From Human Minds to Divine Mind* (West Conshohocken, PA: Templeton Press, 2011), 75.

36. "Apes follow the human's pointing and looking to the bucket, but then they do not make the seemingly straightforward inference that the human is directing their attention there because he thinks it is somehow relevant to their current search for the food. They do not make this relevant inference because it does not occur to them that the human is trying to inform them helpfully—since ape communication is always directive—and this means that they are totally uninterested in why the human is pointing to one of the boring buckets." Tomasello, *A Natural History of Human Thinking*, 52.

37. "Young children begin engaging with others in ways that suggest some form of joint goal from around fourteen to eighteen months of age, when they are still mostly pre-linguistic. Thus, Warneken et al. (2006, 2007) had infants of this age engage in a joint activity with an adult, such as obtaining a toy by each operating one side of an apparatus. Then, the adult simply stopped playing her role for no reason. The children were not happy about this and did various things to attempt to reengage their partner. (They did not do this if her stopping was for a good reason; e.g., she had to attend to something else.) Interesting, when this same situation was arranged for human-raised chimpanzees, they simply ignored the recalcitrant partner and tried to find ways to achieve the goal on their own." Tomasello, *A Natural History of Human Thinking*, 39.

38. "In general, humans are able to coordinate with others, in a way that other primates seemingly are not, to form a 'we' that acts as a kind of plural agent to create everything from a collaborative hunting party to a cultural institution." Tomasello, *A Natural History of Human Thinking*, 3.

39. Mithen adds, "There is indeed evidence in the fossil record that child development of Modern Humans is considerably longer than that of Early Humans. This

We seek a spiritual interconnection with our caregiver, a beckoning for our mother to minister to us, with the promise spoken in looks and gestures of closeness and admiration, that we will minister back to her by loving and needing her.

Building on this ability to read gestures, Tomasello shows how uniquely human beings cooperate—reminding us that it is odd how intuitively we trust each other to give good information, for instance when we ask for directions.[40] To see gestures as meaningful there needs to be a deep presumption that the information the other is giving you is trustworthy and valuable. Tomasello explains that this cooperative form of communication just happens nowhere else in the natural realm. Human beings have their uniqueness in their ability to share each other's mind, to seek out minds and give our mind to other minds.

The capacities for reason and rationality are bound in the unique relational connection of cooperation (they are born from the relational). Tomasello even argues that early humans selected not for traits that would allow for pure survival (strength and sexual attraction), but for kindness. We chose relational connection, minds fluidly able to enter another's mind and love them, over muscle, height, and perfect jawlines. Following Tomasello, we can wonder if the very particles of the second big bang into human uniqueness are the personal realities of kindness, compassion, and empathy. From an evolutionary perspective, what allows for *homo sapiens* to jump into a radical uniqueness is a

comes in the form of the skeletal remains of the few Neanderthal children that exist. These show that Neanderthal children grew up rather quickly, developing robust limbs and a large brain at an early age compared with Modern Humans." *The Prehistory of the Mind*, 193.

40. "For example, humans but not apes engage in cooperative childcare in which all adults do all kinds of things to support developing children (so-called cooperative breeding; Hrdy, 2009). Humans but not apes engage in cooperative communication in which they provide one another with information that they judge to be useful for the recipient. Humans but not apes actively teach one another things helpfully, again for the benefit of the recipient. Humans but not apes make group decisions about group-relevant matters. And humans but not apes create and maintain all kinds of formal social structures such as social norms and institutions and even conventional languages (using agreed-upon means of expression). In all, cooperation is simply a defining feature of human societies in a way that it is not for the societies of the other great apes." Tomasello, *A Natural History of Human Thinking*, 36.

profound choice for connection and togetherness over strength (or as a new form of strength bond in chosen weakness).

In other words, the "relational" understanding of *imago Dei* is right; we have our uniqueness, as evolution says, in our interactions, in our sharing-in one another.[41] We are made in the image of God because the action of God through evolution has made us into embodied *hypostatic* beings. We are persons who want nothing more than to be heard, seen, known, and loved. We have minds forged through the act of God in the second big bang for sharing in the personal. Evolution doesn't oppose this distinct relational/personal reality, but shows how unique it is. We are the strangest of beings who choose kindness, love, mercy, cooperation, and togetherness.

And so, the "substantive" position of image is also accurate. We have the capacities for reason, rationality, and intellect. But these abilities are born from and serve the relational (from the *hypostatic*). We can think about causality, order, and more, because we took the evolutionary jump to seek the personal.[42] Having learned to extend our minds to one another through gestures, trusted communication, and cooperation, our minds became so fluid that, like an echo, we began to hear the mysterious personal reverberations in the universe.[43] We are the only creatures with rationality and reason, but only because we are the creatures who most radically choose weakness over strength,

41. "Humans have created genuine evolutionary novelties via new forms of cooperation, supported and extended by new forms of communication. Further, this has led to new forms of cognitive representation, inference, and self-monitoring together constituting new forms of thinking. And humans have done this twice, the second step building on the first. . . ." Tomasello, *A Natural History of Human Thinking*, 141.

42. This cooperative, hypostatic reality is even seen by more reductionistic scientists. Mithen explains: "To address this question we must return to the issue of consciousness. In this book I am following Nicholas Humphrey's argument that consciousness evolved as a cognitive trick to allow an individual to predict the social behavior of other members of his or her group. Humphrey suggested that it evolved to enable us to use our minds as models for those of other people. At some stage in our evolutionary past we became able to interrogate our own thoughts and feelings, asking ourselves how we would behave in some imagined situation. In other words, consciousness evolved as part of social intelligence." *The Prehistory of the Mind*, 147.

43. This is to give affirmation to Pannenberg's exocentricity. See Wolfhart Pannenberg, *Anthropology in Theological Perspective* (Philadelphia: Westminster, 1985).

deciding or being directed to choose sharing (the *hypostatic*) over immediate survival.

The image of God in us isn't something different than animal; we are animals. But, uniquely, the image is seen in that we are the animals who choose to survive by becoming weak, and binding our being together, creating narratives and moral codes from substantive capacities to fortify relational bonds.

This gives the image of God in us a "function," making it also an accurate way of seeing the *imago Dei*. Yet, its function is directed toward one another and the universe itself. Being the evolutionary creatures that uniquely (and maybe singularly) choose weakness for the sake of togetherness, we are called to be ministers.[44] God is a minister, and because we are in God's image, we are called to receive and give ministry.

The evolution of human animals reflects the *kenotic* nature of God. Just as God humbles Godself to create what is not God, so that God (as the three *hypostases* in one *ousia*) can minister to another, so we human beings, through the *kenotic* evolutionary act of choosing kindness and cooperation (supposedly weaker traits), are called to be ministers. We are in the image of God because our very species wears the *kenotic* marks of the being of God, through the act of God.[45] And having heard the call of this personal God through the relational (*hypostatic*) act of sharing in

44. It is possible that other animals too choose weakness for survival. We can think of forms of empathy and altruism in certain species (see Frans de Waal's *The Age of Empathy*). But what is interesting is that finding empathy and altruism in animals is a challenge to evolution. Yet, even if my statement above isn't right that we are *the only* species that chooses weakness, it does seem clear that we have most radically (and rationally) done so.

45. Unfortunately, I don't have the space to develop it, but I think there is much in Pannenberg's position of exocentricity of the image. I believe we are ministers because of this exocentric reality. Van Huyssteen discusses Pannenberg for the interested reader (see Pannenberg's *Anthropology in Theological Perspective*). "Pannenberg finds in this exocentricity a profound distinction between animals and humans: the 'openness to the world' we share as humans differs not only in degree but also in kind from the 'bondage of animals to [their] environment.' Exocentricity thus means that humans are always open beyond every experience and beyond any given situation, in fact beyond the world itself. We are even open beyond our own cultural constructions: as we transform nature into culture, and constantly replace earlier forms of culture with new ones, we are also open beyond culture to the future, and to finding our ultimate destiny in the future. This restlessness of human nature forms an important root for all religious life." *Alone in the World?*, 140.

the life of others, we are bestowed with reason and rationality, and sent to reflect a ministering God by being the unique animals that are ministers.

FRANCIS COLLINS

If there's a contemporary spokesperson for the overlap of evolution and faith in the US, it's been Francis Collins. Collins is the presidentially appointed director of the National Institute of Health, but is more famously known for leading the efforts to map the human genome. Darwin had no sense of the intricacy of genetics when he sketched out his two big ideas. But since the time of Darwin's theory, genetics has shown him to be largely right. However, the deeper that Collins delved into the genetic coding of our species, the more the commitments of faith spoke to him.

Collins explains that as a young man he thought of himself as an agnostic, ironically a label coined by the Bulldog himself. By agnostic Collins meant that he wasn't sure if there was a God, and didn't really care to think much more about it. What he did care to contemplate was physical chemistry, as he delved into his PhD program at Yale. In the middle of his program, on a lark, he decided to take a course on biochemistry (who hasn't done that!). It was in this course that he was first introduced to DNA, RNA, and protein. And he learned about genetic codes, discovering the new methods for splicing DNA fragments.

Since his youth Collins had been a math nerd, not much different than Einstein, Galileo, and Lemaitre. But, while these epic thinkers saw mathematical elegance in cosmological space, time and motion, through the new study of genetic codes, Collins saw a mathematical grace in biology. Just as there was order, beauty, and novelty in physics, so too in genetic biology. It was an experience of mystery, and one that upended Collins's life.

Finishing his PhD program, instead of taking offers to be a new professor, he applied to med school. The elegance of DNA was a siren's song he needed to follow. Thirty years later, he was decoding the whole of the human genome and being lauded by presidents and dignitaries. Collins more than anyone else could point to a beauty in biology, an order that promised newness out of death. While Darwin saw nature as only red in tooth and claw, Collins saw beneath the battle for resources and into the splendor of genetic patterns.

But while mysterious, math wasn't what moved him to become a world-renowned scientist. Rather, it was ministry.

Collins had pivoted from professor to med student so he could continue to explore genetics. But while his desire was to be in the lab, the required work with patients, and caring for those patients changed him. Standing next to their beds as they died, reaching out to those they loved, finding meaning, hope, and strength in prayer, ministered to Collins. He had a *hypostatic* encounter. Being their doctor and hearing their stories drew him into the personal order of the universe. Their action of ministering to him, and his action of ministering to them, moved the agnostic into the disciple.

Collins now needed to decode and map the human genome, not for the sake of science alone, but for ministry, to participate in the newness coming from death. Genetics made clear that Darwin's ideas were largely right, but when he examined them through the prism of ministry, Collins saw no threat to faith. Instead he saw how this ministering God not only created in the beginning, but continues to create as a minister who promises a coming world where death is no more and creation full and free. Evolution is no threat to the soteriological commitment of faith, because for this God to live and act as minister, this God must be continually creating. Darwin's ideas provide a witness to how God ministers life out of death through a continued creation.[46]

46. Collins tells another beautiful story of ministry in his book which is worth footnoting. Discussing a trip as a Doctor Without Borders, he explains an encounter with a patient after feeling like he hadn't done enough. He says, "With those discouraging thoughts in my head, I approached his bedside the next morning, finding him reading his Bible. He looked at me quizzically, and asked whether I had worked at the hospital for a long time. I admitted that I was new, feeling somewhat irritated and embarrassed that it had been so easy for him to figure that out. But then this young Nigerian farmer, just about as different from me in culture, experience, and ancestry as any two humans could be, spoke the words that will forever be emblazoned in my mind: 'I get the sense you are wondering why you came here,' he said. 'I have an answer for you. You came here for one reason. You came here for me.' I was stunned. Stunned that he could see so clearly into my heart, but even more stunned at the words he was speaking. I had plunged a needle close to

But before we can wrap this all up, we have a problem. While evolution might help us understand God's continued creation, how do we deal with God's original creation in scripture, and the radically different accounts of this original creation presented in evolution and the Bible?

his heart; he had directly impaled mine. With a few simple words he had put my grandiose dreams of being the great white doctor, healing the African millions, to shame. He was right. We are each called to reach out to others. On rare occasions that can happen on a grand scale. But most of the time it happens in simple acts of kindness of one person to another. Those are the events that really matter. The tears of relief that blurred my vision as I digested his words stemmed from indescribable reassurance—reassurance that there in that strange place for just that one moment, I was in harmony with God's will, bonded together with this young man in a most unlikely but marvelous way." *The Language of God: A Scientist Presents Evidence for Belief* (New York: Free Press, 2006), 217.

21.

The Bible, the Ministers, and the End

It was odd that Gus wasn't already there. He was notorious for being earnest and early, and always toting a Bible.

Gus was the church's pastoral assistant. He'd been a solo pastor for more than forty years, and was well known and respected in the denomination. After retirement, Gus and his wife decided to move across the country to be closer to their daughter. When Tanisha heard that Gus had made this move into her community, she asked him to come aboard her church staff in a very part-time capacity, working a handful of hours a week with some specialized ministries. Gus jumped at the opportunity, calling retirement "a prison of boredom." Gus was high energy with an old-school bent. Jared like him. So when Gus suggested the two of them meet weekly to prep the cross-generational Bible studies on Genesis, Jared was all for it. It seemed a particularly interesting opportunity because Gus was working with the over-sixties group. It would be a fascinating chance to find ways of connecting, at least in content, kids like Martin with those over sixty.

This was the third time they'd met at one of the Starbucks in town. There were actually three of them in their mid-sized suburb, making it always a chore to make sure people were clear about the correct rendezvous spot. Gus and Jared had decided to meet up and prep at the biggest one, just blocks from Gus's house. Everyone called it the Star-Ship, not only because it was the largest Starbucks, but also because their chairs looked straight Sci-Fi. It was nothing like The Rusty Spoon; corporate and polished, it lacked all the rough edges.

The first two meetings, by the time Jared arrived, Gus was already on his third cup of coffee with the table in front of him covered in notepads and commentaries. But this time, no Gus. Jared surveyed the room again, shocked by his absence. He looked into every corner, trying to spot a man who looked like the love child of Larry David and Yoda.

On his third scope, Jared saw *her*, sitting quietly in a chair working on her laptop. It was Sarah. Since hearing about her firing, Jared had been thinking about her and praying for her. Maybe this was his excuse. Before he could change his mind, he found himself approaching her. Dipping his head toward her, Jared interrupted with a friendly, "Sarah?"

Startled, Sarah looked up quickly, moving her attention from her computer back to the coffee shop, like awaking from a dream "Jared!"

"Yeah," Jared said, relieved to know that she remembered who he was.

"How are you?" Sarah asked, the standard question.

"I'm okay," Jared said, now remembering why he'd approached her in the first place. "But how are you? I heard things got ugly . . ."

"Oh, you could say that," Sarah said.

"I'm sorry about that."

"So am I."

"Ugly it was," Jared heard proclaimed over his shoulder as if a statement from the great Oz.

Sarah's hard exterior melted when she saw Gus hanging over Jared's shoulder.

"Do you two know each other?" Jared asked with deep surprise.

"Of course; we go way back!" Gus said with his typical hyperbolic energy.

Sarah smiled, and nodded her head. "Actually, we met a few years back. Gus was important in getting my *former* church to move me to full-time. And since my termination, Gus has been

THE BIBLE, THE MINISTERS, AND THE END

meeting with me, helping me pick up the pieces. That's how I found this lovely place," Sarah added with sarcasm.

"What?" Gus said. "I thought I'd just found someone to buy an old man free coffee!"

"Stop!" Sarah said with sad appreciative eyes. "If it weren't for you . . . well, I'm not sure how I'd have made it."

"Well, we've learned a lot together," Gus said. Jared picked up on the ministry in his use of the word "we."

"Yeah, we have," Sarah said with irreverent self-deprecation, "We've learned to be very careful with the Bible."

"What do you mean?" Jared asked.

"I learned too late that the pastor was a concordist and I'm a nonconcordist," Sarah said.[1]

"What?"

"Yeah, those are words that Gus taught me," Sarah said. Gus just shrugged his shoulders and raised his eyes in an "oh gosh" manner.

Sarah continued. "For my former boss, everything in science had to *concord* with Genesis. For me on the other hand, the Bible is truth, and it has complete authority in telling us who God is and how God acts. But it isn't a science book, and doesn't need to be in concord when it comes to science."

"Right," Jared said.

"Well," Gus added, "the church leadership didn't see it that way. They actually said that Sarah was terminated for undercutting the authority of the Bible."

"Yep," said Sarah. "Particularly the senior pastor. He said my view got rid of a historical Adam and minimized sin. And when sin is minimized the gospel is destroyed. So the denomination was told—my paperwork actually says—that I was terminated for 'heresy and corruption of the gospel.' Meaning, I'll never work in this denomination again. I've had three uncles who were pastors in this denomination—one of them went to seminary with

---

1. "In the concordist view God made the earth using the sequence of events described in Genesis 1. . . . According to a nonconcordist view God created the earth using a different timing and order of events than those described Genesis 1." Deborah Haarsma and Loren Haarsma, *Origins: Christian Perspectives on Creation, Evolution, and Intelligent Design* (Grand Rapids, MI: Faith Alive, 2011), 98.

Gus—that's how we met. But now I'll never be welcome there again."

"Wow!" Jared responded. "That's harsh!"

"And painful," Sarah said.

The three of them were silent for a few beats, allowing the heaviness of Sarah's experience to impact them.

"But enough of that!" Sarah said. "What are you guys doing here?"

Almost paralyzed by the irony, Jared said in a low voice, "Preparing for a Bible study . . ."

"On Genesis 1 to 3," Gus added loudly with a smile and a wink.

Sarah cracked up. "Well, watch out!"

SEVERED EARS AND STILL BIBLES

It's all in the colors. Actually it's all in how the unique strokes make the colors pop. They're some of the greatest paintings ever made, but they're as much science as they are art. Vincent Van Gogh is often known as the tortured artist who, after a fight with this hero, Paul Gauguin, cut off his ear and gave it to a prostitute. It's all Quentin Tarantino, before Quentin Tarantino. But what made Van Gogh a genius wasn't necessarily the madness, but like Einstein his infatuation with light. While Einstein looked for equations through thought experiments to find the mystery of light, Van Gogh experimented with colors, pigments, and three-dimensional brushstrokes. He made landscapes that, when standing at the right distance, made you sure sunlight was coming straight through the branches of a tree.

Van Gogh inherited a world after Darwin. Born in the mid-nineteenth century, the opinions of Huxley and others were in the air as he came of age. These new scientific findings were leading some to free themselves from the authority of the Bible—but not the young Van Gogh—not yet at least.

Van Gogh was the son of a pastor, and into his young adulthood a devout and pious believer. But by 1885, things began to change. Just three years after Darwin's death, Van Gogh's own father died. It was March, and the heaviness of the loss led the unknown painter to reflect on the many tense and unhappy moments he'd had with the man. In October of the same year, he sat down and painted, in a mere day, a piece titled *Still Life with Bible.*

In the center of the painting, almost taking up the whole canvas is a large leather-bound Bible, open to Isaiah 53. It speaks of the suffering servant, part of the text saying "a man of sorrows and acquainted with grief . . . he was despised and we esteemed him not." Was Van Gogh referring to Jesus, himself, or his father? We're not sure. But what is clear is that the Bible sits prominently on the table with a candlestick behind it, open to be read.

But below it, and a quarter of its size, is another book. The Bible is too bulky for living with, too heavy to help, but this little book looks made to carry and take into life. Its cover is worn and the binding bent from numerous reads. The book is, actually, Emile Zola's *La joie de vivre.* It's a French novel based in Paris, in which the characters confront the meaninglessness of life and seek significance. Van Gogh, clearly a big fan, wrote to his sister about the book. "If one wants truth," he wrote, "life as it is . . . *La joie de vivre* . . . paint[s] life as we feel it ourselves and thus satisfy that need which we have, that people tell us the truth."

Van Gogh is contrasting the Bible, which weighs so large in his own story, to a modern French novel. The Bible might be big, but it is unworn by life and heaps only sorrow on people. In contrast, this novel speaks the truth. It is useful and its worn corners and creased pages prove that it has a new authority to help us live. Some art historians say Van Gogh asserted that *La joie de vivre* was the Bible for the future. It possessed the truth and authority to help modern people. Or as another art historian says, "In Zola's book it can be argued that Van Gogh was depicting the antithesis of his father's Bible. A fresh and modern way of perceiving the world realistically, rather than the Bible which Van Gogh felt caused 'despair and indignation.' To Van Gogh the Bible was looking backward while modern works by

Zola and other writers he admired looked forward in inventive, new ways."[2]

Between Galileo and Van Gogh a transition happened. Galileo wasn't the first to claim that the Bible was authoritative and trustworthy on subjects of God and salvation, but no scientific treatise.[3] Few said it as elegantly as Galileo, when he asserted, "The Bible told us how to go to heaven, not how the heavens go." Remember, Galileo Galilei was the Steve Jobs of the seventeenth century.[4] But while Galileo wasn't the first to make this distinction, the scientific revolution he helped birth did provide for the unique possibility that someone like Van Gogh could someday discard the Bible, questioning its authority, and seeing a Parisian novel as holding more veracity. The fear of discarding the Bible is what worries most parents and youth pastors about engagement with the scientific. They are scared it will lead young people to cut the Bible out of their lives, like Van Gogh did his ear. So, as much we can take on a new perspective on Darwin's dangerous ideas, seeing an overlap between faith and evolution, we still have the problem of the Bible. The Bible tells a very different story of creation; can these stories be related? Or like Van Gogh, should we assume the Bible is only significant for a past age uninterested in truth?

"TAKE A LITTLE CRITICISM"

The century of Van Gogh and Darwin brought hard times for the Bible. But not really because of art or science. Rather, the

2. http://www.vggallery.com/painting/p_0117.htm.

3. Tertullian and Augustine too make this point.

4. Brooke provides a little background to Galileo's position: "Galileo knew only too well that it could, if the province of biblical authority were not scrupulously defined. In his writings, a mutation occurred in the analogies customarily drawn between the two books. The search for signs of God in nature had often been based on the assumption that the two books had been written in essentially the same language. Galileo, however, achieved a telling differentiation when he argued that nature had a language all its own. The book of nature, he insisted, had been written in the language of mathematics. No amount of theologizing could be a substitute for mathematical analysis. In evaluating the Copernican system, for example, mathematical criteria should take precedence over interpretations of Scripture, which may have become normative but only through ignorance." John Hedley Brooke, *Science and Religion* (London: Cambridge University Press, 2014), 104.

point of the spear that seemed to threaten the importance of the Bible was, ironically, biblical studies itself. The nineteenth century birthed new forms of text criticism. A group of biblical scholars decided to try reading the scriptures *not* for the sake of preaching or devotion, but simply as texts. They sought to discover the world behind the text, the original intent of the author(s), and the historical experience and sources behind them. They showed that there was no such thing as just plainly "reading the Bible." This was right, but a challenge to many. To show what was in the mind of the original writers, these Bible scholars took the Bible apart piece by piece as a mechanic would an old Camaro.

Once something is divided into parts and deconstructed, it loses its enchantment. Darwin's ideas were actually interpreted as *dangerous* in no small part because they came into a time when the Bible (for good or ill) was being deconstructed. In the vacuum of its disenchantment, Darwin's ideas appeared ominous.

But as we saw with Darwin's story, the nineteenth century was a time of global adventure, as well. Those in the colonizing nations of Europe were sending expeditions, like the *Beagle*, to the ends of the earth. And this affected biblical scholarship! In the spirit of Indiana Jones, archeology became a big deal. Particularly, the discovery of Babylonian (and some Egyptian) texts revealed some interesting and shocking things about the Bible. Anyone could see similarities between the stories in Genesis 1–3 and Babylonian myths.[5] The archeology was clearly showing that the ancient Near Eastern creation stories were using similar sources. They were, no doubt, different and unique in themselves, but clearly, they were also somehow aware of (even using) each other. They were like hip-hop artists sampling beats and hooks from other songs to create new forms of expression. The Bible couldn't be confused as a scientific book; it was after something else, it seemed.

---

5. I'm leaning heavily on Peter Enns's work. He explains these similarities more fully in chapter 3 of his book *The Evolution of Adam: What the Bible Does and Doesn't Say About Human Origins* (Grand Rapids, MI: Brazos, 2012).

Seven years before Van Gogh would paint *Still Life with Bible*, another son of a pastor would publish a book called *Prolegomena to the History of Israel*. Julius Wellhausen was a German Old Testament professor using the new text criticism to write a history of the Pentateuch (the first five books of the Hebrew Bible, including—of course—Genesis). Wellhausen, doing an internal analysis of the text, believed that he could see the pattern of sampling. He was able to decipher the different beats and hooks that made up the Pentateuch. There were four of them, he claimed, mixed beautifully into an original song of Israel's origins.[6]

The thing was, at least a few of these samples seemed to show a quite late date. It would be like dating Jay-Z's "Hard Knock Life." You'd know you couldn't date it earlier than the soundtrack of *Annie*. *Annie* would have to come first. In the same way, Wellhausen found structures, vocabulary, and ideas in the Genesis text that could have only been used around the time of the Exile. This led Wellhausen to assert that while parts of the Genesis story were known and used much earlier, it doesn't become a finished song (to keep the analogy going) until after the Israelites returned from the Exile.

And this would make good sense of the archeology. The Israelites had their own distinct beats with their own unique story to tell about their God and God's action. But, it appeared, they sampled the stories of the Babylonians as a way of resistance, as a way of reminding Israelites and Babylonians alike that the God who ministered freedom from the Exodus will come to God's people again and again. For this God of Israel is no regional force, but the very one who makes and sustains the cosmos itself. It is quite a powerful act for a people to take the dominant stories of their captors and recast them, showing their own God as an actor in their captors' own stories. They told a well-known Babylonian tale now with the God of Israel as the single actor. It would be a little like captured American soldiers in a 1950s Soviet prison, when forced to celebrate a communist holiday, retelling the story of Soviet revolt with George Washington in place of Lenin. They'd use the same structure of the

---

6. This is the JEDP structure that most people learn in seminary.

captors' story, but infuse it with the character of a different person, and therefore a completely different point.[7]

This then means, as Peter Enns has said, "The Genesis creation narrative we have in our Bibles today, although surely rooted in much older material, was shaped as a theological response to Israel's national crisis of exile. These stories were not written to speak of 'origins' as we might think of them today (in a natural-science sense). They were written to say something of God and Israel's place in the world as God's chosen people."[8] Enns's point is that making Genesis 1–3 a literal (or even concordist) take on the origins of nature is like assuming that all American mountains are literally purple, because that's what the song "America the Beautiful" says. Israel is using the structure of other people's stories to tell of their own experience of God. Having encountered the ministry of God in returning Israel to its land, making them again a people, they use the structure of Babylonian creation myths to make a larger point: just as this God ministers to God's people, freeing them from Egypt and giving them back a land lost, so this God creates and sustains the whole of the universe, ministering to it life, for this is a God that takes what is dead (what is *not*) and makes things new (what *is*).

So this use of Babylonian myths doesn't lessen the Bible's importance; instead it shows how profound it is. The Bible presents who God is and how this God acts, asserting loudly that this God sets forth a personal order. Israel shows that no matter

7. Enns provides some more texture to this claim: "I recognize that the following is speculative, but I agree with much of contemporary biblical scholarship that the second creation story (Adam) was Israel's original creation story, with some slight universal overtones (still seen, perhaps, in 3:20, where Eve is the 'mother of all living'). It was likely modeled after the pattern of Atrahasis (creation, population growth, flood), as we glimpsed in the previous chapter. A postexilic writer/writers (perhaps the shapers of the Pentateuch) introduced an alternate account of origins, Genesis 1, modeled after common themes found in Enuma Elish, that focused on God's sovereignty and might over his creation, not to mention the rhythm of the week and Sabbath rest. . . . In my opinion, the editors of the Pentateuch subsumed the older story under the newer one so that Genesis 1 became the story of the creation of the cosmos and Genesis 2 became the story of Israel's creation against that universal backdrop. This may be why these two different creation stories are placed next to each other as they are. The editors of the Pentateuch may be expecting their readers to read the two stories sequentially: Genesis 2 presumes the events of Genesis 1." *The Evolution of Adam*, 68.

8. Enns, *The Evolution of Adam*, 5.

what your own story might be, this God that Israel has known as minister comes to us all, holding all together.

What is authoritative for Israel is not the six days of creation, and the order they come in—that's the Babylonian structure they're sampling and remixing. What is authoritative is the proclamation the remixed story makes about the being and act of this God. This God acts to minister to another, liberating the Israelites from Egypt, freeing order from chaos, bringing newness from death and impossibility.

This is what contemporary Old Testament scholar John Walton means by the difference between the "home" vs. "house" story.[9] Israel is using parts of these Babylonian myths *not* to tell a "house story,"[10] how each room is wired for electricity, the thickness of the foundation, the kind of insulation, and the size of studs. Rather, Walton points out that Israel is instead telling a "home story." If a house story tells about impersonal structure, a home tells about Christmases, birthdays, and moments of pain and joy through the years.[11] It tells of the personal order of a family meeting and ministering to each other. Walton's point is that Israel is not trying to tell us about the construction of the house when they use Near Eastern samples, but instead sings a song of encounter. These stories remind the Israelites in exile

9. For full disclosure, Walton is not as convinced by Enns's argument for the postexilic forging of the Genesis texts. However, Walton does believe that Israel is telling a specific story.

10. Scot McKnight summarizes Walton's position nicely, pointing to its implications: "Science, then, encouraged me to think again about the Bible. One recent study, by John Walton, has urged us to think again about what Genesis 1-2 meant in its day. Some elements of Walton's theory are being challenged, but his major idea is reasonable and persuasive: that Genesis 1-2 is not about the origins of the world so much as the function of God's world. That is, Genesis 1-2 presents God fashioning the world as his temple, placing us in it to reflect his glory and to govern his good world on his behalf. That is, the universe is God's temple and we are summoned by God to care for God's temple by worship and work." "Who's Afraid of Science?," in Kathryn Applegate and J. B. Stump, *How I Changed My Mind About Evolution: Evangelicals Reflect on Faith and Science* (Downers Grove, IL: IVP, 2016), 33.

11. John Walton says directly, "Many have believed in the past that the seven days related to the age of the earth because they read the chapter as a house story. The age of the earth pertains to that which is material. If this is a home story, however, it has nothing to do with the age of the physical cosmos. A period of seven days does not pertain to how long it took to build the house; it pertains to the process by which the house became a home." *The Lost World of Adam and Eve: Genesis 2-3 and the Human Origins Debate* (Downers Grove, IL: IVP, 2015), 51.

(and now home) that God too will come and minister to them, creating again a land (home) of their own. The ministry of the Israelite God is so profound that it infuses and possesses the stories of its captors.

A TEMPLE AND A PRIEST

Jared and Gus talked about these ideas. They made sense, and actually in an odd way gave Jared more respect for the Bible, helping him breathe easier. The point wasn't to defend the Bible in the face of evolution, but to recognize and dwell even more on the personhood of God that the Bible reveals. Jared particularly liked the difference between the home and the house stories—he thought he could use it in the Bible study.

Yet just as his confidence was growing, he had a sinking feeling. This perspective, while deeply helpful, was a nonconcordist position. Sarah's experience made Jared pause. Sarah was fired for supposedly minimizing sin because she overlooked the importance of a historical Adam. One of Tanisha's major objectives of this sermon series was to discuss sin. The point was not origins *per se*, but to discuss how sin entered a perfect world. Not thinking about the scientific issues, Tanisha spoke as if Adam was a historical figure. "Was he? And if he wasn't, then what about sin?" Jared thought. These questions also resonated with Martin's concerns about mass extinctions. It appears that the Bible (at least Paul) connects death with sin and the fall of Adam (Romans 6). Evolution, on the other hand, states that death is natural and comes in wave after wave, for hundreds of millions of years, before there was the possibility of *homo sapiens*.

Like a good hip-hop song, the point of sampling isn't to glorify the hook of the original song, but to express something new—to say something original about your experience—using the sample to this end. For instance, to continue with my old-school hip-hop theme, when Puff Daddy (before he was P. Diddy) sampled Sting's "Every Breath You Take" for his song "I'll Be Missing You," it wasn't to introduce a new audience to the British singer or to even give props to Sting's original.

Rather, the point was to express his own experience—in this case, to grieve the loss of Biggie Smalls.

In the same way, Israel samples from ancient Near Eastern myths for their distinct purposes. From within their experience of God's ministry, Israel is claiming that creation is a temple. It is a place to encounter the personhood (*hypostasis*) of God. Just as Solomon took seven years to build the temple that was destroyed as the Southern Kingdom was marched into Exile, so now, back in the land and sampling these myths, the Israelites claim that God creates the universe in seven days! And these seven days take the structure of a temple. The days of creation are not meant to be actual; they are meant to make a larger point. They assert that the universe is the location of God's action, that just as God promises to enter a temple, so this God of Israel is present, sustaining the whole of existence. As Bible scholar William Brown says, "The God of Genesis 1 is a temple builder with an artistic bent."[12] The reader is not to focus on twenty-four-hour days, but on the pillars of creation formed as a temple for persons to encounter a God of ministry.

Brown shows this parallelism in the text that serves like pillars in a temple. For instance, day one and day four revolve around light, day two and day five around water and air, day three and day six around land, animals, and plants. And, finally, day seven, around the holy. These beams, imagined as days, create the temple. Brown reminds us that most ancient Near Eastern temples have three parts—a portico, a nave, and the holy of holies. Days one and four create the first pillars for creation. Stepping out of darkness you enter a portico of light: there is now a universe. There is something instead of nothing. But soon you are moved further across the pillars of day two and day five and you enter the nave. The first pillars of day two and day five separate water and air on one side of the nave. On the other side are the pillars of days three and six, giving us dry land, and filling those waters, skies, and lands with all sorts of creatures. Through the pillars of day three and day six is the Holy of Holies.

The point is clear, this God is a creator, and this universe is

12. William Brown, *The Seven Pillars of Creation: The Bible, Science, and the Ecology of Wonder* (London: Oxford University Press, 2010), 46.

God's temple. It is a place where God is transcendent. Israel's temple cannot hold God, but is nevertheless a place God promises to be present. God is other than creation as a temple, but is nevertheless in it. Israel doesn't care for what *actually* happens, scientifically speaking. Israel's concern is to show that this God is *other*, yet God can be encountered in the world. The whole universe is this God's temple and should be treasured as such. The point isn't to show us exactly how the universe got here (and in what timing). The point is that a ministering God who creates and liberates is in this world, and this universe is God's temple.

THE IMAGE

But there is another piece of creation as temple that pushes us directly into Jared's concerns. When a temple was constructed in the ancient Near East, not only did they have this three-room arrangement but also an image of the god whose temple it was. To show further that Israel is sampling these temple metaphors for their creation story, they too describe an image to the God of Israel. But Israel's image is different. It is no mold, carving, or golden idol. The image of the God of the temple of the universe is these *hypostatic* beings that are called to be priests of creation, reflecting God's image by ministering in the temple as God ministers to them.[13]

13. Brown provides more texture: "The cosmic temple code of Genesis 1 also reveals something significant about humanity's role and identity in the creation account. Many an ancient temple contained an image of its resident deity within its inner sanctum. In Jerusalem, however, the physical representation of God was expressly forbidden, at least by the time of the exile (sixth century BCE), as one finds, for example, conveyed in a certain commandment of the Decalogue: 'You shall not make for yourself an idol.' (Exod 20:4; Deut 5:8). Such is what scholars call Israel's 'aniconic' tradition, a categorical prohibition of divine images, which distinguished ancient Israel's worship practices from some of its more religiously elaborate neighbors. Because God was considered to be without form, at least in some religious circles, the deity could not be represented (see Deut 4:12-18). According to biblical lore, the inner sanctum of the Jerusalem temple contained the 'ark of the covenant' covered by the outstretched wings of two cherubim (I Kgs 6:23-28). The ark was regarded as God's footstool or throne and as the container of the stone tablets of the Decalogue. In place of a statue, the statutes of God were housed." *The Seven Pillars of Creation*, 41.

At the end of the sixth day, the *Adam* [Heb. "earth creature"] is created with a task. This creature is called into ministry. Israel isn't concerned whether this Adam is really the first hominid or even the first *homo sapiens*. Rather, the point of the text is that this creature, this human, is the *first*[14] called to be a priest of this temple.[15] N. T. Wright says that "ever since the scientific revolutions of the eighteenth and nineteenth centuries, Christians have been in danger of focusing on the existence of Adam rather than the vocation of Adam."[16] It is not enough to just be. This Adam

---

14. Walton provides his own perspective that also has the Adam not as the first hominid. "And it leads me to my proposal: that just as God chose Israel from the rest of humankind for a special, strange, demanding vocation, so perhaps what Genesis is telling us is that God chose one pair from the rest of early hominids for a special, strange, demanding vocation. This pair (call them Adam and Eve if you like) were to be the representatives of the whole human race, the ones in whom God's purposes to make the whole world a place of delight and joy and order, eventually colonizing the whole creation, were to be taken forward." Walton, *The Lost World of Adam and Eve*, 178.

15. Van Huyssteen adds to this: "Importantly, however, the imago Dei also includes a priestly or cultic dimension. In the cosmic sanctuary of God's world, humans have pride of place and supreme responsibility, not just as royal stewards and cultural shapers of the environment, but also as 'priests of creation,' actively mediating divine blessing to the nonhuman world and directing a fallen world toward God's purposes for justice and redemption. Instead of a more traditional picture of the imago Dei as a mirror reflecting God, this canonical notion now becomes more like a prism refracting the concentrated light of God's glory through a multitude of human sociocultural activities, as we interact with our earthly environment (cf. Middleton 2005: 89f.) Furthermore, Middleton has argued impressively that Genesis 1 portrays God's relationship to the created order in fundamentally nonviolent terms. In fact, the text depicts God's founding exercise of creative power in such a way that we might appropriately describe it as an act of generosity, even of love. The human responsibility as the imago Dei to imitate the creative act as an act of generosity and love also directly conflicts with any reading of these texts that may want to find in the original text a justification for a scientific or technological conquest over nature, or for violence against women and the environment. On the contrary, Genesis 1 depicts God as a generous creator, sharing power with humans and inviting them to participate in the creative, historical process with responsibility and care." Wentzel van Huyssteen, *Alone in the World? Human Uniqueness in Science and Theology* (Grand Rapids, MI: Eerdmans, 2006), 158.

16. N. T. Wright in Walton's *The Lost World of Adam and Eve*, 170. Wright continues: "The notion of the 'image' doesn't refer to a particular spiritual endowment, a secret 'property' that humans possess somewhere in their genetic makeup, something that might be found by a scientific observation of humans as opposed to chimps. The image is a vocation, a calling. It is the call to be an angled mirror, reflecting God's wise order into the world and reflecting the praises of all creation back to the Creator." *The Lost World of Adam and Eve*, 175.

must be a priest to the universe, reflecting God's own *hypostatic* being, by being the person that ministers to the universe just as God ministers to Adam.[17]

It's possible, though pure speculation, that *homo sapiens* communities that chose for kindness, picking weakness as strength, were those called to reflect the ministering God by being priests in this temple. The story of Adam and Eve [now the image of God reflected in male and female][18] and their children, actually only makes sense next to understanding that they are not the first *homo sapiens*, but the first called into such a deep personal relationship to this ministering God that they can hear this God speak, and are called (ordained) into ministry. After all, when Adam and Eve tragically leave the garden, who will their children marry? But they do. And who are these others that they are scared of and need to be protected from?[19] The first-ness of Adam and Eve is the first-ness of beings called through the unique human capacity for *hypostasis* to reflect this *hypostatic* being of God by being ministers.[20]

17. N. T. Wright says, "Current scientific understanding maintains that there was no first human being because humanity is the result of an evolving population. The evidence of genetics also points to the idea that the genetic diversity that exists in humanity today cannot be traced back to two individuals—a single pair—but that such diversity requires a genetic source population of thousands. If the Bible claims otherwise, then we would have to take a stand against this emerging scientific consensus." *The Lost World of Adam and Eve*, 183.

18. There is only a distinction in gender once Eve is created. The image of God is priest—both male and female. It is in their own *hypostatic* union—together male and female in cooperation—that they are most fully priest for creation.

19. Walton says, "The role of Adam and Eve as priests in sacred space is what sets them apart, not their genetic role. If Genesis 1 features the inauguration center of that sacred space and God taking up his rest, the presence of a *center* of that *sacred space* (i.e., a temple) is implied. If the Garden of Eden serves that temple function, then Genesis 2 must be viewed as taking place in the same general time, though it can come after the seven days rather than within it. In such a scenario, Adam and Eve should likely be considered part of that initial human creation in Genesis 1, though since only corporate humanity is mentioned, the text does not explicitly rule out the idea that there were others. According to my analysis of the *toledot* (account), I would suggest that Genesis 2 is not recursively recounting what happened on day six but is talking about what happened in the *aftermath* of day six." *The Lost World of Adam and Eve*, 115.

20. Walton explains, "Rather than understanding Scripture as necessitating the view that Adam and Eve are the first humans, in light of their specific role concerned with access to God in sacred space and relationship with him, we might alternatively consider the possibility that they are the first significant humans. As with Abram,

So is Adam a historical figure? Yes and no. The biblical text gives us some reason to hold to the historical event. We have genealogies[21] that go back to Adam (though that may be more rhetorical than literal), and Paul uses the singular Adam as a theological device to claim the unique singularity of Jesus. These are big issues that we shouldn't too quickly push aside. But it is also possible that Adam and Eve are representatives for a group of hominids that heard the call of the personal God to build a community of ministers. Regardless whether Adam is a historical figure or not, it seems logical to not place on him the weight of being the first *ever*. Adam was (or Adam's community were) the first minister(s), the first priest called to echo the *hypostatic* nature of God by ministering to others and creation. But we know there were likely many other hominid groups before Adam.

THIS MINIMIZES SIN!

None of this minimizes sin! Adam and Eve (this first community of hominids) reject God and it destroys their ability to be ministers. The Adam sins because the Adam refuses the vocation of the priest. The minister must always enter into nothingness and death—which, as we've seen, is inherited within the evolutionary process—seeking the act of God to come in and through weakness. The Adam brings sin into the world because he

---

who was given a significant role as the ancestor of Israel (though not the first ancestor of Israel), Adam and Eve would be viewed as established as significant by their election. This would be true whether or not other people were around. Their election is to a priestly role, the first to be placed in sacred space. The forming accounts give them insight into the nature of humanity, but they also become the first significant humans because of their role in bringing sin into the world. . . . Adam was the 'first' man, given the opportunity to bring life, but he failed to achieve that goal. Christ, as the 'last' man, succeeded as he provided life and access to the presence of God for all as our great high priest (see 1 Cor 15:45)." *The Lost World of Adam and Eve*, 115.

21. "This same idea seems to be at work in the only other mention of Adam in the entire Old Testament, 1 Chronicles 1:1: Adam is the first name in the nine-chapter genealogy that establishes Israel's unwavering status as God's people from the very beginning. The postexilic community, wishing to affirm its national and religious identity, traced its lineage back to Adam—not the universal first man, but the first man in the chosen line, the first Israelite." Enns, *Evolution of Adam*, 141.

refuses this call and decides he would rather live beyond the risk of nothingness as god-like, free from needing a minister.[22]

The dying inherent in evolution turns to the bloody and at times evil reality of death[23] because the priests have refused the call to minister. They refuse to take on the supposedly weak act of giving their presence to *all* things experiencing dying in the world. Creation is never meant to be perfect in the sense of not dying (this could oppose the scientific), but it is meant to be perfect in the sense that all dying becomes the stage of receiving the deepest form of communion. And it is received as these unique animals called to be ministering priests bear the image of this ministering God, by embracing the nothingness of dying as the birthing of new possibility. The refusal of this call by the Adam, then, has huge ramifications, leading indeed to a fallen world.[24] The natural process of dying is turned into the nightmare of death, because those called to minister to the dying have refused their callings.[25] John Walton says something

22. This is similar to Eberhard Jüngel's position, which I discuss more fully in *Christopraxis*, chapter 6.

23. This contrasting of dying and death is something that Karl Barth explores. See also Ray Anderson, who builds on this in *Theology, Death and Dying* (New York: Basil Blackwell, 1986).

24. Above I use the language of "fall," though it is problematic from both a biblical and scientific perspective. I leave it because it fits with our theological imagination, but quote Walton and Brown's discussion as a way to point to its problems. Walton says, "The Old Testament never refers to the event of Genesis 3 as 'the fall' and does not talk about people or the world as 'fallen.'" *The Lost World of Adam and Eve*, 142. Brown continues: "There is, however, a real collision between science and the traditional interpretation of the biblical 'Fall' that demands a reckoning. By itself, the Yahwist story offers profound reflections concerning the genesis of human sin, about how human violence begets violence leading up to God's grief-stricken resolve to 'blot out' all life on the land by flood (Gen 6:7). But the garden story has been traditionally read, particularly by Christians, as an etiology for all pain and suffering experienced on Earth, from animal predation to earthquakes, all the result of the primal couple's disobedience. Humanity's fall from paradise, it is claimed, brought about nature's fall from perfection. But the story itself is much more limited in scope. Its primary focus is on the human family, not the family of life." *The Seven Pillars of Creation*, 106.

25. I've tried to pick up the call Lamoureux presents here with my assertion about the place of ministry keeping dying part of the 'good' created realm. He explains: "The greatest challenge for evolutionary creation is to explain biblical passages that refer to a causal connection between the sin of Adam and the origin of physical death. Genesis 3 presents death entering the world because God condemned Adam to die in judgment for his sin, Paul in Rom 5 and 1 Cor 15 understood the fall of the

similar when he states, "This, perhaps, is a way of reading the warning of Genesis 2: in the day you eat of it you, too, will die. Not that death, the decay and dissolution of plants, animals and hominids, wasn't a reality already; but you, Adam and Eve, are chosen to be the people through whom God's life-giving reflection will be imaged into the world, and if you choose to worship and serve the creation rather than the Creator, you will merely reflect death back to death, and will share that death yourself."[26]

God, then, desires a history where the universe would be a temple of ministry, overseen by *hypostatic* priests. It is the vocation of those bearing the image to enter the process of dying, representing and reflecting the very care, appreciation, and love of God. Evolution as the process God uses for continually creating makes nothingness and death operative, but dying is to be bound in the spirit of ministry (avoiding turning it into evil) that shares in these natural experiences of dying.[27] God tasks these ministers to make the dying that is inherent in evolution a stage of encounter with meaning, significance, and new possibility—an encounter with the love of God. The Adam creatures are tasked with an ultimately important job; they are to keep

first man to be literal history, and the Church throughout time has firmly upheld the historicity of this event in the garden of Eden. However, evolutionary science reveals overwhelming evidence that death existed for hundreds of millions of years before the appearance of humans. Any Christian approach to evolution must deal with this problem directly." Denis Lamoureux, *Evolutionary Creation: A Christian Approach to Evolution* (Eugene, OR: Wipf & Stock, 2008), 305.

26. Walton, *The Lost World of Adam and Eve*, 178.

27. William Brown nicely discusses the place of dying in creation, pushing the discussion closer to evolution and the call of human being to give beyond competition. "For some biologists, the pervasive feature of death and extinction inherent in evolution's 'progress,' if one can call it that, 'casts doubt on the perfection of God's plan.' It must be repeated, however, that Genesis 1 does not depict a perfect, let alone perfectly micromanaged, creation, only a 'good' one. The distinction is crucial. God enlists the natural elements of creation such as the earth and the waters to participate in the creative process, a conceivably messy, somewhat unregulated affair. The creation narrative, moreover, acknowledges the continuing struggle of life (1:26, 28). To 'fill' the earth involves, from a Darwinian perspective, competition. 'Subduing' the earth, from the perspective of Genesis, is required for the flourishing of human life (1:28). Biologically speaking, the commission to 'subdue' extends to all species for their survival. But 'man' does not live by competition alone, and the same goes for any other species. The flourishing of life also depends upon sustaining various kinds of interdependent relations through cooperation, collectivity, and balance." Brown, *The Seven Pillars of Creation*, 61.

the dying inherent in evolution from becoming the dark evil of death as sin. But as we've said, Adam and Eve refuse the task, and assert that they are beyond ministry. They act as though they can live like God, without nothingness, that they are beyond evolution (not creatures at all). Because they have refused the call of ministry, sin, which is death outside the care and mercy of ministry,[28] has become a dark heavy norm in the universe.

And yet, God still desires this history of ministry for the universe. And so God sends a new priest, who is of the same *hypostasis* as Godself, to come into this fallen history, entering fully the perishing of death, so that this history of death might be redeemed through the ministry of God. Jesus becomes both the full representation of God who is a minister, and the new Adam who does not refuse the call, but fully bears death so that all who experience death in the universe receive the fullness of God's being through the act of ministry. The cross, planted in creation, redeems evolution, turning perishing into promise.

Now all mass extinctions, Martin must hear, bear the ministry of the love of the Father to the Son. And while dying remains, death has lost its sting (1 Corinthians 15:55), for perishing can no longer block the ministry of God. The priests are back practicing ministry in the temple, now empowered by Spirit of the Priest named Christ who *is* the same being (*ousia*) of the ministering creator. And this Christ promises a day in a new temple where the history of death will be evicted for good.

Jared decided to meet up with Martin an hour before the next Bible study. They had a great conversation. Jared talked a little about the temple interpretation and the call to be priests of the temple. Martin connected it nicely to *The Walking Dead*, saying, "It's amazing that when death becomes really full blown there is this great temptation to just try and survive, and you forget other people, and, like, caring for them. I mean, really, when you look at dystopia stuff, its all about, can you keep your humanity and still love people when the world falls apart? I guess, being ministers when death is everywhere. And weirdly, those that actually

---

28. For more about sin, see my chapter in *The Theological Turn in Youth Ministry* and my chapter on sin in *Taking the Cross to Youth Ministry*.

do care for other people, survive. It's kind of like those shows know what you're talking about."

"Yeah," Jared said, shocked at Martin's ability to put pieces together that Jared didn't see.

But Jared couldn't be blamed for being a little slow on the uptake. He had a big night planned for the Bible study and his mind kept racing to the details. He was going to focus on the difference between the home story and the house story. Jared's idea was simple, but brilliant. Christine, Aaron's mom, was an architectural engineer (that's why they had the nice pool!), so Jared ask her if she could get them into a house or building under construction—a place where the beams, studs, and wiring were still exposed—preferably close to her house. Christine found a construction site 50 percent finished five blocks from where they'd been having the Bible study. Jared then pushed his luck and asked Christine if she could give the group, which now had ballooned to seven kids, a ten- to twelve-minute overview of the structural engineering of the building, even showing them the blueprints. Jared told her in advance that as she did this he'd be asking weird questions, like "How tall are the people that will be living here? Where will they put their Christmas tree? In what room will the wife tell her husband that they are expecting a new baby? Where will the baby take its first steps?" Jared knew the kids would think he was nuts. But without any explanation, they'd leave and walk back to Christine and Aaron's place. Then Jared asked Christine if the group could sit in their family room and if she'd take out a photo album and tell the kids about *her* house, answering many of Jared's questions from the construction site.

After these ten to fifteen minutes, Jared planned to read a popular piece on evolution he'd found on the Internet. Next he'd read Genesis 1. Jared would follow this by asking the young people, Which piece was a house story and which was a home story? Which of Christine's stories was more *important*? They were different and important in their own right. Jared hoped this plan would help young people see both the possibilities and the limits of evolution. He also hoped they'd recognize that the Bible has something very different to say than a house story, but speaks of a universe made to be our home, where God calls us to experience and share God's ministering love.

Jared hoped it would all work as he planned. Looking at his phone to get the time, Jared told Martin it was time to go.

That night, when the group grabbed hands to pray and conclude a good night, Jared was happy. Actually, he'd call it joy—a deep sense that he had been given the gift of experiencing the presence of God in and through ministry. For a split second the thought came to him that he wasn't *supposed* to be here. He was *supposed* to have left youth ministry and these young people long behind to became an edgy, hip, senior pastor in Baby Brooklyn. The feeling of gratitude ballooned in his chest when he realized he was indeed right where he was supposed to be.

Epilogue

What about . . . ?

   While Jared bathed in his good feelings and before they could
start their prayer, Tegan spoke up. Tegan had faithfully come
to every Bible study, but always remained quiet and disengaged,
only breaking her frozen face of skepticism when Martin made
an irreverent sarcastic statement. She cleared her throat tentatively, and said, with her head shaking, "Wait . . . wait . . ."

   "What is it, Tegan?," Jared asked, having no idea what she
could possibly be thinking. Tegan had opted out of really saying
anything for the last six weeks.

   "But do you . . ." Tegan said with a slight hesitation, "ever
think that what we believe is just a trick of our brains?"

   "What do you mean?" Aaron asked, confused.

   "It's something I've read on the Internet," Tegan answered.

   "What is?" Jared asked.

Tegan explained: "Well, imagine that your mind is like a
computer and maybe what, like, all religion is, is a programed
work-around, imposed by evolution. Like, we have this amazing consciousness to *think* about *thinking*, but that means we can
think about death, and that thought could crash the whole program of our mind, so we make up gods and spirits as a patch program that keeps the operating system of the brain flowing. So,
like, people still today believe in heaven and stuff, because it is
left over from our more childish minds that couldn't face death.
But now, like, we can be brave enough to face it. I guess I just
feel like evolution made the brain like a computer program."

"That's interesting," Jared returned. "But besides the fear of death, how does that answer our experiences of forgiveness, hope, mercy, belonging, and ultimately love? Even people who don't believe in heaven seem to need those."

"Sure," Tegan said. "But maybe they're not all that special as we think they are. I mean, think about artificial intelligence; I mean, at some point they're going to create programs that allow a machine to hope and love. Will it really be love? Or will that even matter, because we'll *experience* these machines as loving us, and that will be enough? I wonder if 'God' is a made-up thing not that different than machines with artificial intelligence."

Christine, Aaron's mom who so generously helped lead the night, said, "Oh, yeah! That's cognitive science, Tegan! My closest friend from college is a cognitive scientist and she says things just like that." Christine looked at Jared and said, "What do we do with that, Jared?"

Jared could only smile. This was the first time he'd ever heard of cognitive science, but he was sure that delving into Tegan's questions would take them on a journey. These kinds of questions had already taken him into thinking about how the claims of faith meet the findings and theories of evolution, cognitive ethology, physics, Big Bang cosmology, and more. Jared wasn't sure he'd done all these thoughts justice, but he was sure that as an act of ministry he'd joined his young people in wrestling with a complicated world and a big God who meets us in it. He was sure that on this journey Tegan's questions would lead them into a place where again and again, the ministering action of God echoes across the universe. Jared looked forward to where Tegan's questions would lead them . . .